Registered as a charity (No. 266754)

The Association formed by Philip and Mary Carter in 1973,
to promote the interests of users of the South West Coast Path

SOUTH WEST COAST PATH ASSOCIATION
Bowker House, Lee Mill Bridge, Ivybridge, Devon PL21 9EF
Tel: 01752 896237 Fax: 01752 893654 Email: info@swcp.org.uk
Visit our website at www.swcp.org.uk

CHAIRMAN - BRIAN PANTON
5 Nicholas Gardens, Ensbury Park, Bournemouth BH10 4BA
Tel: 01202 526954 Email: brian.panton@ntlworld.com

TREASURER - JOHN MILLS
Bowker House see above. Email: johnmills49@btinternet.com

SECRETARY - STEVE CHURCH
4 Wheal Speed Road, Carbis Bay, St Ives TR26 2QG
Tel: 01736 791777 Email: steve.church1@googlemail.com

ADMINISTRATOR - LIZ WALLIS AND KATE HOLLAND
Bowker House see above

Published by: The South West Coast Path Association

Designed and printed by Swiftprint, Dawlish, Devon www.swiftprintsw.co.uk
ISBN 978-0-907055-19-8

Jacket photography:
Descending to Middle Bottom - photographer Barry Lockwood, South Devon - photographer Fiona Barltrop, Walking Boots - photographer Liz Wallis, Towanroath Engine House, North Cornwall - photographer Dave Westcott

Welcome to the Annual Guide

Welcome to the South West Coast Path Association's Annual Guide to the wonderful experience of England's longest National Trail. This superb walk encircles the coastline of the entire South West Peninsula of England. In its 630 miles it encompasses high cliffs, breezy dunes, wooded estuaries, saltmarshes, picturesque fishing ports, sedate seaside towns, holiday resorts and all the interest of the major seaside city and naval port of Plymouth.

No matter what your interest, be it in the landscape, wildlife, history or just a wish to get away from it all, the South West Coast Path has the answer.

The South West Coast Path Association is the charitable body set up to represent the interests of all those who walk on the Coast Path. It doesn't matter whether you're an afternoon stroller or a long-distance walker who intends to walk all 630 miles, or has done so, the Association is there for you.

The Association campaigns for the best possible standards for the Coast Path and its immediate corridor and financially assists where appropriate to ensure the best possible experience for those using the route. And, of course, it also provides help and information to walkers, including this Guide and the other publications mentioned in these pages.

So, if you've not already done so, why not join 5,000+ Coast Path enthusiasts and become a member. Then -

-your subscription will help the Association promote, protect and enhance the Coast Path, including providing funds for specific improvement projects;

- you will receive your copy of the Annual Guide free and keep up to date with what's happening on the Path via our two free Newsletters each year;

- you will be part of the "family" of those who love the Coast Path by knowing that your input is important to the Path's well-being.

Funding provided by members' subscriptions have enabled the Association to play a vital part in getting bridges replaced, re-constructing the Path when it has been lost to cliff falls, improving its alignment and a host of other improvements. That's all thanks to the Association's members....well done everyone!

In 2013 the Association marks its 40th anniversary. To mark the occasion there is to be a commemorative event during April and May 2013 which will both raise public awareness of the Association and also raise funds to help improve the Coast Path. The event is "The Great South West Walk - putting 40 years of love back into the Coast Path!" The event will provide a series of guided walks along the entire length of the route, acting as two relays from the two ends, Minehead and Poole Harbour, to meet for a birthday party at Land's End on 7th May 2013.

We are aiming to encourage an average of 30 walkers on each of the day legs, each walker being encouraged to raise sponsorship money to fund a series of path improvements.

All the details may be found on the dedicated website www.greatsouthwestwalk.co.uk. We hope as many people as possible, members or not, sign up. Each walk will be a rewarding experience in its own right, being led by a local expert, but will also give the opportunity of enabling some practical help to be given to the Coast Path.

Clovelly Harbour

Contents

Photography courtesy of:
Fiona Barltrop, Ted Forman, Teresa Gomez, Chris Hubury, Barry Lockwood, Lucy Masterton, Jennifer Rowlandson,Paul Zinc, Liz Wallis, Dave Westcott and Steve Pattemore

Introduction to The South West Coast Path

The South West Coast Path National Trail is a 630-mile adventure around the coastline of the south-west peninsula. From Minehead in Somerset all the way to Poole Harbour in Dorset, it is simply the best way to enjoy the scenery, wildlife and heritage of this wonderful coastline.

The sheer variety of the South West Coast Path means that there are plenty of gentle stretches as well as dramatic headlands and steep coastal valleys where the going can be strenuous and demanding. Relaxation, challenge, tranquillity or inspiration - the choice is yours!

National Trails are walking routes (and some also for riding) through the country's finest scenery and heritage. They are created and mainly funded by Natural England and managed by Highway Authorities and the National Trust. They receive a high standard of care and are the flagships of the rights of way network. No one in England and Wales lives more than 50 miles from a National Trail.

As a result of the 1999/2000 survey of the full length of the Coast Path using a global positioning system, we now have access to very precise distances - the Coast Path is 630 miles (1014km) long. The survey carried out by the South West Coast Path Team included the Isle of Portland.

During a survey in 2011-12 of the entire Coast Path, an Association member used a sophisticated altimeter to calculate that the walker who has completed the whole Coast Path will have climbed 115000 feet (35024m), which is just a little short of walking the height of Mount Everest from sea level four times!

The path passes through some of the finest coastal scenery anywhere, and has enormous variety and contrast between bustling resorts and quiet coves. The path is the longest National Trail in the country; we think it is the finest, and hope you will too. We know of no other that has as much contrast and variety as ours and urge you to try it.

So here it is - England's longest and most beautiful walking trail - read about it, then go for it!

Durdle Door

Dedicated to helping everyone enjoy the path

The Association was formed in 1973 by a group of enthusiasts to encourage the development and improvement of the South West Coast Path. This is still one of the main aims of the Association, and it works closely with Natural England, local authorities and other more general user groups such as the Ramblers' Association and the Long Distance Walkers' Association.

Over those years the Association has continuously campaigned for maintenance, signing and alignment improvements.

Of primary importance is to have the Coast Path removed from roads. There have been many improvements as long-standing members will know, and the Association has strongly influenced the implementation of these.

The Association has been instrumental in the placing of markers at each end of the trail, and also a half-way marker.

Today one of the Association's functions is to assist and advise all those who wish to walk along this wonderful coastline - whether in short, relaxing strolls around a headland, or by more demanding long distance walks lasting several days, or by heroic attempts at covering the whole length of 630 miles (1014km) in one go!

The Association currently has a programme of funding improvements to the Coast Path and encourages all who walk and enjoy the trail to join as members and support this very important work. To see how Association funding grants have helped improve the South West Coast Path in recent years see page 182.

Funding provided by our members' subscriptions have enabled the Association to play a vital part in a range of necessary Coast Path projects, including getting bridges replaced, improving the path alignment, replacing the path where it has been lost to cliff falls and other general enhancements. That's all thanks to our members... well done everyone!

So if you haven't already done so, why not join 5,000+ other Coast Path enthusiasts and become a member of the Association? Then...

- Your subscription will help the Association promote, protect and enhance the Coast Path, including providing funding for specific projects;
- You will receive your copy of the Annual Guide free and keep up to date with what's happening on the path via our two free Newsletters each year
- You will be part of the "family" of those who love the Coast Path and know that your input is important to the path's well-being.

And remember, the Association represents ALL Coast Path walkers, not just the hardy long-distance walkers. Whether you plan to walk all 630 miles, or have already done so, or are happy to stroll along the coast on a Sunday afternoon or a couple of days a year when on holiday, if you love the Coast Path the Association is for you.

Aims and Objectives

1. To secure the protection, improvement and preservation of an acceptable South West Coast Path and public access thereto in order to improve the conditions of life of the users of the South West Coast Path.
2. To educate users of the South West Coast Path to a greater knowledge of, respect and care for the coast and the countryside.

In furtherance of these objectives the Association aims to work for and assist in:

1. Providing information about the South West Coast Path and its corridor to the public;
2. The organisation directed at the improvement and maintenance of the South West Coast Path.
3. Providing a forum in which different interests connected with the South West Coast Path (including its corridor) and its use can discuss problems of mutual concern.

Membership

Members receive an Annual Guide as part of their membership plus two Newsletters each year, with up-to-date information on the state of the path.

Subscriptions

Single	**£13.50**
Joint	**£15.00**
Associations & Local Authorities	**£23.00**
Life Membership	**£205.00**
Joint Life Membership	**£227.00**
Non-UK Membership	**£21.00**
Business Membership	**£23.00**

Payment may be made at www.swcp.org.uk or by telephoning 01752 896237 or by using a cheque or postal order made payable to the South West Coast Path Association.

We can accept the credit/debit cards shown below.

A Word to Beginners

Long distance path walking

These words are not for those hardy veterans who have all the gear, have done several paths already, and know all about it. However, we do get a number of letters each year from those who have not ventured before on long distance paths and need some advice. This we are pleased to try and provide and we do hope those who read this will find it helpful. However, it is easy to miss out things that folk wish to know, so if you who are new read this, and are still baffled, please contact us and we will try to provide the answers. As well as perhaps helping you, it will enable us to improve this section for another year and so be of help to more people.

Newcomers to the Coast Path

To get the feel of the Coast Path you are advised to take some day walks along it - there are some very good ones on the coast. Better still, look for the sections marked 'Easy' - start at one end and stop and turn back before you have half had enough. We say before half because it is always better to do a bit less and really enjoy it.

You can soon progress to setting out to walk a whole section either by using two cars or using public transport. One point here - if possible use the public transport to go out and walk back to your car or base; this means that you do not get yourself in a position of having to race the clock if you should take a bit more time than you thought.

If you are walking on your own, do please take additional care, for as you will appreciate, if you fall or twist an ankle there can be problems. If you are on your own therefore, you should leave a note with someone to make sure that you arrive at your destination. Not everyone is happy walking on their own and can feel lonely. There is also an added problem that you may try to do too much, so please bear this in mind.

There is no need to buy expensive equipment for the easy sections at the start; a pair of stout shoes and a rainproof jacket is all you need. As you progress, a small rucksack for 'eats' will be needed next.

Obviously if you can join a walking club and go out with them you will collect lots of friendly advice on all sorts of gear you may care to purchase as you become more serious about walking. Maps, guides, etc., are all listed in their appropriate sections.

For those who have walked, but not on long distance trails

Having stated the two big points, we will elaborate. You will not be able to accomplish in daily distance the same amount you normally cover in a day walk; you will have to settle for less. The first reason is that you will be carrying more equipment; you must for instance, have a complete change of clothing and footwear, possibly nightwear and toilet kit. For this you need a bigger rucksack so you will be carrying quite a bit more weight than you normally do. Secondly, there is what we call the 'wear' factor. For the first few days until you are really fit, it is just simply more tiring having to walk each day. The last point could be called the 'interest' factor. Usually, if you are walking a long distance path, you are further from your home base, in fresh fields and pastures new; there is more to see so you will need more time to look around.

If you usually accomplish 15 miles (24km) a day, aim, say, for 12 miles (19km). This is particularly important if you are booking ahead. You can find yourself tied to a treadmill which you cannot get off. Booking ahead has the advantage that you know there is a bed ahead. On the other hand, it does mean even if you are tired, have developed blisters, and the weather is diabolical, you have to go on. Be guided too by our `Trail Description' section and

The Stacks at Ladram Bay

Gurnard's Head

the terrain you are tackling. 6 miles (10km), say, of a `Severe' section can equal in effort 10-12 miles (16-19km) of an 'Easy' one.

Planning Your Walk

We have stated you must carry more gear and this is true. Having said that, think long and hard about every item you imagine you may need. You will be surprised - you may find you will not want it at all. Watch particularly those extras such as cameras and binoculars - they are often a source of considerable weight. One little additional point, many rucksacks, even modern ones, are not as waterproof as you think. A plastic liner, which can be obtained quite cheaply from rambling shops, etc., as an additional inner layer, may save you that most unpleasant discovery after a long day spent in the rain that your only change of clothing is no longer dry. We would also recommend that in addition to this liner, your dry clothing should then be enclosed in further plastic bags to ensure dryness. Trainer shoes are useful for wearing at the end of the day and can be worn on some parts of the path.

A sensible idea before undertaking a long walking holiday is to take, say, a weekend of two or three days first, walking continuously as a practice.

Another point to watch especially on our Coast Path is the availability of refreshment. At main holiday times, you will get it nearly everywhere, except for the few places we especially mention in our 'Coast Path Walk' section. Out of season, you will find it in surprisingly few places on long stretches of coast. The usual remarks about carrying stand-by supplies, therefore, certainly apply; better to carry an extra couple of bars of chocolate than to go hungry.

Walking alone

The Association has a scheme that enables single female members who are a little nervous about walking alone to team up with other single female members.

Contact the Administrator for information.

Guides, Maps & Books

Guides

Path Descriptions

Path Descriptions written by our Association are detailed accounts on all aspects of short sections of the Coast Path and include hand-drawn maps and illustrations. They cover in detail what cannot be included in our Annual Guide book.

- **Minehead to Porlock Weir** (9.5 miles/15.3km)
- **Porlock Weir to Lynmouth** (12.3 miles/19.8km)
- **Lynmouth to Ilfracombe** (18 miles/30km)
- **Ilfracombe to Croyde Bay** (13.6 miles/21.9km)
- **Croyde Bay to Barnstaple** (14.4 miles/23.1km)
- **Barnstaple to Westward Ho!** (19.1 miles/30.7km)
- **Westward Ho! to Clovelly** (11.2 miles/18km)
- **Clovelly to Hartland Quay** (10.3 miles/16.6km)
- **Hartland Quay to Bude** (15.4 miles/24.8km)
- **Bude to Crackington Haven** (10.2 miles/16.4km)
- **Crackington Haven to Tintagel** (12 miles/20km)
- **Tintagel to Port Isaac** (8 miles/13km)
- **Port Isaac to Padstow** (11.7 miles/18.9km)
- **Padstow to Porthcothan** (13.6 miles/21.8km)
- **Porthcothan to Newquay** (11.1 miles/17.9km)
- **Newquay to Perranporth** (10.8 miles/17.5km)
- **Perranporth to Portreath** (12.2 miles/19.7km)
- **Portreath to Hayle** (12.4 miles/19.9km)
- **Hayle to Pendeen Watch** (19.5 miles/31.3km)
- **Pendeen Watch to Porthcurno** (15.6 miles/25.2km)
- **Porthcurno to Penzance** (11.5 miles/18.5km)
- **Penzance to Porthleven** (14 miles/22.5km)
- **Porthleven to The Lizard** (13.9 miles/22.3km)
- **The Lizard to Coverack** (10.6 miles/17.1km)
- **Coverack to Helford** (13.1 miles/21.1km)
- **Helford to Falmouth** (10 miles/16.1km)
- **Falmouth to Portloe** (13.7 miles/22km)
- **Portloe to Mevagissey** (12.3 miles/19.8km)
- **Mevagissey to Charlestown** (7.2 miles/11.6km)
- **Charlestown to Fowey** (10.3 miles/16.6km)
- **Fowey to Polperro** (7.1 miles/11.5km)
- **Polperro to Looe** (5.0 miles/8.0km)
- **Looe to Portwrinkle** (7.6 miles/12.2km)
- **Portwrinkle to Plymouth** (13.3 miles/21.4km)
- **Plymouth (River Tamar) to Wembury (River Yealm)** (14.8 miles/23.8km)
- **Wembury (Warren Point) to Bigbury-on-Sea** (13.5 miles/21.8km)
- **Bigbury to Salcombe** (13 miles/21km)
- **Salcombe to Torcross** (12.9 miles/20.8km)
- **Torcross to Dartmouth** (10 miles/16km)
- **Dartmouth to Brixham** (10.8 miles/17.3km)
- **Brixham to Torquay** (8.4 miles/13.5km)
- **Torquay to Shaldon** (10.8 miles/17.3km)
- **Shaldon to Exmouth** (7.9 miles/12.7km)
- **Exmouth to Sidmouth** (13.1 miles/21km)
- **Sidmouth to Lyme Regis** (17 miles/27km)
- **Lyme Regis to West Bay** (9.7 miles/15.6km)
- **West Bay to Abbotsbury** (9.4 miles/15.2km)
- **Abbotsbury to Ferry Bridge** (10.9 miles/17.5km)
- **Isle of Portland** (13.2 miles/21.3km)
- **Ferry Bridge to Lulworth Cove** (13.2 miles/21.3km)
- **Lulworth to Kimmeridge, Lulworth Range** (7 miles/11km)
- **Kimmeridge to South Haven Point, Poole Harbour** (20.9 miles/33.6km)
- **Alternative Inland Route, West Bexington to Osmington Mills** (18 miles/28km)

These Path Descriptions are all priced at £1.00 including UK postage. A complete set of Path Descriptions is priced £45.00. All are available to purchase online or from the Administrator (see page 3). *(Please note that Path Descriptions are continually revised. Updates of certain distances and route details are in the process of being produced.)*

The Reverse Guide

The Association has written a description of the Trail for those walking in the Poole to Minehead direction. It deals only with the path so this Annual Guide will be necessary for all the other information. Our Reverse Guide supplement was comprehensively revised in 2008.

Price £4.00 including UK postage

Maps

We are sometimes asked if you require a map sheet as well as a guide book and our advice is certainly yes. One does not get as badly lost on the Coast Path as you can on inland paths, but a map is an asset nonetheless. Furthermore many walkers derive much interest from looking at their route in relation to the rest of the countryside on ordinary walks, and the same applies just as much, if not more so, on our Coast Path. The National Trail Guides offer a partial solution with their maps, but even these are not as useful as a map sheet.

Harvey Maps

Walk for a week with just one map - those who have walked in the Scottish Highlands or the Lake District will know of Harvey Maps.

Produced at a scale of 1:40 000 the walkers' maps for the South West Coast Path are ideal for this National Trail which, because it is following a geographic feature, i.e. the coast, route finding does not usually present any real difficulties.

Six maps cover the entire route of the Coast Path compared with fourteen OS Landranger maps or seventeen OS Explorer/Outdoor Leisure maps. The maps have a similar amount of detail as Landranger maps for the walker yet without the administrative symbols that sometimes obscure the detail. The maps are of a more manageable size (folding to approx 240 x 120mm or 9.52" x 4.68") and are waterproof. Weight wise (without the wallet) they are a mere 84g compared with Landrangers at 74g and Explorers at 110g (without their card covers). Another useful feature is the provision on areas of the map not needed for walking (in this case the sea) of much important information about the Trail and services along the way.

Map 1 Minehead to Bude
Map 2 Bude to Portreath
Map 3 Portreath to Lizard
Map 4 Lizard to Plymouth
Map 5 Plymouth to Sidmouth
Map 6 Sidmouth to Poole

They are priced at £9.95 each and are becoming more widely available at branches of Waterstone's and Cotswold Outdoors (or direct from Harvey Maps). For further details visit www.harveymaps.co.uk or telephone 01786 841202, fax 01786 841098, sales@harveymaps.co.uk

They offer the complete set for £49.75.

1:50 000 Ordnance Survey Maps

The Metric 1:50 000 Landranger Series needed to cover the coast from Minehead in Somerset to Poole Harbour in Dorset are as follows, working round the coast from Minehead.

181 Minehead & Brendon Hills
180 Barnstaple & Ilfracombe
190 Bude & Clovelly
200 Newquay & Bodmin
204 Truro & Falmouth
203 Land's End & The Lizard
204 Truro & Falmouth
200 Newquay & Bodmin
201 Plymouth & Launceston
202 Torbay & South Dartmoor
192 Exeter & Sidmouth
193 Taunton & Lyme Regis
194 Dorchester & Weymouth
195 Bournemouth & Purbeck

Geevor Mines

Geographers A-Z Maps

The Geographers A-Z Map Company has now mapped the entire 630 miles of the South West Coast Path and covered the entire route in five new and convenient Adventure Atlases.

The maps use 1:25,000 mapping, updated by A-Z cartographers, and each one includes a comprehensive index, outdoor information and QR barcodes to provide an instant connection to the latest local information including weather and tide times.

The five maps cover North Devon and Somerset (Minehead to Bude), North Cornwall (Bude to Land's End), South Cornwall (Land's End to Plymouth), South Devon (Plymouth to Lyme Regis) and Dorset (Lyme Regis to Poole). The maps cost £7.95 each – check them out and order them at www.az.co.uk/adventure.

1:25 000 Ordnance Survey Maps

In path order, from Minehead the Coast Path is on 2½" maps.

- **Outdoor Leisure 9** Exmoor
- **Explorer 139** Bideford, Ilfracombe and Barnstaple
- **Explorer 126** Clovelly and Hartland
- **Explorer 111** Bude, Boscastle and Tintagel
- **Explorer 109** Bodmin Moor (depicts Coast Path from Boscastle to Portgaverne)
- **Explorer 106** Newquay and Padstow
- **Explorer 104** Redruth, St Agnes, Camborne and Perranporth
- **Explorer 102** Land's End
- **Explorer 103** The Lizard
- **Explorer 105** Falmouth and Mevagissey
- **Explorer 107** St Austell and Liskeard
- **Explorer 108** Lower Tamar Valley and Plymouth
- **Explorer OL20** South Devon
- **Explorer 110** Torquay and Dawlish
- **Explorer 115** Exmouth and Sidmouth
- **Explorer 116** Lyme Regis and Bridport
- **Outdoor Leisure 15** Purbeck and South Dorset

All Harvey and OS maps can be obtained from most bookshops. They, including Harvey Maps, may also be obtained from KenRoy Thompson Limited, 25 Cobourg Street, Plymouth PL1 1SR
Tel: 01752 227693
Email: maps@kenroythompson.co.uk
Website: kenroythompson.co.uk

POST FREE TO UK MEMBERS OF THE SOUTH WEST COAST PATH ASSOCIATION (Credit cards accepted).

The above is a comprehensive list of maps for the South West Coast Path. In Section 3 you will also find the relevant maps listed for each section of the Coast Path.

Books

These publications are available from bookshops.

This list is not exhaustive; there are a number of other books available but we have tried hard to list all those which are really useful and even those not really useful that you might think would be.

South West Coast Path - Minehead to South Haven Point (ISBN 1-85284-379-9)

An excellent pocket sized book by Paddy Dillon (March 2003). We can recommend it as most useful. It has stunning photographs and OS maps. Available from Cicerone Press, 2 Police Square, Milnthorpe, Cumbria LA7 7PY at £12.95 and bookshops. Third print 2007 ISBN 978-1-85284-379-3.

National Trail Guides -

published by Aurum Press in association with Natural England. They are available from bookshops, or in case of difficulty, from Aurum Press, 25 Bedford Avenue, London WC1B 3AT. These are good guide books with good maps. An excellent venture by those involved.

Minehead to Padstow
by Roland Tarr (May 2011)

Padstow to Falmouth
by John Macadam (May 2011)

Falmouth to Exmouth
by Brian Le Messurier (May 2011)

Exmouth to Poole
by Roland Tarr (May 2011)

Most Tourist Information Centres (see our Accommodation section) have good supplies of leaflets and books relating to their local areas. We suggest you telephone or write to them and ask what is available.

Please also see the Association's shop on pages 186-189 and remember that Tourist Information Centres (see page 179) are a source of local leaflets and books.

Railways

Help in planning your journey to the south west can be obtained at www.transportdirect.info

Throughout the year there is a regular service of direct First Great Western High Speed services linking London Paddington with Taunton, Exeter St. David's, Newton Abbot, Plymouth and Cornwall. There are also regular Arriva Cross Country Trains services linking Birmingham, the North West, North East and Scotland with Taunton, Exeter St. David's, Plymouth, Cornwall and Bournemouth.

There is also a First Great Western overnight sleeper service between Paddington and Penzance.

All these services offer a range of on-train facilities including catering and on most First Great Western High Speed services during the school holidays, coach E is dedicated for the use of families. During the high season (May to September), demand for seats is high so it is recommended that seats are reserved in advance to ensure a comfortable journey. There is a half hourly South West Trains service linking London Waterloo, Woking, Basingstoke and Southampton with Bournemouth, Poole, Wareham (for Swanage), Dorchester (for Bridport and Lyme Regis) and Weymouth for those intending to walk the Dorset end of the Coast Path.

East Devon is also served by South West Trains with an hourly service from London Waterloo to Exeter St David's calling at Woking, Basingstoke and Salisbury to Axminster (for Lyme Regis & Seaton), Honiton (for Sidmouth), and Exeter Central (for Exmouth branch).

First Great Western West offers long distance and most local trains in the South West. The long distance trains link Cardiff and Bristol with Exeter, Penzance, Plymouth, Portsmouth, Salisbury, Southampton and Weymouth. The local services on the branch lines of Devon and Cornwall offer connections into and out of First Great Western and Arriva Cross Country services, and South West Trains at Exeter for the Exmouth branch.

For those walking the Coast Path in the far west, why not consider using the First Great Western night sleeper service from Paddington to Penzance? This is a unique way to arrive on the Coast Path ready to walk fully refreshed.

First Great Western West local routes run Sunday services on the routes listed below

- **Westbury - Yeovil - Weymouth**
- **Liskeard - Looe**
- **Exeter - Barnstaple**
- **Par - Newquay**
- **Exeter - Exmouth**
- **Truro - Falmouth**
- **Newton Abbot -Torquay - Paignton**
- **St Erth - St Ives**
- **Plymouth - Gunnislake**

The web address for First Great Western High Speed and West services is **www.firstgreatwestern.co.uk**

To obtain train information, book tickets and reserve seats call the National Rail Enquiries Service on 08457 484950 (24 hours a day) or via the website **www.nationalrail.co.uk**

The web address for Arriva is **www.crosscountrytrains.co.uk**

The web address for South West Trains is **www.southwesttrains.co.uk**

Bus Services

A National Transport Enquiry Service has been established. For all timetable enquiries in South West England, call Traveline on 0871 200 2233 or www.travelinesw.com

The main bus operative contact details are: First Devon and Cornwall Tel: 0845 600 1420 **www.firstgroup.com.**

Tourist Information Centres can be very helpful with bus enquiries. For details of all coastal TICs see our Accommodation section at the back of this book.

Access to the start of the Path

Access to the start of the path can be made locally and from outside the region, with First's bus service 28 linking Minehead to the mainline railway station at Taunton. Service 28 Taunton - Minehead currently operates on an half-hourly frequency up to the early evenings from Monday to Saturdays.

On Sundays service 28 operates less frequently. For service 28 timetable enquiries telephone First - Taunton. Tel: 01823 272033. National Express operates some direct services to Minehead and others to Taunton where passengers can change to First Service 28 for Minehead. For more information about national coach services to the South West, telephone National Express Tel: 0870 580 8080 (this is charged at local call rates).

Getting to the South West

Airports

There are airports in or near towns close to the Coast Path. In path order, they are:

Newquay Airport
For flights to and from the Isles of Scilly, Glasgow, Edinburgh, Gatwick, Manchester & East Midlands; also Dusseldorf:
St Mawgan, Newquay TR8 4RQ
Tel: 01637 860600
www.newquaycornwallairport.com

Land's End
For flights to the Isles of Scilly:
Information from Isles of Scilly Travel, Steamship House, Quay Street, Penzance TR18 4BZ
Tel: 01736 334220
www.islesofscilly-travel.co.uk

Exeter
Exeter International Airport, Exeter, EX5 2BD
Tel: 01392 446446
www.exeter-airport.co.uk

Bournemouth
Bournemouth Airport Ltd., Christchurch, Bournemouth BH23 6SE
Tel: 01202 364000
www.bournemouthairport.com

Sea Transport & Coastal Cruises

Brittany Ferries provide a ferry link as follows to the South West Coast Path: Plymouth/Roscoff; Poole/Cherbourg (Summer only); Plymouth/Santander.
Tel: 0871 244 0744
www.brittany-ferries.co.uk, or contact by mail to Brittany Ferries, Millbay, Plymouth, Devon, PL1 3EW

The famous pleasure steamers Waverley and Balmoral provide both cruises and transport, to and from the Exmoor Coast.

From May until late September these sea-going ships provide transport to South Wales, Bristol, North Somerset, Lundy Island and the Exmoor Coast.

Sailings are to and from Ilfracombe, Bideford & Minehead. The timetable is subject to the Bristol Channel tides which have the second highest rise and fall in the world. Free copies of the full programme are available from:
Waverley Excursions Ltd.,
The Waverley Terminal,
36 Lancefield Quay, Glasgow G3 8HA
www.waverleyexcursions.co.uk
Tel: 0845 1304647, or from Tourist Information Centres in West Somerset and North Devon.

Pen Enys Point

Planning your walking holiday in the south west can be helped at www.travelinesw.com or telephone 0871 200 2233 (calls cost 10 per minute from a BT landline; other providers and mobiles may vary).

Private Branch Line Railways

Bishops Lydeard to Minehead

The West Somerset Railway runs steam trains through 20 scenic miles (32 km) to Minehead. Bishops Lydeard is 4 miles (6 km) outside Taunton and easily accessible by bus. The service operates between March and October. For details contact the company at 'The Railway Station', Minehead TA24 5BG
Tel: 01643 704996 Book online at
www.west-somerset-railway.co.uk

Paignton to Kingswear (Dartmouth)

For the rambler who is also a railway enthusiast, the Paignton and Dartmouth Steam Railway is a `must'. This most attractive line runs from Paignton to Goodrington, Churston and Kingswear and operates preserved Great Western steam locomotives and rolling-stock. The line passes through some delightful coastal and river scenery, and a trip on the railway could easily be combined with a walk to make a very pleasant day out. Steam trains operate on selected dates in April, May and October; daily June - September; Santa specials in December. For details contact Queens Park Station, Torbay Road, Paignton TQ4 6AF
Tel: 01803 555872
www.paignton-steamrailway.co.uk.

The Bodmin & Wenford Railway

runs between Bodmin Parkway to Bodmin General is a service that could prove useful for those requiring bus transport to the coast.
Tel: 0845 125 9678
www.bodminandwenfordrailway.co.uk

The Swanage Railway

which links a large park and ride facility at Norden, north west of Corfe Castle to Swanage, could also prove useful for those requiring car parking (not long stay) with access by rail to the Coast Path. If you require information contact the enquiry line on
Tel: 01929 425800
www.swanagerailway.co.uk

Bus Information

Listed below, in path order, are details of services and information available from County Councils and local bus operators; it is intended for guidance use only. All information provided is correct at the time of going to print; responsibility for any inaccuracies or changes cannot be accepted by County Councils or bus operators. For up to date bus service information, telephone the relevant numbers given in the following paragraphs.

Somerset

For service 28 from Taunton to Minehead and services 30/30A from Taunton to Lyme Regis and Weymouth via Axminster (change buses) contact First, The Bus Station, Tower Street, Taunton, TA1 4AF
Tel: 0845 602 0156
www.firstgroup.com

For service 18 from Taunton to Minehead contact Webberbus, Unit 8C, Beech Business Park, Bristol Road, Bridgwater, TA6 4FF
Tel: 0800 096 3039
www.webberbus.com

For service 39/300 from Minehead to Porlock/ Lynmouth contact Quantock Motor Services, The Coal Yard, Broadgauge Business Park, Station Road, Bishops Lydeard, TA4 3BU
Tel: 01823 430202.
www.quantockmotorservices.co.uk

Somerset County Council produces booklets detailing the timetables of all public bus services in Somerset which can be downloaded at www.somerset.gov.uk/timetables, or requested from Transporting Somerset, PPC302A, County Hall, Taunton, TA1 4DY
Tel: 0845 345 9155
Email: transport@somerset.gov.uk
www.somerset.gov.uk

North Devon

The North Devon coast has a range of bus services which may be of use to coastal walkers. The greatest choice of coastal destinations is provided from Barnstaple. The principal services are: 309/310 Barnstaple to Lynton; Services 3, 30, 301 Barnstaple to llfracombe and Combe Martin; 308 Barnstaple to Georgeham; 303 Barnstaple, to Woolacombe; 1, Barnstaple to Bideford and Westward Ho!; 2, Barnstaple to Bideford and Appledore and 319 Barnstaple to Bideford,

Clovelly and Hartland. Also 21 Barnstaple to Bideford and Westward Ho! and 21A Ilfracombe, Barnstaple to Bideford and Appledore. Note that the number prefix refers to the bus route number. During the Summer, Exmoor Coastlink 300 operates daily from Ilfracombe to Lynton, Lynmouth (changing at Lynmouth) for Porlock and Minehead, with glorious coastal views along much of the route.

Those who are walking between North Devon and North Cornwall may find First Devon and Cornwall X9 service or Western Greyhound 599 from Exeter to Bude a useful link.

The above services are operated by First Devon and Cornwall, Filers Travel, Quantock Motor Services, Stagecoach South West, TW Coaches and Western Greyhound. For timetable enquiries telephone Traveline - 0871 2002233, 0700-2100 daily, www.traveline.org.uk

Devon County Council produces an annual timetable guide from May each year, entitled 'North Devon Public Transport Guide'. They are available from Tourist Information Centres, Libraries, bus operators or by telephoning the DevonBus enquiry line Barnstaple: 01271 382800 or Exeter 01392 382800, Monday - Friday 0900-1700. Email: devonbus@devon.gov.uk www.devon.gov.uk.
Also see www.devon.gov.uk where there is a new interactive bus map.

Cornwall

Cornwall Council, in conjunction with local bus operators, produces a public transport guide, published in May each year, covering the whole of Cornwall. It is available by post, price £2.50, from The Passenger Transport Unit, Carrick House, Pydar Street, Truro, Cornwall, TR1 1EB. Telephone 0300 1234 222. The timetable can also be obtained, free of charge, locally from bus stations, tourist information centres and libraries as can a county public transport map showing all bus and rail routes with a summary of frequencies. Full details on all the services contained in the guide can also be obtained from www.cornwallpublictransport.info

Public transport information can also be obtained from Traveline 0871 200 22 33, www.traveline.org.uk. The main bus operator contact details are: First Devon and Cornwall, Tel: 0845 600 1420 www.firstgroup.com Western Greyhound, Tel: 01637 871871, www.westerngreyhound.com

The principal routes serving coastal areas are:

First Services: 1 Penzance - Land's End, 2 Penzance - Helston - Falmouth/Truro, 10 Penzance - St Just, 16 Penzance - Nancledra - St Ives, 17 St Ives - Penzance, 27 Truro - St Austell - Par , 34 Helston - Redruth, 35 Helston - Helford Passage - Falmouth, 36 Helston - Coverack, 37 Helston - The Lizard, 81 Cremyll to Plymouth, 85 Truro - St Agnes, 88 Truro - Falmouth, 300 Penzance - Land's End - St Just - St Ives (summer only), 500 Truro - Falmouth - Helford Passage

Western Greyhound services:
501 Penzance - Land's End,
504 Penzance - Mousehole - Porthcurno - Land's End - St Just, 508 Penzance - Zennor - St Ives, 510 Wadebridge - Camelford - Exeter 515 Penzance - Hayle - Gwithian - St Ives, 524/526 Fowey - Par - St Austell - Mevagissey - Gorran Haven, 525/526 Fowey - Par - Charlestown - Mevagissey - Gorran Haven, 547 Newquay - Perranporth - St Agnes - St Ives, 550/551 Truro - Veryan - St Mawes, 555 Bodmin Parkway - Bodmin - Wadebridge - Padstow, 556 Newquay - Padstow, 572 Polperro - Looe - Plymouth, 573/574 Polperro - Looe - Liskeard - Callington, 584 Wadebridge - Port Isaac - Camelford, 591/592/594/597/598 Newquay - Perranporth - St Agnes - Truro - Newquay 595 Wadebridge - Camelford - Boscastle - Tintagel - Bude, 599 Bude - Exeter

Travel Cornwall:
403 Newquay - Perranporth - St Agnes - Truro

Stagecoach:
X9 Bude - Exeter
Information correct as of December 2012

South Devon

The coastline between Plymouth and Exeter is accessible by bus from many inland towns. The principal services are:

80/81 Plymouth to Torpoint; 34 Plymouth City Centre and Admirals Hard for Cremyll Ferry (buses meet ferry and through ticket available); 2 Plymouth City Centre to Mount Batten; 54 Plymouth to Bovisand (Summer only); 49 Plymouth to Heybrook Bay; 48 Plymouth to Wembury; 94 Plymouth to Noss Mayo; 93 Plymouth to Kingsbridge & Dartmouth; X80 Plymouth to Paignton & Torquay; X38 Plymouth to Exeter; X64 Exeter to Totnes (Kingsbridge and Salcombe on Sundays), 164 Totnes to Kingsbridge; X81 Torquay and Totnes to Dartmouth; 162 Kingsbridge to Hope Cove; 606 Kingsbridge to Salcombe; 120 Kingswear to Paignton;

22, 24 Kingswear to Brixham; 12 Brixham & Paignton to Torquay and Newton Abbot; 11 Torquay to Teignmouth; 2 Newton Abbot to Teignmouth, Dawlish and Exeter. 25 Goodrington to Paignton and Stoke Gabriel; 17 Brixham to Furzeham, Wall Park and The Quay; X46 Paignton to Torquay and Exeter; 88 Paignton to Totnes, Buckfastleigh, Ashburton and Newton Abbot; X80 Torquay to Paignton, Totnes, Ivybridge and Plymouth.

The above services are operated by First, Tally Ho, Plymouth Citybus, Stagecoach South West and Dart Pleasure Craft.
For timetable enquiries telephone Traveline on 0871 200 2233.

Devon County Council produces annual timetable guides, from May each year for the South Hams and Teignbridge areas. They are available from Devon bus on Traveline 0871 200 2233, or from Salcombe TIC 01548 843927.

Plymouth Citybus map and services are available from from Plymouth Citybus on 01752 662271 or www.citycoach.co.uk
Also see www.devon.gov.uk where there is a new interactive bus map.

East Devon

The East Devon coastline is accessible by bus from Exeter, Ottery St. Mary, Honiton and Axminster. The principal services are:

X53 Exeter to Beer, Seaton, (summer only) Lyme Regis, Bridport, West Bay and Weymouth;
X53 Exeter to Wareham, Poole, 20 Taunton to Seaton; 57 Exeter to Exmouth, change Exmouth for service 157 (through fares available) to Budleigh Salterton and Sidmouth; 52A Exeter to Sidmouth & Seaton; 52B Exeter to Sidmouth & Honiton; 382 Ottery St. Mary to Sidmouth; 885 Axminster to Seaton;
30 Taunton to Axminster change at Axminster for service 31, 31 Axminster to Lyme Regis (and continues to Bridport, Dorchester and Weymouth); 899 Sidmouth to Branscombe, Beer and Seaton. On Summer Sundays service 56B operates between Sidmouth, Honiton, Ottery St Mary & Exeter.

The above services are operated by Stagecoach South West, Axe Valley Mini-Travel and First Hampshire and Dorset. For timetable enquiries telephone Traveline public transport info.(Tel: 0871 200 2233) daily 0700-2100.

Devon County Council produces an annual timetable guide from May each year, entitled `East Devon Public Transport Guide'- they are available from Tourist Information Centres, libraries, bus operators or by telephoning the DevonBus enquiry line on Exeter (Tel: 01392 382800) Monday-Friday 0900-1700.

Bus Map - Other useful information provided by Devon County Council includes the public transport map. This depicts all bus routes and railway lines throughout the county and gives a summary of service frequency. It is available from Tourist Information Centres, libraries and bus stations or by telephoning the DevonBus enquiry line on Barnstaple (Tel: 01271 382800) or Exeter (Tel: 01392 382800) Monday-Friday 0900-1700 or www.devon.gov.uk.

Dorset

The Dorset Coast is accessible by bus from various inland points with train connections for the distant traveller. The principal routes are listed below.

Service 31 provides hourly journeys from Mondays to Saturdays between Weymouth-Dorchester-Bridport-Lyme Regis and Axminster, calling at Axminster and Dorchester South rail stations for onward travel. The service operates until late in the evening. There is a two hourly service along the same route on Sundays. Passengers benefit from low floor buses that provide easy access and greater comfort. Contact First Hampshire and Dorset. Tel: 0870 010 60 22.

Services 103 and 104 provide journeys between Dorchester-Wool-Bovington/ Wareham. Operated by Damory Coaches and Dorset Community Transport respectively the services run Monday to Saturday with four services a day serving Lulworth Cove.

Service X53 is fully accessible and operates several journeys each day between Poole-Wareham-Weymouth-Lyme Regis and Exeter. During the winter, the Sunday service is reduced and operates until December between Weymouth and Lyme Regis. Details from First Hampshire and Dorset, see above.

Service X43 operates between Weymouth, Wareham and Swanage during the summer months.

Service 40 runs daily between Poole, Swanage and Wareham. Service 44 operates between Swanage, Harmans Cross and Worth Matravers from Monday to Saturday. Details from Wilts & Dorset Bus Company, Tel: 01202 673555.

Service 50 operates daily between Bournemouth and Swanage via the Sandbanks Ferry. Service 52 runs from the Sandbanks ferry into Poole town centre daily, (not winter Sundays) details from Wilts & Dorset Bus Company,
Tel: 01983 827005.

Frequent services run to Portland from Weymouth and Dorchester. They are mainly operated by First Hampshire and Dorset and South West Coaches, details above.

Dorset County Council produces comprehensive timetable information including a countywide Bus and Rail Map.

All information is available from Tourist Information Centres or Dorset Passenger Transport, County Hall, Dorchester, DT1 1XJ. Tel: 01305 225165 or Email: publictransport@dorsetcc.gov.uk

Timetables can be downloaded at www.dorsetforyou.com/bustimes

Important Information: There may be changes to services and/or operators from April 2012. For up to date information, visit www.dorsetforyou.com/bustimes or contact Dorset Passenger Transport - details as above.

Ferries & River Crossings

The nature of the Coast Path means that many ferries must be used to cross estuaries along the length of the path. It is recommended the ferry operator be contacted direct for the service to be used. Please do this especially when a fairly late timing is expected and it is necessary to confirm the time of the last run. Also do this when using outside the main tourist season or if use by a party of walkers is planned.

Full ferry details are shown here. Less detailed ferry information is also included in the relevant Walk Section text.

The walker tends to view feet as the only certain method of progress - and why not? Unfortunately, the absolute purist would need to be an olympic-class swimmer not to have to use ferries on the South West Coast Path. However, a certain amount of scepticism is helpful, absolute reliance on ferries is not advised. There are other ferries available on the path which walkers may wish to use for diversions or shortcuts. We have attempted to list those directly necessary.

The ferry crossings encountered, in path order, are: River Torridge (Instow/Appledore) (optional); River Camel (Rock/Padstow); River Gannel (Newquay/Crantock); Helford River (Helford/Helford Passage); Fal Estuary (Falmouth/St Mawes and St Mawes/Place); River Fowey (Fowey/Polruan); River Tamar (Cremyll/Plymouth); River Yealm (Wembury/Noss Mayo); River Avon (Bigbury-on-Sea/Bantham); River Dart (Dartmouth/Kingswear); River Teign (Shaldon/Teignmouth); River Exe (Starcross/Exmouth, Turf/Topsham); Weymouth Harbour.

Instow/Appledore (River Torridge)

This ferry service, an optional means of crossing the Torridge without passing through Bideford, has recently been revived after many years. Tel: 07757 620999
Website: www.appledoreinstowferry.com
Email: contact@appledoreinstowferry.com
The ferry will operate from early April 2013 until October.

Rock/Padstow (River Camel)

Black Tor Ferry, Padstow Harbour Commissioners, Harbour Office, West Quay, Padstow, Cornwall PL28 8AQ
Tel: 01841 532239 Mobile: 07773 081574
Fax: 01841 5333346
Website: www.padstow-harbour.co.uk
Email: padstowharbour@btconnect.com
Ferry operates all year at 20 min intervals
08:00 to 18:50 (Summer)
08:00 to 19:50 (mid July-end August)
08:00 to 16:50 (winter)

Water taxi

A water taxi service operates between Rock and Padstow between 19:00 and midnight from Easter to 31st October, weather and tides permitting. Contact: GB Smith&Son
Tel: 01208 862815 (office hours)
Fax: 01208 863090
Website: www.rock-watertaxi.co.uk
Email: info@rock-watertaxi.co.uk
Or contact the boat direct on 07778 105297.

Newquay/Crantock (River Gannel)

Fern Pit Café & Ferry, G A Northey and G King (Proprietors), Fern Pit, Riverside Crescent, Newquay, Cornwall TR7 1PJ
Tel: 01637 873181 Website: www.fernpit.co.uk
Email: mail@fernpit.co.uk
Ferry operates as follows: 18th May to mid September continuous, 7 days a week, 10:00-18:00. Weather dependant.

Gillan Creek

Anthony Jenkin Tel: 01326 231357
Ferry operates most days Easter, and April 1st to 30th October
Website: www.stanthony.co.uk
Email: anthony@stanthony.co.uk

Helford River
River Boats, Helford Passage, Falmouth, Cornwall Tel: 01326 250770
Website: www.helford-river-boats.co.uk
Email: info@helford-river-boats.co.uk
Ferry operates Easter to 31st October 09:30 to 17:30 daily on demand.
It is possible to use local taxi services if the ferry is not operating - Autocabs, tel: 01326 573773 or Cove Cars, tel: 07980 814058.

Falmouth/St Mawes (River Fal)
Cornwall Ferries, 2 Ferry Cottages, Feock, Truro, Cornwall TR3 6QT
Tel: 01326 313201 - Kiosk (summer)
Tel: 01872 861910
Website: www.falriver.co.uk
Ferry operates all year.
June-October inclusive 3 ferries per hour, fewer at other times. Ferries operate from Falmouth Prince of Wales Pier all year and Custom House Quay summer only.

St Mawes/Place (Percuil River)
Cornwall Ferries (see above)
Mobile: 07791 283884
Ferry operates Easter to 31st October 09:30 to 17:00, every half hour.
There is also Falmouth Water Taxi service which operates between Falmouth and St Mawes or Place, weather permitting, between March and October, 12:00 to 15:00. If needed, it is best to telephone a day in advance.
Tel: Brian Kneebone, 07970 242258 or 07522 446659.
www.falmouthwatertaxi.co.uk

Fowey/Polruan (River Fowey)
Polruan Ferry Co Ltd, Toms Yard, East Street Polruan-by-Fowey, Cornwall PL23 1PB
Tel: 01726 870232
Ferry operates all year at 5-10 min intervals.
07:15 to 23:00 1st May-30th September (Saturdays 07:30 start, Sundays 09:00 start)
07:15 to 19:00 1st October-30th April (Saturdays 07:30 start, Sundays 10:00 to 17:00). Website: ctomsandson.co.uk
enquiries@ctomsandson.co.uk

Cremyll/Plymouth
Cremyll Ferry, Cremyll Quay, Cremyll, Torpoint, Cornwall PL10 1HX
Tel: 01752 822105 (full timetable available - phone above no.) www.tamarcruising.com
Email: info@tamarcruising.com
The ferry operates depending on weather, tides and other circumstances permitting.
All year round at 30 minute intervals.
Summer Service from 1st April to 30th September.
From Mt Edgcumbe:
Weekdays 06:45 to 20:30, Saturdays 08:00 to 21:30, Sundays 09:00 to 21:00.
From Plymouth: Weekdays 07:15 to 20:45. Saturdays 08:15 to 21:45, Sundays 09:15 to 21:15.
Winter Service from 1st October to 31st March.
From Mt Edgcumbe:
Weekdays 06:45 to 18:30. Saturdays 08:00 to 18:30, Sundays 09:00 to 18:00.
From Plymouth:
Weekdays 07:15 to 18:45, Saturdays 08:15 to 18:45, Sundays 09:15 to 18:15.
Closed Christmas, Boxing & New Year's Days
We urge you to contact the ferry operator direct if you are relying on this service, particularly if you are anticipating a fairly late finish and need to confirm the time of its last run. Further information about the Cremyll ferry can be found at www.plymouth.gov.uk/cremyllferry

Sutton Harbour/Mount Batten
Mount Batten Ferry 07930 838614
www.mountbattenferry.com
info@soundcruising.com
All year round. Runs 15 and 45 minutes past the hour from The Barbican, and on the hour and 30 minutes past from Mount Batten Point. Ferry starts at 07:45 from The Barbican on weekdays, and from 08:45 at weekends. Last ferry departs Mount Batten at 18:15 in winter, and 22:30 in summer.
We urge you to contact the ferry operator direct if you are relying on this service, particularly if you are anticipating a fairly late finish and need to confirm the time of its last run.

Wembury (Warren Point)/Noss Mayo (River Yealm)
Bill Gregor, 1 Underhaye, Yealmpton, Plymouth, Devon PL8 2JR
Tel: 01752 880079 Mobile: 07817 132757
Ferry operates 2nd April to 30th September, on demand, 10:00 to 12:00 and 15:00 to 16:00. During fine weather, weekends, and school holidays ferry will operate 10:00 to 16:00 daily, but please phone first to confirm.
Eco-Taxi based in Kingsbridge will carry walkers between Plymouth and Dartmouth and from all estuaries in South Devon.
Tel: 01548 856347 or 07811 385275.
regal7@hotmail.co.uk
Alternatively, Ivy Cabs may also carry walkers round the South Hams estuaries.
Tel: 01752 696969

Bigbury/Bantham (River Avon)

Marsh Dawes, The Boathouse,
Bantham, Kingsbridge, Devon.
Tel: 01548 561196 Mobile: 07837 361306
Ferry operates 29th April - 28th September, daily except Sundays, 10:00 to 11:00 and 15:00 to 16:00. Eco-Taxi based in Kingsbridge will carry walkers between Plymouth and Dartmouth
and from all estuaries in South Devon.
Tel: 01548 856347 or 07811 385275
regal7@hotmail.co.uk
Alternatively, Ivy Cabs may also carry walkers round the South Hams estuaries.
Tel: 01752 696969

Salcombe to East Portlemouth Ferry

The Salcombe Ferry
Tel: 01548 842061/560558
Mobile: 06679319375 Simon Shortman
All year round.
Winter: ½ hourly between 08:00 to 17:30 hrs.
Summer: Continuous service 08:00 to 19:00 hrs. (July & August) 08:30 hrs start weekends and bank holidays. Please note that the ferry point is located at the steps from the Ferry Hotel. We urge you to contact the ferry operator direct if you are relying on this service, particularly if you are anticipating a fairly late finish and need to confirm the time of its last run.

Dartmouth/Kingswear (River Dart)

South Hams District Council,
Lower Ferry Office, The Square,
Kingswear, Dartmouth TQ6 0AA
Tel: 01803 752342 Fax: 01803 752227
www.southhams.gov.uk/
sp-dartmouthlowerferry
Ferry operates all year on a continuous service 07:00 to 22:45, Sundays 08:00 to 22:45

Dartmouth Passenger Ferry (River Dart)

Dartmouth Steam Railway & River Boat Co.
5 Lower Street, Dartmouth TQ6 9AJ
Tel: 01803 555872
www.dartmouthrailriver.co.uk
Ferry operates all year on a continuous service 07:30 to 23:10, Sundays 09:00 to 23:10.

Shaldon/Teignmouth

The ferry operates:

April - Mid July	08:00 to 18:00
Mid July - End August	08:00 to Dusk
September - October	08:00 to 18:00
November - January	08:00 to 16:30*
February - March	08:00 to 17:00*

Special event finish time is posted on the day on the ferry notice board.
*Winter weekends from November to March the ferry starts at 1000.
Ferry mobile: 07896 711822
Tel: 01626 215617
www.teignbridge.gov.uk/riverteignferry
leisure@teignbridge.gov.uk
If operating, the ferry runs from the beach opposite the Ferry Boat Inn.

Starcross/Exmouth (River Exe)

Mr Mark Rackley, Starcross Pier and Pleasure Company, 26 Marine Parade, Dawlish,
Devon EX7 9DL
Tel: 01626 862452 or 07974 022536
Ferry operates mid-April - end October, hourly, 7 days a week. From Starcross, on the hour from 10:10 until 16:10 (Easter and October), until 17:10 (mid-May, and June-mid September), until 18:00 (August). From Exmouth, on the half hour from 10:40 until 16:40 (Easter and October), until 17:40 (mid-May and June-mid September), until 18:15 (August).

Turf/Topsham (River Exe)

Steve Garrett Tel: 07778 370582
www.topshamtoturfferry.co.uk
Email: seadreamferry@btinternet.com
Ferry operates 7 days a week, Easter holiday, mid-May - mid-September and weekends April-October; from Turf 11:45 to 16:00 and from Topsham 11:30 to 15:15.

Topsham Ferry (River Exe) (between Topsham Quay riverside and Topsham Lock canalside)

Exeter City Council
Canals and Rivers Department
Tel: 01392 274306 (office); 07801 203338 (ferryman).
Ferry operates Easter-September daily except Tuesdays, 11:00 to 17:00; October-March Saturdays, Sundays and Bank Holidays 11:00 to 17:00 or sunset. Wave or phone for service. Between April and September the ferry may be available outside these hours, weather and tides permitting; phone for details.

Weymouth Harbour

Weymouth and Portland Borough Council,
Harbour Master's Office,
3 Custom House Quay, Weymouth DT4 8BG
Tel: 01305 838423
Ferry operates (rowing boat):

Easter-June	11:00 to 15:00
July	09:30 to 17:00
August	09:30 to 19:00
September-October	11.00 to 15.00

All weather permitting.
www.harbour.weymouth.gov.uk
www.harbour.weymouth.gov.uk

South Haven Point to Sandbanks, Poole
See end of Walk 70, page 130.

South Haven Point/Sandbanks
Shell Bay/Sandbanks
(Mouth of Poole Harbour) Bournemouth - Swanage Motor Road & Ferry Company, Shell Bay, Studland BH19 3BA
Tel: 01929 450203 Fax: 01929 450498
www.sandbanksferry.co.uk
All year round. Daily every 20 mins.
Sandbanks 07:00 to 23:00 hrs
Shell Bay 07:10 to 23:10 hrs
Christmas Day every half hour.

The ferry is scheduled to have a refit at the end of October to early November. If you intend to use the ferry at this time check the Association's website under Path News or the ferry company's website.

If you are relying on a ferry service we urge you to contact the ferry operator direct, particularly if you anticpate a fairly late finish and need to confirm the time of its last run.

Tide Times

The tide tables included in this edition refer to the times of low water at Devonport.

These tables will act as a guide for those wishing to paddle across the Gannel (Newquay) or the Erme. Please be sure to read the warnings given under each section. We have been criticised for being too cautious over the times we suggest for paddling across the rivers, and know that some walkers cross at other times.

We believe our attitude is correct as there certainly are dangers, but you may wish to try at low tide on other occasions to see if conditions will permit a safe crossing. Variations in barometric pressure can affect tide levels. Remember there are different levels daily of low water; if in doubt seek local knowledge.

- Newquay (The Gannel) deduct 30 minutes
- River Erme as at Devonport

The tidal information for the port of Devonport is reproduced by permission of the Controller of Her Majesty's Stationery Office and the UK Hydrographic Office (www.ukho.gov.uk)

MARCH 2013 LOW WATER *From 31st March add 1 hour for BST*			
1	Fri	0145	1406
2	Sat	0219	1439
3	Sun	0255	1516
4	Mon	0336	1600
5	Tues	0429	1700
6	Weds	0543	1829
7	Thurs	0730	2018
8	Fri	0902	2133
9	Sat	1005	2229
10	Sun	1056	2318
11	Mon	1142	****
12	Tues	0001	1225
13	Weds	0042	1303
14	Thurs	0118	1338
15	Fri	0151	1409
16	Sat	0220	1436
17	Sun	0247	1501
18	Mon	0314	1527
19	Tues	0343	1601
20	Weds	0436	1713
21	Thurs	0603	1839
22	Fri	0723	1955
23	Sat	0835	2103
24	Sun	0936	2159
25	Mon	1027	2247
26	Tues	1112	2331
27	Weds	1154	****
28	Thurs	0012	1235
29	Fri	0052	1313
30	Sat	0129	1350
31	Sun	0206	1427

APRIL 2013 LOW WATER *Add 1 hour for BST*			
1	Mon	0245	1506
2	Tues	0329	1553
3	Weds	0424	1653
4	Thurs	0537	1819
5	Fri	0717	2000
6	Sat	0842	2112
7	Sun	0943	2207
8	Mon	1033	2254
9	Tues	1118	2337
10	Weds	1158	****
11	Thurs	0016	1236
12	Fri	0052	1310
13	Sat	0124	1339
14	Sun	0152	1406
15	Mon	0219	1430
16	Tues	0244	1454
17	Weds	0311	1525
18	Thurs	0355	1621
19	Fri	0517	1753
20	Sat	0639	1911
21	Sun	0749	2018
22	Mon	0852	2118
23	Tues	0947	2212
24	Weds	1038	2301
25	Thurs	1125	2347
26	Fri	****	1210
27	Sat	0031	1253
28	Sun	0114	1335
29	Mon	0157	1417
30	Tues	0240	1501

MAY 2013 LOW WATER *Add 1 hour for BST*			
1	Weds	0328	1550
2	Thurs	0422	1648
3	Fri	0529	1801
4	Sat	0650	1926
5	Sun	0809	2038
6	Mon	0911	2136
7	Tues	1003	2225
8	Weds	1048	2309
9	Thurs	1130	2349
10	Fri	****	1208
11	Sat	0025	1242
12	Sun	0058	1312
13	Mon	0128	1340
14	Tues	0156	1406
15	Weds	0223	1434
16	Thurs	0253	1506
17	Fri	0332	1552
18	Sat	0430	1700
19	Sun	0548	1821
20	Mon	0701	1932
21	Tues	0808	2037
22	Weds	0908	2137
23	Thurs	1005	2232
24	Fri	1058	2324
25	Sat	1148	****
26	Sun	0013	1237
27	Mon	0102	1324
28	Tues	0149	1410
29	Weds	0236	1457
30	Thurs	0323	1544
31	Fri	0413	1635

JUNE 2013 LOW WATER *Add 1 hour for BST*			
1	Sat	0509	1733
2	Sun	0612	1841
3	Mon	0721	1953
4	Tues	0829	2058
5	Weds	0927	2153
6	Thurs	1017	2240
7	Fri	1101	2323
8	Sat	1141	****
9	Sun	0001	1217
10	Mon	0036	1249
11	Tues	0108	1320
12	Weds	0138	1349
13	Thurs	0207	1419
14	Fri	0238	1451
15	Sat	0313	1530
16	Sun	0357	1619
17	Mon	0455	1725
18	Tues	0607	1843
19	Weds	0723	1958
20	Thurs	0833	2106
21	Fri	0937	2208
22	Sat	1036	2306
23	Sun	1132	****
24	Mon	0000	1225
25	Tues	0051	1314
26	Weds	0140	1401
27	Thurs	0226	1445
28	Fri	0311	1529
29	Sat	0354	1612
30	Sun	0439	1659

JULY 2013 LOW WATER *Add 1 hour for BST*			
1	Mon	0529	1752
2	Tues	0626	1856
3	Weds	0733	2009
4	Thurs	0843	2117
5	Fri	0943	2212
6	Sat	1033	2258
7	Sun	1116	2339
8	Mon	1154	****
9	Tues	0016	1230
10	Weds	0050	1302
11	Thurs	0121	1333
12	Fri	0151	1403
13	Sat	0221	1434
14	Sun	0254	1508
15	Mon	0331	1550
16	Tues	0417	1643
17	Weds	0518	1755
18	Thurs	0639	1923
19	Fri	0804	2043
20	Sat	0918	2152
21	Sun	1022	2253
22	Mon	1120	2348
23	Tues	****	1212
24	Weds	0038	1301
25	Thurs	0126	1345
26	Fri	0209	1427
27	Sat	0249	1506
28	Sun	0327	1543
29	Mon	0405	1622
30	Tues	0445	1707
31	Weds	0534	1804

AUGUST 2013 LOW WATER *Add 1 hour for BST*			
1	Thurs	0636	1915
2	Fri	0751	2036
3	Sat	0907	2144
4	Sun	1005	2234
5	Mon	1051	2316
6	Tues	1132	2354
7	Weds	****	1208
8	Thurs	0029	1242
9	Fri	0101	1314
10	Sat	0132	1344
11	Sun	0202	1415
12	Mon	0233	1448
13	Tues	0307	1526
14	Weds	0349	1615
15	Thurs	0444	1723
16	Fri	0605	1900
17	Sat	0746	2030
18	Sun	0907	2143
19	Mon	1012	2242
20	Tues	1107	2334
21	Weds	1157	****
22	Thurs	0021	1242
23	Fri	0106	1324
24	Sat	0146	1402
25	Sun	0222	1437
26	Mon	0256	1510
27	Tues	0328	1544
28	Weds	0401	1623
29	Thurs	0445	1718
30	Fri	0549	1830
31	Sat	0705	1951

SEPTEMBER 2013 LOW WATER *Add 1 hour for BST*			
1	Sun	0826	2110
2	Mon	0932	2203
3	Tues	1021	2246
4	Weds	1103	2325
5	Thurs	1141	****
6	Fri	0002	1218
7	Sat	0037	1252
8	Sun	0110	1325
9	Mon	0142	1357
10	Tues	0214	1431
11	Weds	0249	1509
12	Thurs	0330	1558
13	Fri	0424	1707
14	Sat	0548	1849
15	Sun	0737	2023
16	Mon	0858	2131
17	Tues	0959	2227
18	Weds	1050	2315
19	Thurs	1137	****
20	Fri	0000	1220
21	Sat	0041	1259
22	Sun	0119	1335
23	Mon	0152	1408
24	Tues	0223	1438
25	Weds	0251	1507
26	Thurs	0319	1541
27	Fri	0355	1632
28	Sat	0500	1748
29	Sun	0623	1908
30	Mon	0741	2022

OCTOBER 2013 LOW WATER *Add 1 hour until 27th for BST*			
1	Tues	0849	2121
2	Weds	0943	2208
3	Thurs	1028	2251
4	Fri	1110	2331
5	Sat	1150	****
6	Sun	0010	1229
7	Mon	0047	1305
8	Tues	0123	1342
9	Weds	0159	1419
10	Thurs	0237	1501
11	Fri	0321	1552
12	Sat	0417	1702
13	Sun	0539	1838
14	Mon	0723	2007
15	Tues	0840	2112
16	Weds	0938	2205
17	Thurs	1028	2252
18	Fri	1113	2335
19	Sat	1155	****
20	Sun	0014	1234
21	Mon	0051	1308
22	Tues	0123	1340
23	Weds	0152	1409
24	Thurs	0219	1437
25	Fri	0244	1506
26	Sat	0313	1547
27	Sun	0403	1659
28	Mon	0532	1820
29	Tues	0652	1931
30	Weds	0801	2033
31	Thurs	0900	2127

NOVEMBER 2013 LOW WATER			
1	Fri	0951	2215
2	Sat	1038	2301
3	Sun	1123	2344
4	Mon	****	1206
5	Tues	0026	1249
6	Weds	0108	1331
7	Thurs	0149	1414
8	Fri	0232	1500
9	Sat	0319	1552
10	Sun	0415	1656
11	Mon	0525	1814
12	Tues	0652	1936
13	Weds	0809	2042
14	Thurs	0911	2137
15	Fri	1002	2225
16	Sat	1048	2309
17	Sun	1131	2349
18	Mon	****	1209
19	Tues	0025	1245
20	Weds	0058	1317
21	Thurs	0127	1346
22	Fri	0155	1415
23	Sat	0222	1444
24	Sun	0251	1518
25	Mon	0329	1606
26	Tues	0427	1719
27	Weds	0551	1836
28	Thurs	0708	1944
29	Fri	0815	2045
30	Sat	0914	2141

DECEMBER 2013 LOW WATER			
1	Sun	1008	2233
2	Mon	1059	2322
3	Tues	1149	****
4	Weds	0010	1237
5	Thurs	0057	1324
6	Fri	0143	1411
7	Sat	0229	1457
8	Sun	0315	1546
9	Mon	0405	1639
10	Tues	0500	1739
11	Weds	0606	1849
12	Thurs	0724	2002
13	Fri	0835	2105
14	Sat	0934	2158
15	Sun	1024	2245
16	Mon	1109	2326
17	Tues	1149	****
18	Weds	0004	1226
19	Thurs	0038	1300
20	Fri	0109	1330
21	Sat	0138	1358
22	Sun	0205	1427
23	Mon	0234	1457
24	Tues	0306	1533
25	Weds	0348	1620
26	Thurs	0444	1726
27	Fri	0602	1849
28	Sat	0726	2004
29	Sun	0838	2110
30	Mon	0942	2210
31	Tues	1041	2306

The Crowns

On long trips it is a good idea to:

Send guides, maps etc. ahead to larger post offices Poste Restante.

The only snag is if you arrive on a Saturday evening.

Start out with a few map-sized envelopes and the smallest available roll of sellotape so that you can despatch finished guides, maps, books etc. home.

Kit Transfer

Coast Path walking can be arduous in places but some of the hard work can be eliminated. One of the harder tasks can be having to carry a heavy pack from one B&B to the next. There are, however, potential ways around this.

1. Many of the B&Bs are willing to move kit for a fee. Look in the accommodation section of this Guide and check for the code KT (for Kit Transfer) under the Facilities column.
2. The Association holds a list of Holiday Walking Companies on our website. Many of these offer Kit Transfer, usually along certain lengths of the Path. Go to our website at www.swcp.org.uk and click on Holiday Walking Companies to see what is available. The Association also has a small booklet with these companies listed - see the Walking Holiday Companies paragraph below.
3. For transfer of kit anywhere on the Coast Path, the Association has an agreement with Luggage Transfers Ltd.

Luggage Transfers South West

Luggage Transfers Ltd, started in 2008 by two SWCPA members, moves up to 10,000 bags a month for walkers on the Coast Path, and is the only comprehensive service covering the entire Path.

The large volume of deliveries means that they can combine and "daisy chain" transfers which has kept the cost of the service low at an average of £8 for each bag movement. The effect of volume delivery also saves an estimated 200 tons of carbon emissions each season.

In addition, Luggage Transfers encourages walkers to donate 25p per transfer to the Association in order to raise funds for the Path. It also encourages its accommodation providers to become Business Members of the Association, which brings us a membership fee to be used for Path improvements. In return, Business Members get an enhanced entry in the accommodation list of the Annual Guide and on the website. Try and use them if you can to repay their support for us.

To book your luggage transfers with them, go to their website at www.luggagetransfers.co.uk. Alternatively, click on the accommodation list at the Association's own website. For telephone enquiries, call 01326 567247. The office is open 9.00am to 7.00pm 7 days a week from March until October inclusive, and office hours November until February.

Walking Holiday Companies

For those who require a Coast Path walk without carrying rucksacks and have their accommodation fixed in advance there are several businesses that will arrange everything. All you have to do is let them know your requirements and pay them. Also there are some excellent organisations that run walking holidays with guides. The South West Coast Path Association realised that there are too many to be listed in this guide so we have created a small booklet with these companies listed. We will supply it at a cost of £1.50. Contact the Administrator at Bowker House, see page 3.

The Countryside Code

- Be safe - plan ahead and follow any signs
- Leave gates and property as you find them
- Protect plants and animals, and take your litter home
- Keep dogs under close control
- Consider other people

Because our Coast Path is so special and so popular, it is important to treat it with care and to use it in an environmentally sensitive way by employing the following principles:

- Use guidebooks and information
- Keep to the path to minimise erosion
- Report problems to the South West Coast Path Association
- Always consider the interests of landowners and other users
- Take special care where the Coast Path is routed onto roads

Supporting Local Businesses

- Use public transport to reach the path wherever possible
- Support local shops and services

Website News

Any news concerning the state of the Coast Path received after this book is printed will be published in newsletters and on our web site www.swcp.org.uk

Coast Path Safety Advice

Your safety is your responsibility - please look after yourself and other members of your group. Keep to the path and stay away from cliff edges - please follow advisory signs and waymarks. Supervise children and dogs - please look out for your children and pets at all times. Be prepared and well equipped - wear suitable clothing and footwear and be ready for possible changes in the weather.

Stay within your capabilities - some sections of the Coast Path can be strenuous and/or remote. In an emergency dial 999 and ask for the coastguard.

Weather

The South West Coast Path is more exposed to wind than any other long distance trail, so please pay attention to gale forecasts as well as rain. Along some sections, strong winds can be dangerous, especially when rounding exposed headlands and crossing bridges; a high backpack can act like a sail.

Always use sun protection especially on bright cloudy or breezy days when the risk of sunburn seems lower.

Detailed local forecasts are available from the UK Meteorological Office on 0870 900 0100 (24 hours) or www.metoffice.gov.uk/weather/uk

Military Ranges

Two lengths of the Coast Path may be affected by the use or otherwise of military ranges. The use of one, at Tregantle in south east Cornwall, only means that a more inland and less pleasant route must be used for a length of some 1.25 miles/2km in Section 46, Portwrinkle-Cremyll (Plymouth Ferry). However, if there is military use of the other, east of Lulworth Cove in Dorset, this means the whole of Section 67 between Lulworth Cove and Kimmeridge Bay will be impossible. Generally the Lulworth ranges are closed to walkers Monday to Friday during school term time and also up to six times a year at weekends. Try to arrange your walk so as not to miss this superb but tough section.

Information details for the ranges are included in the relevant Section descriptions.

Telephones

Mobile phones sometimes will not work in remote places and it's reassuring to see a public telephone box just when you need it. However, many of these remote telephones have recently been converted to only take debit cards. You can use the following cards in these boxes - Switch; Maestro; Delta; Solo; Visa Debit but not Electron. There are still some telephone boxes which will accept BT Phonecards and all boxes will accept BT Chargecards (these are only available to BT landline customers). Mobile phones are always useful to have whilst on the Coast Path. However, do not rely on them as coverage is not always good in the South West. You may also have difficulty in obtaining top-up in some areas.

Banks

There are small Post Offices in most villages. Overseas visitors, we suggest, will find their cashpoint cards very useful. ATM machines are widely available along the Coast Path and can be sourced at www.link.co.uk/atmlocator/Pages/ATMLocator.aspx

Dogs

1. Beaches

Most district councils and unitary authorities have implemented dog bans on beaches generally from 1st May to 31st October. Our Association and most of the general public regard this as a sensible measure.

There are several sections of the South West Coast Path that cross beaches and are officially marked as such. These beaches are Croyde Bay in Devon, Harlyn Bay, Constantine, Treyarnon, Perranporth and Penberth slipway in Cornwall, and Studland in Dorset. The routing of the Coast Path (with its designation as a National Trail) across these beaches means that they are public rights of way. A public right of way DOES carry precedence over seasonal regulations banning dogs, and ultimately any walker in the process of walking along, but not stopping on, these sections of the path may be accompanied by a dog under TOTAL control.

However we strongly recommend the following:

a) If an alternative route is provided and signposted, that you use it.

b) That residents near to dog ban beaches use other walks and do not use the beach path during the ban period.

c) Total control means that the dog should be on a short (not extendable) lead.

d) That your progress should be as unobtrusive as possible to other beach users. To aid this, close attention should be paid to the actual route marked on the map.

e) Lastly, but most importantly, should the worst happen, any dog mess MUST be removed from the beach.

2. Along the Coast Path

Many walk the Coast Path with their dogs and all have an enjoyable time and we receive many reports of dogs completing the whole path.

However we do urge caution because the Coast Path is very high along many sections, and it takes only an excited dog to go chasing after a rabbit, to cause much grief if it goes over the edge. If your dog is well-trained and you can trust it, then please enjoy your Coast Path walk with your four-legged friend. If it is not and you cannot, then do take care.

Many sections along the South West Coast Path will have farm livestock grazing.

Again, walkers should maintain proper control of their dogs.

Important - Please Note

Information included or available through the South West Coast Path Association (SWCPA) is given in good faith and is believed to be accurate and correct at the time of going to print - however it cannot be guaranteed not to include inaccuracies or typographical errors.

Advice received via the SWCPA should not be relied upon for personal decisions and you should take into account the weather and your own capabilities before following the walks set out in this Guide. It is for the individual concerned to weigh up the risks of each of the walks described in this book.

The SWCPA makes no representations about the suitability of walks to any one person and will accept no liability for any loss or damage suffered as a result of relying on this book; it should be used for guidance only.

In no event shall the SWCPA be liable for any personal injury or any loss suffered as a result of using this publication.

Week 1 (Seven days)

Day	Distance		From - to
1	10mi	15km	**Minehead - Porlock Weir** *Take National Rail main line to Taunton; bus Taunton - Minehead; or National Express coach to Minehead*
2	12mi	20km	**Porlock Weir - Lynton**
3	13mi	21km	**Lynton - Combe Martin**
4	13mi	20km	**Combe Martin - Woolacombe**
5	16mi	27km	**Woolacombe - Braunton**
6	12mi	20km	**Braunton - Instow**
7	11mi	18km	**Instow - Westward Ho!**
Total	**87mi**	**141km**	*Take bus Westward Ho! - Barnstaple; train Barnstaple - Exeter; National Rail main line from Exeter; or National Express coach from Westward Ho!*

Week 2 (Seven days)

Day	Distance		From - to
1	11mi	18km	**Westward Ho! - Clovelly** *National Rail main line to Exeter; train Exeter - Barnstaple; bus Barnstaple - Westward Ho!; or National Express coach to Westward Ho!*
2	10mi	16km	**Clovelly - Hartland Quay**
3	15mi	25km	**Hartland Quay - Bude**
4	10mi	16km	**Bude - Crackington Haven**
5	11mi	18km	**Crackington Haven - Tintagel**
6	9mi	15km	**Tintagel - Port Isaac**
7	12mi	19km	**Port Isaac - Padstow**
Total	**78mi**	**127km**	*Bus to Bodmin Parkway; National Rail main line from Bodmin Parkway.*

Week 3 (Six days)

Day	Distance		From - to
1	14mi	22km	Padstow - Porthcothan *National Rail main line to Bodmin Parkway; bus Bodmin Parkway - Padstow.*
2	11mi	18km	Porthcothan - Newquay
3	11mi	18km	Newquay - Perranporth
4	12mi	20km	Perranporth - Portreath
5	12mi	20km	Portreath - Hayle
6	6mi	9km	Hayle - St Ives
Total	**66mi**	**107km**	*Train St Ives-St Erth; National Rail main line from St Erth; or National Express coach from St Ives.*

Week 4 (Six days)

Day	Distance		From - to
1	14mi	22km	**St Ives - Pendeen Watch** *National Rail main line to St Erth; train St Erth - St Ives; or National Express coach to St Ives.*
2	9mi	15km	**Pendeen Watch - Sennen Cove**
3	12mi	19km	**Sennen Cove - Lamorna Cove**
4	9mi	15km	**Lamorna Cove - Marazion**
5	11mi	17km	**Marazion - Porthleven**
6	13mi	22km	**Porthleven - Lizard**
Total	**68mi**	**110km**	*Bus Lizard Town - Helston; bus Helston - Redruth; National Rail main line from Redruth*

It is possible to use one accommodation base in summer between St Ives and Marazion as summer bus service 300 travels in a circuit both ways around the Land's End peninsula. See page 15 Local Transport.

Week 5 (Six days)

Day	Distance		From - to
1	11mi	17km	**Lizard - Coverack** *National Rail main line to Redruth; bus Redruth-Helston; bus Helston - Lizard Town.*
2	13mi	21km	**Coverack - Helford**
3	10mi	16km	**Helford - Falmouth**
4	14mi	22km	**Falmouth - Portloe**
5	12mi	20km	**Portloe - Mevagissey**
6	12mi	19km	**Mevagissey - Par**
Total	**72mi**	**115km**	*National Rail main line from Par.*

Week 6 (Seven days)

Day	Distance		From - to
1	13mi	21km	**Par - Polperro** *National Rail main line to Par.*
2	12mi	20km	**Polperro - Portwrinkle**
3	13mi	21km	**Portwrinkle - Plymouth**
4	15mi	24km	**Plymouth - Wembury (ferry crossing)**
5	14mi	22km	**Wembury (ferry crossing) - Bigbury on Sea**
6	14mi	22km	**Bigbury on Sea - Salcombe**
7	13mi	21km	**Salcombe - Torcross**
Total	**94mi**	**151km**	*Bus Torcross - Plymouth; National Rail main line or National Express coach from Plymouth.*

Week 7 (Six days)

Day	Distance		From - to
1	10mi	16km	**Torcross - Dartmouth** *National rail main line or National Express coach to Plymouth; bus Plymouth - Torcross.*
2	11mi	17km	**Dartmouth - Brixham**
3	11mi	17km	**Brixham - Babbacombe**
4	16mi	27km	**Babbacombe - Exmouth**
5	13mi	21km	**Exmouth - Sidmouth**
6	11mi	17km	**Sidmouth - Seaton (Devon)**
Total	**72mi**	**115km**	*Bus Seaton - Exeter; National Rail main line or National Express Coach from Exeter.*

Week 8 (Seven days)

Day	Distance		From - to
1	14	23	**Seaton (Devon) - Seatown (Dorset)** *National Rail main line or National Express coach to Exeter; bus Exeter - Seaton.*
2	12	19	**Seatown (Dorset) - Abbotsbury**
3	11	17	**Abbotsbury - Ferry Bridge (Wyke Regis)**
4	13	21	**Isle of Portland**
5	14	23	**Ferry Bridge (Wyke Regis) - Lulworth Cove**
6	14	23	**Lulworth Cove - Worth Matravers**
7	14	22	**Worth Matravers - South Haven Point (Poole Harbour)**
Total	**92mi**	**148km**	*Ferry South Haven Point-Sandbanks; bus Sandbanks-Poole or Bournemouth; National Rail main line or National Express coach from Poole or Bournemouth.* 630 miles of path to cover, it is

Other breakdowns are obviously possible, although the above is probably the best one for individual full weeks. A good alternative to use with direct nationwide public transport access at both ends of each stage would be:-

- Stage 1: Minehead to Barnstaple (68 miles/110km)
- Stage 2: Barnstaple to Bude (56 miles/90km)
- Stage 3: Bude to St Ives (108 miles/174km)
- Stage 4: St Ives to Falmouth (103 miles/165km)
- Stage 5:Falmouth to Plymouth (81 miles/131km)
- Stage 6: Plymouth to Exmouth (98 miles/158km)
- Stage 7: Exmouth to Weymouth (60 miles/97km)
- Stage 8: Weymouth to Poole (via Portland) (56 miles/90km)

Those interested in devising their own lengths might wish to know the locations of train access points on the Coast Path. On the national network, these are at Barnstaple (branch line from Exeter), Newquay (branch line from Par), St Ives (branch line from St Erth), Penzance, Falmouth (branch line from Truro), Par, Looe (branch line from Liskeard), Plymouth, Paignton, Torquay, Teignmouth, Dawlish, Exmouth (branch line from Exeter), Weymouth and Poole (for access to South Haven Point). Other locations are served during the summer by private railways, usually with steam-powered trains - Minehead (West Somerset Railway), Kingswear and Paignton (Dartmouth Steam Railway) and Swanage (Swanage Railway).

Reporting Problems on the Path

Be our Eyes and Ears on the Ground

With 630 miles of path to cover, it is impossible for the path wardens and rangers or the Association's local representatives to keep up with everything on the path at all times. So, if you encounter any problems, be they broken or missing signposts or waymarks, broken stiles or gates, real difficulties with the path surface, or anything else you think we should know about, contact us at our office address or phone number on page 3, or e-mail us. We will get in touch with the relevant path ranger with your concerns.

Background

The South West Coast Path is one of the "family" of National Trails. It is generally well signposted and waymarked, using the National Trail symbol of the acorn. In some parts of the Coast Path waymarking relates to the local environment, for example the use of granite waymarks in parts of West Cornwall and Purbeck stone signs in Dorset. Be sure when walking the route to follow any such directions on the ground rather than relying on literature - things change over time, even including the route of the South West Coast Path, literature can become out-of-date.

Those who set out to walk all or any of this beautiful trail should remember that much of it is a cliff-top path - in places a very high cliff top. Those who manage the Coast Path want to keep it safe, but walkers should be reminded that it is unwise to leave the path at any point on the seaward side. Sometimes the edges of cliff tops away from the path can be unstable and unsafe.

Now and again the descriptions suggest an alternative path away from the officially designated route. These alternatives will themselves follow rights of way or, occasionally, "permitted routes" maintained by the landowner for use by the public. They are suggested for a more scenic and enjoyable experience than the formal route.

Once again, the Association stresses that ANYONE USING THE PATH SHOULD NOT WANDER OFF IT, ESPECIALLY ON THE SEAWARD SIDE. TO DO SO WOULD BE PUTTING YOURSELF AND POSSIBLY OTHERS IN DANGER OF SEVERE PERSONAL INJURY, OR EVEN DEATH.

Always follow the National Trail Waymark.

That said, the South West Coast Path is a wonderful environment enjoyed by millions. Choose a length, long or short, and undertake one of the greatest walking experiences the country has to offer.

The Environment of the South West Coast Path

The South West Coast Path is one of the country's National Trails; it is, indeed, the longest of them at 630 miles/1,105km. In common with all National Trails, the Coast Path passes through an outstanding environment. In the Coast Path's case, this outstanding environment is recognised by the large number of formal designations throughout its length. These include both international and national designations.

International Designations

i. **North Devon Biosphere Reserve**

   Biosphere Reserves are places with world-class environments designated by UNESCO to promote and demonstrate a balanced relationship between nature and people. They are places where conservation and sustainable development go hand in hand. North Devon is a UNESCO Biosphere Reserve because of its blend of special landscapes and wildlife areas, rich cultural heritage and communities that care about it and want to sustain it into the future. The core area of the Biosphere Reserve is at Braunton Burrows (Section 7 of the Trail Descriptions following), but including the outer areas the Reserve covers the Coast Path between Lynmouth and Marsland Mouth (Sections 3-13).

ii. **Cornwall and West Devon Mining Landscape World Heritage Site**

   World Heritage Sites are designated by UNESCO for their "Outstanding Universal Value". This World Heritage Site is defined by the mining landscape which was formed by the cultural tradition of non-ferrous hard-rock mining. It contributed to developing the Industrial Revolution in Britain and pioneered its transfer overseas. The designation covers ten distinct areas, of which five relate to the Coast Path. These are the St Agnes Mining District (Section 24), the Port of Hayle (Sections 25 and 26), the St Just Mining District (Sections 27 and 28), the Tregonning and Gwinear Mining District with Trewavas (Section 32) and the Luxulyan Valley and Charlestown (Section 41).

iii. **Jurassic Coast World Heritage Site**

   This was England's first World Heritage Site designated for its natural properties. Is it designated as it clearly depicts a geological "walk through time" of 185 million years of Earth's history in 95 miles/152km. Geological history of the Triassic, Jurassic and Cretaceous periods are successively exposed and are accessible over the length of the Site, which stretches between Exmouth and Swanage (Sections 58-70).

National Designations

Most of the South West Coast Path is covered by the national landscape designations of National Park or Area of Outstanding Natural Beauty (AONB). In landscape terms these designations are regarded as equal, representing the country's finest landscapes.

i. **Exmoor National Park**
   Minehead - Combe Martin (Sections 1-3).

ii. **North Devon AONB**
   Combe Martin - Marsland Mouth, excluding Ilfracombe, the Taw-Torridge Estuary and Westward Ho! (Sections 4-8, 11-13).

iii. **Cornwall AONB**
   The entire coast of Cornwall, excluding Bude and its environs, Polzeath and Rock, Carnewas - Newquay, Gwithian - St Ives, Newlyn - Marazion, Charlestown - Par and Looe - Rame Head (Sections 13-25, 27-44, 46).

iv. **South Devon AONB**
   Plymouth - Brixham (Sections 48-54).

v. **East Devon AONB**
   Exmouth - Lyme Regis, excluding Sidmouth and Beer - Seaton (Sections 58-61).

vi. **Dorset AONB**
   The entire coast of Dorset, excluding Weymouth - Portland (Sections 62-64, 66-70). The South Dorset Ridgeway (Section 71) also falls within this designation.

The Landscape of the South West Coast Path

The wealth of landscape and environmental designations outlined above gives some idea of the quality of the landscape through which the South West Coast Path passes. However, this hides the fact there is a wide range of landscape types to be experienced. For those not over-familiar with the South West, we have divided the Coast Path into seven areas, shown on the map on page 2, and noted on each of the Section descriptions. This will help to pinpoint geographically the various path Sections, but can also be used to describe the path's landscapes.

The various areas are identified by using a colour coding system as shown on the map on page 2 and set out in the Contents page 5. The colour code is used on the corner tabs of the Walk Sections, the title information and the page numbers.

i. Exmoor

Minehead - Combe Martin (Sections 1-3)

The Exmoor length is characterised by two main landscape types. The first is the meeting of the rolling expanse of high moorland and the sea. The coastline itself is one of high cliffs, some of them among the highest sea cliffs in England, but this height is sometimes disguised by the cliffs' convex shape, usually referred to as "hog's back". Views are often extensive inland, over the undulating moorland, while seaward in good visibility the coast of Wales may be seen across the Bristol Channel. In contrast, substantial lengths of the Exmoor coast comprise deep and steep valleys cutting across the high land. These valleys, locally known as "combes", are typically wooded, often with ancient oak woodland. Often this woodland spreads along the adjacent cliff faces, also convex in shape. Views from the Coast Path here are inevitably less extensive, and sometimes quite limited by the woodland, but the nature of the ancient woodland makes for an environment of considerable ecological interest. The combes and the height of the cliffs in this length result in some notable gradients in places.

ii. North Devon

Combe Martin - Marsland Mouth (Sections 4-13)

Most of the North Devon coast faces north over the Bristol Channel. Much of this length comprises cliffs of moderate height with, in the east, some prominent headlands like Morte Point and Baggy Point which offer fine coastal vistas. In the centre of this length is the large joint estuary of the Taw and Torridge Rivers, flanked by areas of sand dunes and marshland. Adjacent to the estuary and just east of it are extensive sandy beaches, popular with surfers and families. Seascapes typically have the coast of Wales beyond the Bristol Channel as the backdrop in the east of this length. In the centre and west the offshore island of Lundy, at the "mouth" of the Bristol Channel, is the focal point. At the west end of this length is Hartland Point, one of the Coast Path's major headlands (referred to as the Point of Hercules in a Roman geography). It marks an abrupt change in direction from the east-west typical of most of North Devon (and Exmoor) to the north-south length beyond. This north-south length is very dramatic, with high cliffs fronted by jagged fingers of rock stretching into the Atlantic. Deep and steep valleys cut into this coastline, but there are no bays or harbours - an historic attempt to make a harbour at Hartland Quay was foiled by the elements. This is a section of great atmosphere.

iii. North Cornwall

Marsland Mouth - Portreath (Sections 13-24)

This section of coast trends either north-south or north east-south west. As such, it faces the prevailing Atlantic westerlies, making for a sometimes exposed landscape. This is exacerbated by the fact that much of the length comprises high cliffs, often quite sheer, with prominent headlands giving excellent coastal vistas. In places the feet of these cliffs are fronted by extensive sandy beaches, as north of Bude or at Watergate and Perran Beaches, north and south of Newquay. The cliff line is also punctuated by numerous sandy coves. There are also two main breaches in the cliff where river estuaries reach the sea, the Camel at Padstow and the Gannel at Newquay. These estuaries are also flanked by extensive sandy beaches. The uncompromising nature of the cliffs means there are few ports or harbours. Padstow, sheltered within the Camel estuary, is an ancient port and Newquay has a medieval origin, sheltered behind the promontory of Towan Head. Newquay has now, of course, expanded into a major holiday centre. Smaller 19th century harbours at the north-east end at Bude, originally largely based on its canal, and at the south-west end at Portreath, originally based on exporting mineral ores, have also expanded into tourism centres. These are very much exceptional settlements on this coast.

iv. West Cornwall

Portreath - Falmouth (Sections 25-37)

Most of this part of the coast is occupied by the two great peninsulas of Penwith, the westernmost part of England, and the Lizard, the southernmost. Both are composed of hard, resistant rocks making for a rugged cliff coastline, but their characters differ. Penwith is largely granite and inland of its impressive cliffs, frequently marked by rock pinnacles and solid jointed slabs, is a rough semi-moorland landscape. The Lizard has a much smoother profile, with its inland landscape an unusual flat-topped plateau. The exposed locations of these two peninsulas result in harsh, weather-beaten coastlines with a lack of large-scale tree cover, though both are magnificently dramatic. Only on the eastern, lee side of the Lizard does the coastline become a little more lush. Flanking these two peninsulas are lower, more sheltered lengths - St Ives Bay on the north-east side of Penwith, Mount's Bay between Penwith and the Lizard and the Helford - Fal estuaries east of the Lizard. It is in these sheltered areas the only ports and harbours of any size are found, principally Penzance and Falmouth.

v. South Cornwall

Falmouth - the Tamar (Sections 38-46)

The South Cornwall stretch of coast is relatively sheltered being either south-east or south-facing and being largely in the lee of the large peninsula of the Lizard. Cliffs of moderate height are found along most of the length, and there are numerous intimate little bays and some quite prominent headlands. In the eastern half of the length the coast is cut by wooded river valleys, at Fowey, Looe and Seaton. In the centre is the major feature of St Austell Bay, the only part that lacks the otherwise ubiquitous cliffs. This bay also has the only major length of coastal development in South Cornwall, based on the town of St Austell and its extensions. Elsewhere, small ancient fishing ports such as Mevagissey, Fowey and Looe are scattered along the coast, all of them very picturesque. Major estuaries, of the Fal and Tamar, mark the two ends, each of them of great historic maritime importance.

vi. South Devon

Plymouth - Lyme Regis (Sections 47-61)

This section of coast may be conveniently subdivided into three landscape types. In the west, between the Rivers Tamar and Dart, is an area of largely slate cliffs, sometimes quite rugged, these being cut by the drowned mouths of wooded river valleys. This area is usually referred to as the South Hams and extends south to the major headland of Prawle Point, west of this headland being relatively exposed and the east of it much more sheltered. To the east, between the Dart and the Exe, is an area of low, mostly red sandstone cliffs. This length, the "Riviera", is largely occupied by towns based on tourism such

South Haven Point

as Paignton, Torquay, Teignmouth and Dawlish, and being east-facing is mainly sheltered. Much of this length presents an almost continuously developed coastline. Further east still, between the Exe and the Dorset border at Lyme Regis, the cliffs rise again. This section, East Devon, has a slightly different character to the rest of the south coast of Devon. The red sandstone cliffs continue across the Exe for a while. Then, halfway along the East Devon coast, chalk and greensand make for a change in the landscape, to a mixture of white cliffs and extensive undercliffs and landslips. South Devon has many holiday resorts, some of the earliest in the country such as Exmouth and Teignmouth, some famed for their elegance such as Torquay, and some based on historic towns and villages such as Dartmouth and Beer. The biggest urban area of all on the South West Coast Path is Plymouth. Its historic importance is, of course, largely based on the Royal Navy.

vii. Dorset

Lyme Regis - South Haven Point (Poole Harbour) (Sections 62-70)

South Dorset Ridgeway (Section 71)

Geology is both the curse and the boon of the Dorset part of the South West Coast Path. As a curse, the geology means the Dorset cliffs are vulnerable to slippage, especially at the western end. This has meant that several diversions, necessary but hardly ideal, have had to be put in place for the Coast Path. There is currently no clear idea of when permanent solutions will be found for these problems. The Marine and Coastal Access Act 2010 may resolve the matter of replacement or alternative routes in the longer term but, apart from the Weymouth area, there is currently no programme for implementation. However, as a boon, Dorset's exposed and accessible layers of geological history have made it a textbook example for a wide range of coastal features. These features are also landscape highlights - the great shingle bar of Chesil Beach backed by the semi-freshwater lagoon of the Fleet; the fortress-like monolith of the Isle of Portland, jutting into the English Channel; the textbook arch of Durdle Door; the erosion of soft rock once the harder limestone has been broken through forming hollowed-out bays, as at Lulworth Cove; the offshore Purbeck stone stacks at Handfast Point. Inland, the rolling green hills evoke the spirit and landscape of Thomas Hardy, a worthy addition to the range of South West Coast Path landscapes.

Spekes Mill Mouth

Key to Walk Descriptions

Based on the Suggested Itinerary on page 27, the South West Coast Path has been divided into 70 Sections. Each Section represents a day's or half-day's walk of the Itinerary. However, it must be emphasised that these Sections should not be confined to use by those walking long stretches of the Coast Path. Each Section is designed to be used on its own as a one-off if so wished, as well as by those planning long walks of several days. The Sections are arranged in anti-clockwise order, from Minehead to Poole, with an additional Section 71 for the alternative inland South Dorset Ridgeway.

Each Section entry follows in the following format:

Distance - length of the Section in miles and kilometres;

Cumulative distance - total length of the Coast Path from Minehead to the end of the Section in miles and kilometres;

Ascent - height climbed during the Section in feet and metres;

Cumulative ascent - total height climbed on the Coast Path from Minehead to the end of the Section in feet and metres;

Grading - each Section is graded as Easy, Moderate, Strenuous or Severe. Inevitably, such grading is subjective to an extent, and not all of any Section will be identical throughout, but the grading will give an idea of the effort required;

Timing - this is an estimated fair average for completing the Section. Times will vary depending on weather, number in party, gear carried, number of refreshment or photograph stops. The estimate should be an aide in planning.

OS Maps - the reference numbers of the OS Maps needed to walk the Section are given. Both Landranger (1:50,000) and Explorer (1:25,000) maps are given;

Area - for those not geographically acquainted with the South West, the Coast Path has been sub-divided into seven areas for ease of identification of each Section's location; see map on page 2 and area descriptions on pages 31-33.

Path Description booklet - the Association has published a series of Path Description booklets which give detailed walking directions as well as pointing out items of interest along the route; see page 10. The relevant Path Description booklet title for the Section is given.

There is then an overview of each Section. This covers the landscape, its general character and some of its highlights.

Next, there is a short description of how the Section can be undertaken as a day or part-day walk with public transport or a local circular walk. For more details about local public transport see pages 15-21.

Finally, the main body of the Section description contains simplified instructions for walking in a Minehead - Poole direction, generally only highlighting those locations where it is possible to go astray.

Remember, as a National Trail, the South West Coast Path is usually well signed and waymarked throughout its length, using the National Trail acorn symbol. Bear in mind that things change over the years, including the actual route of the Coast Path, so using out-of-date literature can be misleading. If in doubt, follow the signs and waymarks on the ground.

The various areas are identified by using a colour coding system as shown on the map on page 2 and set out in the Contents page 5. The colour code is used on the corner tabs of the Walk Sections, the title information and the page numbers.

Week 1 - Day 1

OS Maps: Landranger 181; Explorer OL9

	This Walk	Cumulative	This Walk	Cumulative	Grading	Timing
Ascent	1,824ft	1,824ft	556m	556m	Official: Moderate Alternative: Strenuous	4.5 hours
Distance	9.5mi	9.5mi	15.3km	15.3km		

For detailed directions see our Minehead to Porlock Weir Path description booklet.

This is a classic example of where moorland meets the sea. Inland, the high expanse of Exmoor rolls away, broken by deep wooded valleys; where it meets the Bristol Channel there are high, convex cliffs, cut by deep and narrow "coombes". This is a lonely, remote length, away from main roads and settlements, with often the only evidence of modern life being development far away on the opposite shore of the Bristol Channel on the South Wales coast. At the western end is the contrasting landscape of Porlock Vale, a flat-floored area of farmland and marshland behind its shingle ridge, quite different in character from the rest of this Section.

Directions

Minehead and Porlock Weir are connected by a year-round bus service. However, there are no "staging posts" along this length although there are possible circular walks based on Minehead or Porlock via Selworthy Beacon, on the inland "official route".

The South West Coast Path starts from the celebratory marker on the sea front, approximately 100 yards/91m beyond the Quay Inn. The current route, which may not be shown on older maps, proceeds along the sea front, past the quay. Just before Greenaleigh Farm it turns left on ascending zigzags to North Hill.

At the summit of North Hill follow the acorn sign towards Selworthy and Bossington. At the next Coast Path sign there is a fork, the route to the right being marked "Rugged Cliff Top Path", and either option can be taken. Do not be put off by the description of the seaward path as "rugged" - it is a splendid alternative and not difficult, and gives much better sea views than the inland "official" path. It is well waymarked, and dogs are permitted but must be under very close control. There is likely to be cattle grazing.

On the "rugged" path, at the stile, take the left fork towards a bench, then continue downhill to take the lower path by a "Rugged Path" signpost. From Grexy Combe (GR 937 481) take the well-defined diagonal path up the hill to a wall, which is then followed first towards the sea then parallel to it to Western Brockholes. Here it turns inland to re-join the inland "official" path behind Hurlstone Point. (This seaward path will add about an hour to the estimated time.)

The inland route, meanwhile, follows good tracks parallel to the sea. Joining the "rugged" path on Bossington Hill, the now-combined route descends Hurlstone

SWCP marker, Minehead

Combe. There is an optional diversion out to Hurlstone Point which gives a superb view. From Hurlstone, take care not to follow the obvious path to the left which contours round Bossington Hill.

The path descends and goes inland to Bossington village and then just past the car park out towards the sea again. The route now crosses the marsh to Porlock Weir, easy to follow the whole way. At high spring tides it can become impassable, and signs to Porlock village should be followed. (For tidal information consult Minehead TIC.) If the diversion via Porlock village is taken, leave the village on the Toll Road then bear right on a footpath that goes behind West Porlock to Porlock Weir.

Week 1 - Day 2

OS Maps: Landranger 181 (eastern half); Landranger 180 (western half); Explorer OL9

	This Walk	Cumulative	This Walk	Cumulative	Grading	Timing
Ascent	3,156ft	4,980ft	962m	1,518m	Moderate, strenuous in parts	5.5 hours
Distance	12.3mi	21.8mi	19.8km	35.1km		

For detailed directions see our Porlock Weir to Lynmouth Path Description booklet.

Culbone Church

This is a Section of two halves. In the east, approximately between Porlock Weir and the Devon/Somerset border, Exmoor meets the sea at a run of high, convex but well-wooded cliffs. The Coast Path here is a woodland walk with frequent glimpses of the sea, quiet and remote in character. To the west the cliffs become more open and steeper and the area around The Foreland and Countisbury is a spectacular viewpoint with panoramas over the double-decker towns of Lynton and Lynmouth.

Directions

A summer bus service links Porlock Weir to Lynton. It is possible to divide the walk at County Gate, mid-way along, which is on the bus route.

The official route is signposted left of the Anchor Hotel at Porlock Weir but it is possible to go in front of the hotel, past the shops then left signposted to Culbone. Reaching Culbone turn right to visit the charming tiny church, which is recommended. From the church retrace steps and turn right uphill on the Coast Path. After about 300 yards/275m bear right into Culbone, Embelle and Yenworthy Woods. This route may not be shown on some older maps. Unfortunately, recent land slippages towards the end of Yenworthy Wood have forced an inland diversion via Yenworthy Combe.

Continue to Sister's Fountain, where the access path to the bus route at County Gate on the A39 leaves the Coast Path. Go uphill through a pair of wild boar head gateposts, then take care not to miss the narrow signposted path 300 yards/275m past the cottage as the drive bears left.

An alternative waymarked route may be taken between Culbone and Yenworthy Wood. Although slightly more inland, it offers better views than the mainly woodland more coastal route.

At Coddow Combe, the route is signposted left off the lighthouse track "Countisbury 1.5 miles". From Countisbury the now spectacular path continues down the seaward side of the A39 road. Lower down it joins the road for a short way before descending on zigzags to the foreshore. Walk into Lynmouth, crossing the footbridge, then turn right to the sea front. Lynton is vertically above Lynmouth and is reached by turning left up the steps before the cliff railway (which can be taken as an interesting alternative). A new route is also available past the Esplanade car park at the end of the sea front, where a pleasant path, signposted to Lynton, goes left up the steep wooded hillside to emerge on the Coast Path west of Lynton. Both Lynmouth and Lynton have all facilities.

It is interesting to know that from Lynmouth it is possible to walk Devon's Coast to Coast route using the Two Moors Way and its southern extension to the south coast at Wembury. Guide books are available from Lynton TIC.

Week 1 - Day 3

OS Maps: **Landranger 180; Explorer OL9**

	This Walk	Cumulative	This Walk	Cumulative	Grading	Timing
Ascent	3,766ft	8,746ft	1,148m	2,666m	Strenuous	7 hours
Distance	13.3mi	35.1mi	21.4km	56.5km		

For detailed directions, see our Lynmouth to Ilfracombe Path Description booklet.

This generally quiet and remote Section passes through a series of spectacular coastal landscapes: the Valley of Rocks with its rocky crags and pinnacles; the steep wooded cliffs at Woody Bay; the breathtaking scenery of the deep and steep crevice carved through the cliffs at Heddon's Mouth; the wide open spaces of Holdstone Down; and the heights of the Great Hangman, the highest point on the entire Coast Path and one of the highest coastal locations in the country.

Directions

Lynton and Combe Martin are connected by a summer bus service (year-round at weekends). Heddon's Mouth (6.5 miles/10.5km from Lynton) makes a good break in this length (though not on the bus route). It has refreshment facilities at Hunter's Inn and as there is a parallel higher path between here and Woody Bay there is scope for a scenic circular walk.

The Coast Path out of Lynton is on North Walk, and this path leads to Castle Rock in the Valley of Rocks. The next section follows a minor but sometimes busy road, but a diversion to the right from the turning circle at the end of the Valley avoids its first length. Continue past the Toll House and up the hill. A permissive path on the right to Crock Point then avoids another length, and also gives stunning views.

The Coast Path leaves the road just before the Woody Bay Hotel opposite the Red House. Arriving at another road turn left uphill. Follow the next Coast Path sign ahead. When this superb stretch reaches the dramatic Heddon's Mouth valley follow it down to the valley floor. On reaching the stone bridge over the Heddon River turn right, over the river, and at the next path turn hard left. Continue for 100 yards/91m to the signpost on the right to Combe Martin. (Inland on either side of the river the path leads to the pub and shop at Hunter's Inn.)

Climb steeply away from the valley floor, keeping right at the top where the path levels off. Continue round the headland (take care in windy conditions) then the path heads inland to reach a stone wall; this is followed parallel to the sea. The wall ends and the signed path continues across the heathland of Holdstone Down. At Sherrycombe the route follows the grass track along the top of the combe to the inland end and then down. Ascending Great Hangman from Sherrycombe bear away from the wall on the left and ignore the many paths going to the right, meeting the wall higher up. From Great Hangman the path is obvious to Little Hangman and beyond to Combe Martin.

Castle Rock

Week 1 - Day 4 (half day)

OS Maps: Landranger 180; Explorer 139 or OL9

	This Walk	Cumulative	This Walk	Cumulative	Grading	Timing
Ascent	1,280ft	10,026ft	390m	3,056m	Moderate, strenuous in parts	2.5 hours
Distance	5.3mi	40.4mi	8.6km	65.1km		

For detailed directions see our Lynmouth to Ilfracombe Path description booklet.

This is a Section of rocky inlets, one of which, Watermouth, is spacious enough for boats to be moored. These bays are divided by rugged headlands. The cliffs here are grey and slatey, making for a forbidding looking coastline, notwithstanding the little bays. At the western end the site of a prehistoric hill fort gives a panoramic view over Ilfracombe. This Section is never far from the A399 coast road and various tourist facilities, so despite the impressive cliffs it is not a lonely length.

Watermouth Harbour

Directions

Combe Martin and Ilfracombe are linked by a regular bus service, allowing a bus-walk to be easily undertaken on this Section.

The Coast Path leaves the Lime Kiln car park in Combe Martin, passing the TIC, then forks right to join the A399 road. Turn right (Seaside Hill Road) above the beach. Turn right onto a narrow tarmac lane which climbs steeply to re-join the A399 road. Walk on the slightly raised path along the roadside through two gates. Go along a path beside a field to a flight of steps, then turn left up the slip road back to the main road and on to the brow, passing the bus shelter. Turn right to follow the road down to the old main road, with a bus shelter, now used as an Information Point, over to the right. Here turn left beside the entrance to the Sandy Cove Hotel to follow a track towards Watermouth Cove.

At Watermouth it is possible to cross the foreshore for some 110 yards/100m to a flight of steps at most states of the tide; take care, as the rocks can be slippery. However, if the tide is high, it is necessary to walk along the main road; in this case be especially careful. (Check the Watermouth tide timings by contacting Ilfracombe or Combe Martin TICs.)

If it is necessary to walk the road route it is recommended to cross the road at Watermouth Cove Caravan Park entrance, in order to get a good view of the traffic. Then walk along the grass verge past Watermouth Castle. When the verge peters out there is a good view to cross back. Then walk facing the traffic to the cut-through on the right to the signed Coast Path.

(For those walking eastwards on the road route, it is recommended to cross the road immediately from the cut-through, then along the elevated verge to pass Watermouth Castle. It is then possible to cross back with a better view along the road.)

NB. The Association is awaiting final plans from Devon County Council for a safe improvement here. The Association has offered to part-fund this much-needed and long awaited work. If complete, new signing will indicate the improved route.

The next pleasant section of path passes the western side of Watermouth Cove and on around Widmouth Head and then Rillage Point. There is then a roadside section into Hele. Turn right here then climb some steps on the far left of the beach. The path zigzags up past Beacon Point to the top of Hillsborough. Follow the waymarks down the hill to Ilfracombe Harbour.

Week 1 - Day 4 (half day)

OS Maps: **Landranger 180; Explorer 139**

	This Walk	Cumulative	This Walk	Cumulative	Grading	Timing
Ascent	2,037ft	12,063ft	621m	3,677m	Easy to moderate; strenuous west of Lee Bay	3.5 hours
Distance	7.3mi	47.7mi	11.7km	76.8km		

For detailed directions see our Ilfracombe to Croyde Bay Path Description booklet.

Most of this Section is characterised by grass-topped cliffs fronting numerous small coves and a foreshore of rock ledges. Half-way along is the focal point of Bull Point lighthouse. At Morte Point the character of the coastline changes abruptly as the enormous beach of Woolacombe Sands in its vast bay comes into view, often dotted with surfers. The dark jagged rocks of Morte Point give this headland a superb brooding atmosphere.

Directions

From Ilfracombe Harbour pass the Sandpiper Inn into Capstone Road. After some 170 yards/150m turn right to pass around Capstone Point. At the far end take a flight of steps that goes up behind the back of the Landmark Theatre. Follow this path to the top of the gardens and through a gate by a shelter. Bear right along Granville Road then right again onto an unmetalled road which leads to the Torrs Walk on the right; the Torrs Walk is well waymarked.

At the top of the Torrs Walk bear right and follow the path down the field to the stile in the corner. Continue ahead around the hill to another stile then cross the field to meet the old coach road ahead. Bear right on this track, which later becomes a minor road into Lee Bay. Refreshments are available year-round at the Grampus Inn in Lee village, a short way inland.

The next length from Lee Bay is quite strenuous. Proceed up the road from Lee, turning right at the top of the hill through a brick-pillared gate. Two steep valleys are crossed before Bull Point and its lighthouse are reached. The path continues on and out around Morte Point, a spectacular jagged slate ridge like a dinosaur's back emerging from the sea. The path leaves Morte Point and continues beneath the cliffs past small sandy bays to arrive at Woolacombe.

Lee Bay

Week 1 - Day 5 (half day)

OS Maps: Landranger 180; Explorer 139

	This Walk	Cumulative	This Walk	Cumulative	Grading	Timing
Ascent	725ft	12,788ft	221m	3,898m	Moderate	3 hours
Distance	6.3mi	54.0mi	10.2km	87.0km		

For detailed directions see our Ilfracombe to Croyde Bay Path Description booklet.

The main feature of this Section is the vast sandy beach of Woolacombe Sands, backed by a substantial line of dunes. Busy with families and surfers close to the town, it becomes surprisingly empty away from the facilities. Beyond the beach is the superb headland of Baggy Point, a contrast to the beach with its steep cliffs and broad, grassy top. Rounding the headland another, smaller sandy bay comes into view, Croyde Bay, with the wider vista of Bideford Bay beyond.

Directions

Croyde Bay is an excellent centre for a circular walk using the Coast Path, around Baggy Point to Putsborough, giving views over Woolacombe Sands while experiencing the superb character of the headland.

At Woolacombe the Coast Path leaves the Watersmeet Hotel parallel to the Esplanade road, then turns up Challacombe Road. It leaves this road on the right at approximately the National Trust sign - there may be no waymark here. The path continues through the enormous dunes of Woolacombe Warren - the waymarking means that going astray is unlikely. An alternative is to follow Marine Drive and the track beyond, which gives better views. If the tide is low many walk the length of Woolacombe Sands but this should not be attempted on a high or rising tide.

The official path leaves the Warren by a set of steep steps, joining the extension to Marine Drive and the alternative route. It continues along the track then a road, leaving it to the right after the caravan site. As an alternative, take the earlier path on the right to the car park at Putsborough, where there are seasonal refreshments and toilets (the beach route joins here). Go left of the caravan site to a stile and up the cliff slope to re-join the official path.

The excellent high level path continues to the end of Baggy Point, giving superb views. At the end of the headland, bear right to join the lower path towards Croyde. Follow the road, partly on a parallel path. Do not leave the road at the first slipway. The official path leaves the road a little further on to cross the beach, but many will continue on to visit Croyde and its facilities.

Baggy Point wreck post

Week 1 - Day 5 (half day)

OS Maps: Landranger 180; Explorer 139

	This Walk	Cumulative	This Walk	Cumulative	Grading	Timing
Ascent	506ft	13,294ft	154m	4,052m	Easy	3.25 hours
Distance	8.8mi	62.8mi	14.0km	101.0km		

For detailed description see our Croyde Bay to Barnstaple Path Description booklet.

The length immediately adjacent to Croyde Bay follows a low cliff and gives stunning views over the truly enormous length of Saunton Sands with the dune complex of Braunton Burrows behind. Beyond is the sweep of Bideford Bay, with the possibility of seeing as far as Hartland Point lighthouse, many miles away. Offshore on the horizon is the isle of Lundy. The remainder of this Section is low and level, through a huge range of dunes (the official route) or along the seemingly endless Saunton Sands. Then comes the twin estuary of the Rivers Taw and Torridge, with mudbanks and reclaimed marshes making for a birdwatcher's delight. This is a length displaying a relatively rare aspect of the South West coast.

Directions

Croyde Bay and Braunton are linked by a regular year-round bus service, making this a good bus-walk possibility.

The Coast Path leaves Croyde Bay via the beach (no dogs May-September) and on to the low cliffs at Down End. Turn left at the old coastguard lookout to the B3231 road. Cross the road with care here, turn left then climb some stone steps. The path now contours round Saunton Down, parallel to and above the road. This ends opposite the large white building of the Saunton Sands Hotel.

From here there are optional routes. The first option is to cross the road and pass around the hotel to the Saunton Sands car park, where there are toilets and seasonal refreshments. Leave the car park by the entrance road and after 55 yards/50m bear right along a sandy lane to the B3231. Continue carefully along the road for some 400 yards/365m, past the Golf Club driveway, turning right at a red brick partially rendered house.

If there is no need for the toilets or refreshments, a better option is to turn left uphill opposite the hotel, away from the road. Follow the path as it bears round to the right until it arrives at the B3231 opposite the red brick house described above. Cross the road to continue on the same route as above.

This route now enters the Braunton Burrows nature reserve, designated a UNESCO Biosphere Reserve for its nature conservation importance. The route through the Burrows is well waymarked; it then follows a clear track to arrive at the car park at Broad Sands, at the mouth of the estuary of the Taw and Torridge rivers. From here head for the white cottage on the estuary side, a well-known local landmark known as the White House.

Many walkers prefer to miss the Burrows and walk from Saunton Sands car park the length of the beach, for some 3.5 miles/5.5km. Near the end of the beach, just after a wooden groyne, look out for a slatted wooden catwalk entering the dunes to the left. Follow this to arrive at the Broad Sands car park. This beach route keeps the sea in sight, not the case with the Burrows route.

From the White House follow the estuary side on top of the Great Sea Bank. This is followed, between estuary and reclaimed marshes, to the old quay at Velator on the edge of Braunton. To visit Braunton and its facilities, turn left at Velator along the footpath and cycleway, following the former railway track.

Towards Baggy Point

Week 1 - Day 6 (half day)

OS Maps: **Landranger 180; Explorer 139**

	This Walk	Cumulative	This Walk	Cumulative	Grading	Timing
Ascent	16ft	13,310ft	5m	4,057m	Easy	2 hours
Distance	5.6mi	68.4mi	9.1km	110.1km		

For detailed directions, see our Croyde Bay to Barnstaple Path Description booklet.

This is a flat, low-level Section, following the line of the former railway track once used by the Atlantic Coast Express. As well as the Coast Path, it is also used by Devon's Coast to Coast Cycle Route. At the Braunton end, the main item of interest is the Royal Marines air base at Chivenor, next to the path, but further on the path runs alongside the estuary of the River Taw, with its interplay of water and sand and mud banks. This makes for a pleasant environment; in character, however, this length is semi-urban.

Directions

There is a regular and year-round bus service between Braunton and Barnstaple, which can also be accessed at Chivenor and at the Braunton Inn, approximately mid-way along the route, giving various short walks options.

From Braunton's main car park the signed route to Barnstaple leads to the Coast Path at Velator and from here the path follows the former railway past Chivenor Royal Marines base and then alongside the Taw Estuary all the way to Barnstaple.

A new bridge over the river offers an alternative crossing point, but using this misses Barnstaple and its facilities though it does give a superb view down the river.

Approaching Barnstaple on the former railway the path crosses a bridge over the tributary River Yeo and then passes the old railway station to a riverside embankment. Leave this at steps climbing to Barnstaple's Long Bridge. Barnstaple, North Devon's major centre, is a pleasant and interesting historic town well worth exploring, as well as offering a range of facilities, including a branch line railway to the main line at Exeter.

Barnstaple New Bridge

Week 1 - Day 6 (half day)

OS Maps: **Landranger 180; Explorer 139**

	This Walk	Cumulative	This Walk	Cumulative	Grading	Timing
Ascent	36ft	13,346ft	11m	4,068m	Easy	2.5 hours
Distance	7.4mi	75.8mi	11.9km	122.0km		

For detailed directions see our Barnstaple to Westward Ho! Path Description booklet.

This is a flat, low-level Section, much of it following a former railway line on the south side of the Taw Estuary. It passes through a landscape of marshland and pastures, with the tidal expanses and sand banks of the river never far away. This is an area of great value for birdlife. Approaching Instow the estuary opens out as the Taw's sister river, the Torridge, joins and there are wide areas of sand bars and dunes. This Section, despite its proximity to "civilisation" and the use of the former railway as part of the Devon Coast to Coast Cycle Route, is nevertheless one of much interest and character.

Directions

There is a regular and frequent all-year bus service between Barnstaple and Instow, which can also be accessed at Fremington, approximately mid-way along the route. A variety of short walk options is therefore available.

Cross Barnstaple's Long Bridge then keep to the right of the large roundabout, pass the factory buildings, then cross a mini-roundabout to a path which curves around to a subway under the approach road for the high-level bridge. A link path to the railway station goes off to the left here. In addition, this link path gives access to the Station Master's Cafe, which usefully also carries a range of local walking information. The main path, signed Coast Path and Tarka Trail, then links to the former railway line. The short cut across the high-level bridge joins here.

The former railway continues past the delightfully restored Fremington Quay, with its all-year cafe and Information Point. At Yelland look out for the path leaving the railway to the right which takes the Coast Path behind the site of an old power station. It then crosses an area of dunes to arrive at the estuary-side road through Instow, which has all facilities.

Week 1 - Day 7

OS Maps: Landranger 180; Explorer 139

	This Walk	Cumulative	This Walk	Cumulative	Grading	Timing
Ascent	528ft	13,871ft	160m	4, 228 m	Easy	4.5 hours
Distance	11.7mi	87.5mi	18.8km	140.8km		

For detailed directions see our Barnstaple to Westward Ho! Path Description booklet.

Much of this Section follows the estuary of the River Torridge, first on its east bank then turning back on its west. The estuary is largely enclosed by green hills, but houses and roads are ever-present and a high-level road bridge over the estuary is a major feature. The Coast Path crosses the river at the charming old port of Bideford. Passing beyond the estuary and through the characterful old fishing town of Appledore, the path crosses the open spaces of Northam Burrows and its surrounding marshlands and then alongside an enormous pebble ridge as it arrives again at the open sea. As an alternative option, missing out Bideford, a ferry service is now operating from April to October between Instow and Appledore; tel: 07757 620999 for details (and see page 18).

Directions

A regular bus service links Instow and Westward Ho! and another connects Instow to Appledore, both via Bideford. These services allow for a range of Coast Path-based walk options.

From Instow go through the old railway station and follow the former railway, passing underneath the high-level bridge, to the restored Bideford station. Leave the station to cross Bideford Long Bridge, then turn right along the bustling quay. Bideford has all facilities. Keep alongside the river past the car park then next to the rugby club to a lane which passes under the high-level bridge. Follow the waymarked tracks to a riverside lane then, after the old tank traps, fork right to a small woodland area.

Descend to a boardwalk then, if the tide is low, continue on the old sea wall. At high tide a well waymarked route circles the marshy area. Follow the waymarked route round Appledore shipyard and at the road turn right into Appledore via Myrtle Street. Continue along the quay and on into the charming old part of the town, along Irsha Street and past the lifeboat station to a path along the edge of low cliffs and across a field to a slipway, where the route joins a road. Follow the road for approximately 0.3 mile/0.5km to a crossroads and here turn right.

Follow the track ahead alongside the marshes then on the seaward side of the dunes to the pebble ridge. Continue ahead on the landward side of the ridge to Westward Ho! (At most states of the tide it is possible to walk along the beach next to the ridge.)

Week 2 - Day 1

OS Maps: Landranger 180 (eastern half) ; Explorer 139 (eastern half); Landranger 190 (western half); Explorer 126 (western half)

	This Walk	Cumulative	This Walk	Cumulative	Grading	Timing
Ascent	2,995ft	16,866ft	913m	5,141m	Strenuous	6 hours
Distance	11.2mi	98.7mi	18.0km	158.8km		

For detailed directions see our Westward Ho! to Clovelly Path Description booklet.

This Section is one of cliffs and woods. The eastern half is an area of undulating cliffs, cut in places by substantial valleys, though in the length closest to Westward Ho!, where the line of an old railway is used, the path is generally level. The western half passes through lengthy wooded stretches, much of it along the old carriage road known as the Hobby Drive. At the western end, Clovelly is probably one of the most picturesque villages in England.

Directions

There is no direct bus route between Westward Ho! and Clovelly. However, there is one between Bideford and Clovelly, as well as a frequent link to Bideford from Westward Ho! Buck's Mills, about two thirds of the way along this length towards Clovelly, is on the Bideford-Clovelly bus route, giving a possible bus-walk at this end.

At Westward Ho! walk along the path above the beach. After passing the last of the holiday chalets, the path follows the track of the long-disused Bideford to Westward Ho! railway. This makes a fine easy scenic walk. Where the railway turns inland, the path continues along the cliffs, rising and falling to cross a short pebble beach before climbing again. At Peppercombe turn inland to cross the stream and then continue through woodland. Note that some old maps may not show the correct route at Worthygate Wood. The path drops to Buck's Mills, a picturesque little spot, then climbs again into more woods. On leaving Barton Wood, keep to the bottom edge of the field until crossing a bridge to the Hobby Drive at the end of a second field. The Hobby Drive section is nearly 3 miles/5km long, and although very pleasant offers sea glimpses rather than sea views. The path arrives at Clovelly at the top of the steep village street. Clovelly is very picturesque and has most facilities, though perhaps limited in range.

Bucks Mills

12 • Clovelly to Hartland Quay

Week 2 - Day 2

OS Maps: Landranger 190; Explorer 126

	This Walk	Cumulative	This Walk	Cumulative	Grading	Timing
Ascent	2,382ft	19,248ft	726m	5,867m	Moderate to strenuous	5 hours
Distance	10.3mi	109.0mi	16.6km	175.4km		

For detailed directions see our Clovelly to Hartland Quay Path Description booklet.

There is a great contrast in this Section between east and west. In the east the landscape is one of parkland, the domesticated and partly ornamental landscape of the grounds of Clovelly Court. After leaving the parkland a run of high cliffs culminates at Hartland Point, one of the great defining headlands of the Coast Path. Here the coast turns from east-west to north-south and its character changes into one of the Coast Path's most breathtaking stretches, with dark brooding cliffs behind jagged fingers of rock stretching into the Atlantic Ocean. Experiencing its magnificent scenery is well worth the effort of crossing the spectacular deep valleys which cut the coast. The Section ends at the pub and hotel at Hartland Quay, which has a wonderful remote atmosphere.

Angel Wings Shelter

Directions

Hartland Quay has no public transport. However, there are numerous walking links from the Coast Path to Hartland village, 2.5 miles/4km inland, which is on the bus route to Clovelly.

If using Clovelly as a base, it is requested that walkers use the main car park. Following negotiations, a special lower parking charge is available for Coast Path walkers. Enquire at the Visitor Centre.

From the main car park walk out of the entrance and turn right down the road for some 220 yards/200m to a black gate on the left. Go through and follow the track first right and through a gap in the wall, then leave the track and follow the marked path down to the right. After a while go through a kissing-gate then follow the fence on the right to another gate into shrubbery. Continue through the shrubbery through more gates. Turn right at a T-junction and right again at the next fork. Soon the path arrives at an unusual seat known as the "Angel's Wings". At the track, turn hard right - not along the track. After passing a superb viewpoint the path descends steeply into a valley to another track. Go right here. The signed detour to the viewpoint is well worth the effort.

The Coast Path goes down the valley to the shore at Mouth Mill. Cross the stream then follow the grass track inland past the lime kiln.

Shortly, turn right and climb the valley side. Half-way up, follow the steps to the right. On reaching the top pass through fields to a stile on the right leading to some descending zigzags. Cross the bridge at the bottom, turn left then take the first right.

After the prehistoric earthwork of Windbury Castle the path continues on the cliff-top to Shipload Bay and then on to Hartland Point, where there are seasonal refreshments. The Coast Path turns sharp left off the lighthouse track towards the coastguard lookout before the lighthouse gate. A short diversion gives a good view of a wreck on the rocks below.

From Hartland Point the path descends into an unusual valley, almost parallel to the coast, at Smoothlands, before climbing again. Descending then to the valley at the Abbey River the path goes inland to cross at a stone bridge. At the next cliff top, past an old folly tower, the path arrives at a road by the old Rocket House. Bear right to follow the path downhill to Hartland Quay, a lonely outpost with car park, toilets and refreshments, as well as an hotel.

Week 2 - Day 3

OS Maps: Landranger 190; Explorer 126 (most of length); Explorer 111 (Bude)

	This Walk	Cumulative	This Walk	Cumulative	Grading	Timing
Ascent	4,170ft	23,418ft	1,271m	7,138m	Severe	8.5 hours
Distance	15.4mi	124.4mi	24.8km	200.2km		

For detailed directions see our Hartland Quay to Bude Path Description booklet.

This is an awe-inspiring and dramatic coastline. Great jagged ridges of rock stretch out into the Atlantic Ocean, backed by high, surf-fringed cliffs. The coast is punctuated by jutting headlands and tiny, often inaccessible beaches. In the south, towards Bude, the coast softens a little and, at low tide, long sandy beaches appear. This is a spectacular Section.

Directions

Hartland Quay has no public transport connections. There is, however, an infrequent bus service between Bude and Morwenstow, half-way along, which could be used for a bus-walk on the southern half of this Section.

Note that this is probably the most arduous of all the days in the suggested itinerary. It is necessary to cross ten river valleys to complete the length, all of them steep and deep. Because of this, many may prefer to split the length at Morwenstow.

From Hartland Quay a track then a grassy path passes behind St Catherine's Tor. There is a climb then the cliff path reaches the dramatic waterfall at Speke's Mill Mouth. Keep to the eastern side of the stream here for some 150 yards/135m then cross by the wooden footbridge. Follow the signs up the valley inland of Swansford Hill. Take care at Sandhole Cliff, after joining the metalled road, to look out for the signpost after about 0.3 mile/0.5km indicating the turn right back to the coast. (It is hoped this length of road may be eliminated in the near future.)

After Welcombe Mouth, Marsland Mouth marks the Cornish border, indicated by a wooden sign. The ascents and descents continue, and a diversion to Morwenstow might be worth considering. The church is picturesque and interesting and there are seasonal refreshments nearby.

At the radio dishes do not miss the sign directing right towards the cliff edge. Descending to Duckpool, cross the stream by a footbridge. There are toilets here. Continue on to Sandy Mouth where there are more toilets and seasonal refreshments. The going now eases at last and after passing over the open cliffs at Maer Down the path arrives at Crooklets Beach at Bude. Follow the path along the low cliffs behind the beaches into the town, which has all facilities.

Back from Hartland Quay

Week 2 - Day 4

OS Maps: **Landranger 190; Explorer 111**

	This Walk	Cumulative	This Walk	Cumulative	Grading	Timing
Ascent	2,494ft	25,912ft	760m	7,898m	Easy then strenuous	4.75 hours
Distance	10.2mi	134.6mi	16.4km	216.6km		

For detailed directions see our Bude to Crackington Haven Path Description booklet.

Low grassy cliffs and surfing beaches south of Bude give way to an ever higher and more rugged coastline fronted by rough rock ledges and cut by deep and steep valleys. There are some superb viewpoints along this later quiet and remote-feeling length which reward the effort. Crackington Haven is a pleasant spot and on the cliffs above, St Gennys Church is a superb spot for contemplation.

Directions

A regular bus service links Bude with Crackington Haven, and also serves Widemouth Bay, about 3 miles/7km from Bude, thus offering a number of bus-walk options.

The path south from Bude starts at the sea lock on the historic Bude Canal, then climbs to the cliff top at Compass Point and on to Efford Beacon. There are excellent views from here. The path over Efford Down to Upton and on to Widemouth Bay is easy to follow. Widemouth has toilets and refreshments, the last before Crackington Haven.

South of Widemouth the path follows the low cliff for a short distance then diverts inland slightly at Wanson Mouth to join the coast road in the stream valley. Turn right and follow the road as it climbs steeply to Penhalt Cliff. There are more magnificent views from the cliff-top car park.

From the southern end of the car park the Coast Path crosses a field and descends steeply to Millook Haven. Now follow the steep road uphill for a short distance then turn right onto the cliff top at Raven's Beak. From here the path climbs steadily past the stunted oak woodland at Dizzard Point and on to Chipman Point. Two further deep and steep valleys are crossed, then a ridge walk leads to Castle Point, which gives tremendous views. Another steep valley crossing leads on to Pencannow Point and views over Crackington Haven. The path descends easily into the cove, where there are toilets, refreshments, buses and accommodation.

Bude Canal

Week 2 - Day 5 (half day)

OS Maps: **Landranger 190; Explorer 111**

	This Walk	Cumulative	This Walk	Cumulative	Grading	Timing
Ascent	2,264ft	28,176ft	690m	8,588m	Strenuous	3.75 hours
Distance	6.8mi	141.4mi	10.9km	227.5km		

For detailed directions see our Crackington Haven to Tintagel Path Description booklet.

This is a Section of high cliffs, the highest, indeed in Cornwall. Not only are they high, but they also present an appearance of bulk, of being literally massive, and the walker will often feel dwarfed by them, especially on a climb or descent or perhaps on a headland. Much of this Section is also quite lonely, and this combination makes this a coast with an imposing character.

Directions

Crackington Haven and Boscastle are linked by a regular bus service, making this an option for a bus-walk.

There are toilets and seasonal shops, cafes and a pub at Crackington Haven. Leave behind the beach near the toilets and head out for the headland of Cambeak. Rounding the headland, keep away from its high and sheer cliff edges. Beyond Cambeak the path is relatively level, passing above the landslip zone at Strangles Beach. Ahead looms High Cliff, the appropriately-named highest cliff in Cornwall. There is a steady ascent but the descent on the south side is very steep. The path then climbs through a landfall at Rusey Cliff, twisting and turning to the top. A cliff top section through fields follows to the sheer black cliff at Buckator. The path then dips slightly before continuing at high level to Fire Beacon Point. Here the descent is steep, but helped by attractive slate steps. The path then follows the cliff face into the inlet of Pentargon, with its impressive waterfall. This is best seen from the southern side - do not be tempted to leave the path for a better view.

The now easy path continues on to Boscastle. Aim for the white mast on Penally Hill, then follow the path alongside the beautiful harbour inlet into Boscastle, now happily restored after its 2004 experiences.

Boscastle

Week 2 - Day 5 (half day)

OS Maps: Landranger 190 (eastern half); Landranger 200 (western half); Explorer 111

	This Walk	Cumulative	This Walk	Cumulative	Grading	Timing
Ascent	1,230ft	29,406ft	375m	8,963m	Moderate	2.25 hours
Distance	4.6mi	146.0mi	7.4km	234.9km		

For detailed directions see our Crackington Haven to Tintagel Path Description booklet.

This fairly short Section is a great local favourite, as it combines all the best of the Coast Path - headlands, sandy bays, historic features and, yes, steep valleys, all in a manageable but picturesque length which is not too taxing. In addition, although popular, it never seems crowded and is, indeed, a "real" walk. With all this and its convenient bus links it is a perfect Coast Path taster.

Directions

Boscastle and Tintagel are linked by a regular bus service. It also serves Rocky Valley, half-way between the two, enabling a variety of bus-walks to be undertaken.

Boscastle has been attractively rebuilt after the floods of 2004, and has all facilities.

The Coast Path leaves the south side of the harbour over the new stone bridge and climbs towards the headland of Willapark, with its prominent white watch tower. The path cuts across the neck of the headland, but a diversion to the end is worthwhile.

After a steep descent and climb at Grower Gut the path continues easily, turning seaward of the Manor House at Trevalga. The headland beyond gives views over the rocky offshore islands important for breeding seabirds. The path continues past Firebeacon Hill - look out for the Ladies Window rock arch in the gully to the right - then passes seaward of a cliff-top caravan and camping site. There is then a des cent into the exquisite Rocky Valley. There is a path up the valley to a bus stop on the coast road, passing prehistoric carvings in the cliff wall.

From the footbridge in the valley the path climbs again, round the edge of the grassy Bossiney Common and above the sandy bay at Bossiney Haven. Another climb then leads to another headland also, confusingly, called Willapark. Again the Coast Path cuts across the neck of the headland and, again, a diversion to the end is worthwhile.

The path now continues to Barras Nose headland, from where it descends to Tintagel Haven below the castle ruins. Here are toilets, cafe and English Heritage gift shop. A good but steep path leads inland to the village.

The Ladies Window

17 • Tintagel to Port Isaac

Week 2 - Day 6

OS Maps: Landranger 200; Explorer 111 (eastern half); Explorer 106 (western half)

	This Walk	Cumulative	This Walk	Cumulative	Grading	Timing
Ascent	2,589ft	31,995ft	789m	9,752m	Severe	4.75 hours
Distance	9.1mi	155.1mi	14.7km	249.6km		

For detailed directions see our Tintagel to Port Isaac Path Description booklet.

Both ends of this Section are relatively popular and accessible. At Tintagel the Coast Path passes the remains of the medieval castle perched on its isolated headland then the atmospherically located cliff-top church and the now picturesque evidence of coastal slate quarrying. At the other end is the beautifully quaint village of Port Isaac in its scenic bay. The long central length, though, comprises high cliffs cut by sometimes precipitously steep valleys. It is remote, lonely and often tough, and will be especially appreciated by those who relish an empty, arduous and dramatic coastline.

Near Tintagel

Directions

There is a regular bus service between Tintagel and Port Isaac; occasionally a change at Camelford is needed. A bus-walk is therefore possible on this Section.

Tintagel has all necessary facilities. Surprisingly, however, little in the village is very old other than the Old Post Office, once a local manor house.

From the village walk down the path to Tintagel Haven. From here the Coast Path climbs past the entrance to the Castle and gives excellent views over the headland which forms the castle site. A good path continues seaward of the church and on beyond past the Youth Hostel in its former quarry building and round Penhallic Point with its superb views.

The path drops steeply to Trebarwith Strand, where there are toilets, refreshments and pub, the last facilities before Port Isaac. The next part is particularly tough as it climbs steeply out of the Trebarwith valley then almost immediately drops down to sea level and up again at Backways Cove. There follows a level stretch of about a mile/1.5km to the stream valley behind Tregardock Beach. Descend on the inland side of the detached piece of cliff known as The Mountain, then climb again to Tregardock Cliff. Another level length follows, before the deepest and steepest valley yet at Jacket's Point. At the top yet another deep valley almost immediately follows. Then comes a further valley, at Barrett's Zawn. This is an area of massive rock falls. The next valley follows, this one with exceptionally steep and stony sides.

At last the path levels out again through cliff-top meadows, with just a small valley to cross at St Illickswell Gug. Eventually, the path reaches the road at Cartway Cove. Take the path on the right and round the headland to Port Gaverne, a charming spot. Follow the road uphill to the car park at the edge of Port Isaac. Go through this and follow the well-signed path above the attractive harbour inlet into the village.

Port Isaac is a very picturesque village clustered round the little harbour at the head of a sheltered bay. It has all facilities.

Port Isaac

Week 2 - Day 7

OS Maps: **Landranger 200; Explorer 106**

	This Walk	Cumulative	This Walk	Cumulative	Grading	Timing
Ascent	2,923ft	34,918ft	891m	10,643m	Strenuous then easy	5.5 hours
Distance	11.7mi	166.8mi	18.9km	268.5km		

For detailed directions see our Port Isaac to Padstow Path Description booklet.

This Section can be divided into three distinct characters. From Port Isaac to Port Quin is a rollercoaster of a path, closely following the ups and downs and ins and outs of the quiet, scenic but energy-sapping coast. From Port Quin to Polzeath the character becomes rather more open, if still very scenic, including the broad headland of The Rumps and Pentire Point, a wonderful airy lookout. From Polzeath to the Padstow ferry the landscape is tamer, more domesticated, often with housing or tourist development and more estuarine than maritime as it reaches the mouth of the River Camel.

Directions

There is a regular bus service between Port Isaac and Rock, the ferry point for Padstow. This service also passes through Polzeath at the mouth of the Camel estuary, giving several scenic bus-walk options, including an almost level estuary-side one. There is a popular circuit using the Coast Path between Port Isaac and Port Quin and others from Polzeath around Pentire Point.

Port Isaac has all necessary facilities, and is a scenic gem. To leave the village, take the road to the right behind the fish market. Climbing, it bears right and becomes a cliff path, soon dropping into Pine Haven. From here to Port Quin the path is magnificent and clear, but tough as it follows the cliff edge next to a prominent fence line. There is an optional diversion to the end of Varley Head.

Near Polzeath

The path enters the beautiful Port Quin inlet, descending to what was once a busy pilchard port, though there are no facilities here now. Follow the road westbound up the steep hill and a little way up the Coast Path leaves to the right, towards Doyden Point. The path follows above the cove, keeping seaward of and below the large house. Head to a prominent stone cairn, then continue ahead on a grassy path and past some old mineshafts. From the cairn a diversion to the right goes to the folly of Doyden Castle and to Doyden Point, where there is a superb view back to Port Quin.

Padstow Ferry at Rock

There is a sharp descent to Epphaven Cove then the path passes through a delightful little wooded valley before climbing past the impressive Lundy Hole. The clear cliff path now heads for the Iron Age fortress on The Rumps headland. A detour to the end is well worthwhile.

From The Rumps the path climbs through a little former quarry area then continues at high level round Pentire Point, giving spectacular views. An easy descent follows to Polzeath, all well marked. Polzeath has all necessary facilities, including now an all-year café, "Tubestation", open Wednesday-Saturday during the winter. The path follows the road past the beach car park then goes right by the cottages, where the road bends sharp left on the steep hill. It now follows a low cliff to Daymer Bay, where there are toilets and a seasonal cafe, then down steps to the beach. At the far end of the beach it leaves through dunes and over a footbridge below Brea Hill. It is possible to detour to visit the little St Enodoc Church from here.

To continue on the Coast Path follow the path clinging to the side of Brea Hill, though it is possible to go over the top or, at low tide, along the beach. On the far, south, side of Brea Hill the well-signed path continues through dunes to arrive at Rock car park. The ferry to Padstow is in the estuary just below. However, be warned that at exceptionally low tides the ferry may sail from some way downstream, in front of the dunes.

The ferry operates all year at 20 minute intervals, 08:00 to 18:50 (June-mid July); 08:00 to 19:50 (mid July-end August); 08:00 to 16:50 (winter) - telephone 01841 532239 or 07773 081574.

For ferry details see page 18.

A water taxi service operates between Rock and Padstow between 19:00 and midnight from Easter to 31st October, weather and tides permitting - telephone 01208 862815 (office hours) or mobile 07778 105297. For further details see page 18.

Note that it is possible to walk Coast to Coast across Cornwall between Padstow and Fowey on the south coast, using the Saints' Way. A guidebook is available from Padstow TIC.

Week 3 - Day 1 (half day)

OS Maps: Landranger 200: Explorer 106

	This Walk	Cumulative	This Walk	Cumulative	Grading	Timing
Ascent	744ft	35,662ft	227m	10,870m	Easy	2.5 hours
Distance	5.7mi	172.5mi	9.1km	277.6km		

For detailed directions see our Padstow to Porthcothan Path Description booklet.

The length from Padstow to Stepper Point, at the mouth of the Camel, is a scenic length of ever-changing estuarine views with sandy stretches, especially at low tide. Beyond, the coast is an easy but picturesque length of cliffs, which include occasional views right across the headland at the mouth of the estuary and up the Camel as well as west to Trevose Head. The two elements of this Section combine to form a popular local walk.

Directions

A regular bus service links Padstow with the inland end of Trevone, about one mile/1.5 km from the Coast Path. This allows for a possible bus-walk. There are also a number of possible circular walks from Padstow using the Coast Path which take in the Stepper Point headland.

Padstow is a charming and bustling little harbour town a short way up the Camel Estuary. If arriving from Rock, notice that normally this arrives in Padstow at the harbour, but at low tide it lands a short distance downstream at St Saviour's Point. In either event, it is well worthwhile taking time to explore the town.

The Coast Path leaves the north end of the harbour past the TIC and proceeds on low cliffs alongside the estuary. After passing a wooded little stream valley at St George's Cove the path heads inland of a marshy area before going back to the cliffs and on to Hawker's Cove. Refreshments are available at Hawker's Cove at the "Rest a While" tea garden. Only outside seating is available so it may not be available in bad weather. It may be best to telephone 01841 532919 to check opening times. Pass behind the old pilots' houses here then fork right to climb to Stepper Point, with its Daymark tower. From here there are remarkable views, inland to Bodmin Moor as well as along the coast.

The path is now on the exposed Atlantic coast. Go round the precipitous inlet of Butter Hole Cove, looking out for the small Pepper Hole to the right of the path just before. An easy length to Gunver Head follows, with excellent sea views. Approaching Trevone the path skirts the impressive Round Hole collapsed cave - approach this with caution as the sides are sheer. Follow the cliffs round into the bay at Trevone, which has toilets, cafe and pub, as well as a car park.

Sea Pink & Cowslips

Week 3 - Day 1 (half day)

OS Maps: Landranger 200; Explorer 106

	This Walk	Cumulative	This Walk	Cumulative	Grading	Timing
Ascent	817ft	36,479ft	249m	11,119m	Easy	3.5 hours
Distance	7.9mi	180.4mi	12.7km	290.3km		

For detailed directions see our Padstow to Porthcothan Path description booklet.

This is a popular Section, never far from a variety of holiday accommodation. It is perhaps most associated with a range of scenic sandy surfing beaches, some of them quite extensive. As a contrast, around the middle of the length is the great landmark of Trevose Head and its lighthouse, visible from great swathes of the North Cornwall coast and an atmospheric location.

Directions

A regular bus service passes the inland end of Trevone, about one mile/1.6km from the Coast Path, and links to Porthcothan. The same route serves Constantine Bay, about two-thirds of the way along the coast from Trevone, giving a potential for a variety of bus-walks.

Trevone has all necessary facilities. The path crosses the rear of the beach and leaves behind the little headland on the south-west side of the bay, following the cliff edge round rocky Newtrain Bay. Reaching Harlyn there are refreshments and toilets. Cross the stream on the road bridge then follow the beach below the low cliff for some 330 yards/300m before climbing left onto the cliff and then continuing to the headland at Cataclews Point.

The path passes inland of Padstow's lifeboat station, accessible by a cul-de-sac path, and then goes on to Trevose Head, passing the lighthouse. On a clear day the coastal views are incredibly extensive, ranging from the satellite dishes north of Bude to the granite hills of West Penwith behind St Ives. This is an atmospheric headland.

After an old quarry the path passes a Round Hole collapsed cave and descends to the partly rocky Booby's Bay. Continue on to the rear of Constantine Bay, a very attractive and extensive beach at low tide. Walk the length of the beach. There are toilets and seasonal refreshments at the far end and a bus stop a little way inland. Beyond the dunes the path rounds Treyarnon Head to cross another attractive beach at Treyarnon Bay, with seasonal toilets and refreshments.

An unusually indented coastline follows, with sheer-sided headlands and impressive coves. Near Pepper Cove the ramparts of an Iron Age cliff fort may be seen, and the whole coastline is quite spectacular. The path then turns into another sandy cove, at Porthcothan Bay, which has toilets and refreshments and also has a pub, the Tredrea Inn, about 500 yards/458m inland up the road.

Trevose Head

Week 3 - Day 2

OS Maps: **Landranger 200; Explorer 106**

	This Walk	Cumulative	This Walk	Cumulative	Grading	Timing
Ascent	1,447ft	37,926ft	441m	11,560m	Moderate	5 hours
Distance	11.1mi	191.5mi	17.9km	308.2km		

For detailed directions see our Porthcothan to Newquay Path Description booklet.

This is a relatively well-used Section, particularly around Newquay. It shows the interplay of high cliffs and sandy beaches particularly well. Almost the whole length is characterised by high, flat-topped cliffs, sometimes with prominent headlands, which for long stretches form the back of extensive attractive sandy beaches, many of them popular with surfers. While never a lonely Section, its cliffs and bays make it one well worth exploring, helped by the relatively easy terrain.

Directions

Porthcothan and Newquay are linked by a regular bus service. This route follows a road parallel and close to the coast, meaning that there are a number of possible links to the Coast Path from this bus, allowing for quite a range of possible bus-walks.

Porthcothan has all facilities that may be needed. The Coast Path leaves past the shop and keeps in front of the houses and on around the headland. After a short steep descent and climb, an easy level walk leads to Park Head, an excellent viewpoint. There have been numerous landslips here so keep to the path inland of the white posts. The whole headland is worth wandering over and exploring. Ahead now is the National Trust's Carnewas property, with its spectacular beach. The Trust's cafe and Information Centre are open through the summer. On the beach below are the massive stacks forming Bedruthan Steps.

The Bedruthan Steps area can be busy, but a quieter length follows to Trenance Point and into the sandy bay of Mawgan Porth, where there are toilets, refreshments and a pub as well as a bus stop. Surprisingly, this was once the site of an unfinished canal project.

Cross the stream using the road then leave it to the right on the sharp bend on the hill out of Mawgan Porth. There then follows a long high level length to Watergate Bay on airy flat-topped cliffs, cut by a couple of minor descents. The path passes Iron Age remains here while inland is the contrast of Newquay Airport. The path continues on the cliff top behind the magnificent Watergate Beach, much used for surfing and other activities. The path then descends to the road by the Watergate Bay Hotel, and here there are toilets, refreshments and another bus stop.

Cross the stream at the road then turn right by the car park and climb back to the cliffs, which are now followed to the outskirts of Newquay. The coastal view ahead to the town and its headlands is excellent. The Coast Path leaves the road to

Sea Pinks on wall

pass round the headland of Trevelgue Head, an important prehistoric location. Although the path bypasses the island at the very end, this can be visited via the footbridge, and is worth the diversion for the views. The path returns to the road by Porth Beach before leaving it at steps down on the left, to pass underneath the main road and cross the next little headland to emerge above Lusty Glaze beach - look for the information board here relating to the canal previously encountered at Mawgan Porth.

The path continues into the park at Barrowfields, skirting its seaward side, to reach the main road into Newquay town centre. Follow this just past the railway station then take the old tramway road on the right. At the overbridge climb the steps on the right and go down to Trebarwith Crescent. Go left here then right into Island Crescent. Follow this then turn right along the footpath above Towan Beach.

At the corner go down the steps on the right then from the car park cross Beach Road and follow the tarmac path ahead. At the end follow the steps on the left to pass a bowling green and public toilets to Fore Street. Turn right here as far as the Red Lion and here turn right again to the harbour down North Quay Hill.

As well as all facilities, Newquay has a branch line railway station linking to the main line to Penzance and is the centre of a network of local bus routes.

Week 3 - Day 3 (half day)

OS Maps: **Landranger 200; Explorer 104**

	This Walk	Cumulative	This Walk	Cumulative	Grading	Timing
Ascent	1,145ft	39,071ft	349m	11,909m	Moderate	3.5 hours
Distance	6.3mi	197.8mi	10.2km	318.4km		

For detailed directions see our Newquay to Perranporth Path Description booklet.

This Section includes some superb viewpoints from headlands in and around Newquay, the panoramas quite unspoiled by the proximity of the large town. Beyond Newquay a range of landscapes is experienced, from wide sandy beaches to exposed cliff tops to small sandy bays to dune systems. In addition, unexpectedly, the wooded estuary valley of the river known as The Gannel is crossed at the edge of Newquay. This variety, and the proximity to a range of facilities and accommodation, make this a popular, well-used length.

Directions

A regular bus service links Newquay with Holywell Bay, and also serves Crantock, between the two. This gives a number of bus-walk possibilities.

Newquay is the biggest town on Cornwall's north coast. Although usually busy, being especially popular with surfers and also with groups of young holidaymakers, it is in a very attractive setting of beaches and headlands. All the facilities are here, and there is a branch railway linking to the main line to Penzance.

From Newquay Harbour the Coast Path climbs past the old Huer's Hut to Towan Head. This is a good lookout spot, and is excellent for seabird watching. From Towan Head the path then follows the back of Fistral Beach. This is probably the country's most popular surfing beach and international competitions are held here. The path climbs to the cliffs at the southern end and then crosses the road to go along Pentire Crescent which leads into Penmere Drive. The path then arrives above the Gannel Estuary. However, this misses the major headland of Pentire Point East, which is well worth the diversion to the end. (If following the diversion round the headland, on returning from the end aim for the far bottom of the car park at the neck of the headland. From here head along the suburban road parallel to the Gannel. Follow this to the Fern Pit Cafe.)

There are four options from here for crossing the Gannel, depending on the tide and time of year.

OPTION 1: FERN PIT FERRY (deduct 2 miles/3km from total mileage)
The first option is to use the Fern Pit Ferry from behind the cafe. The cafe is approximately 0.7 mile/1.1km west of Penmere Drive along Pentire Crescent. The ferry operates continuously, 7 days a week, 10.00-18.00 18th May until mid September weather dependent - telephone 01637 873181. For further details see page 18.

OPTION 2: PENPOL CROSSING (official route)

Go along Penmere Drive and take the next close on the right (even nos 6-16), bearing left down the footpath between gardens. This descends to the Gannel and to a tidal footbridge. This can be used 3-4 hours either side of low water. Cross the Gannel here. (If coming from the headland circuit, continue past the Fern Pit Cafe and on along Riverside Avenue, then ahead and right. At a junction where there is a footpath to the right keep ahead, ignoring the footpath. Bear right into Penmere Drive, again ignoring the footpath on the right. Go along Penmere Drive and take the next close on the right, bearing left down the footpath between gardens. This joins the main route to descend to the Gannel.)

OPTION 3: TRENANCE FOOTBRIDGE (add 3 miles/4.8km to total mileage)

This route is usable at most states of the tide. From the Newquay side of the Penpol crossing continue upstream on the path parallel to the river until it arrives at the A392 Gannel Road. There is a footbridge on the right just before the junction with the A3058 Trevemper Road. Cross the bridge and continue ahead, following the bridleway to Trevemper. Turn right just before reaching the tarmac and follow the footpath through Treringey to arrive at the south side of the Penpol tidal footbridge.

OPTION 4: MAIN ROAD ROUTE (add 4.5 miles/7.2km to total mileage)

Continue past the Trenance footbridge and along the A392 Trevemper Road from the roundabout. At the next roundabout turn right and after about 100 yards/90m take the little unsigned lane on the right. This leads to Trevemper, going forward and right as the lane goes left. After the gate turn left on the route described under Option 3 through Treringey.

Options 2, 3 and 4 come together at Penpol. Follow the lane then take the signed path on the right above the estuary. After passing the ferry landing for Option 1 this path leads to Crantock Beach car park. Crantock village with its facilities and bus stop is a little way inland. Cross the car park to the dunes; bear left at the junction of grassy paths on entering the dune area and follow this inland of the main dune area to re-emerge at a coastal path which leads to the cliffs of Pentire Point West where the Bowgie Inn provides meals and refreshments. The path goes round Porth Joke (known locally as Polly Joke), then on around Kelsey Head to Holywell Bay, descending across more dunes either into the village or to cross the river on a seaward footbridge. There are facilities, some seasonal, here.

Crantock Ferry

Week 3 - Day 3 (half day)

OS Maps: **Landranger 200; Explorer 104**

	This Walk	Cumulative	This Walk	Cumulative	Grading	Timing
Ascent	755ft	39,826ft	230m	12,139m	Moderate	2 hours
Distance	4.5mi	202.3mi	7.3km	325.7km		

For detailed directions see our Newquay to Perranporth Path Description booklet.

Perranporth sundial

The theme of this Section is sand, in the form of both dunes and beaches, although it begins by rounding headlands at Penhale and Ligger Points. However, even at Penhale the inland vista is dominated by dunes, although the adjacent Army camp is also prominent. For the bulk of this Section sand is everywhere around, on the seemingly endless length of Perran Beach and the dunes which back it. Both ends, Holywell and Perranporth, are busy holiday settlements but the more remote areas of Perran Beach can be surprisingly quiet.

Directions

Holywell Bay and Perranporth are linked by a regular bus service, making a bus-walk a feasible option here.

Holywell Bay has all facilities, some seasonal.

From Holywell Bay the path rounds Penhale Point, skirting the seaward edge of the somewhat unattractive Penhale army camp. It then goes on out to Ligger Point, where there is a panoramic view of the length of Perran Beach. The path heads towards the dunes then descends behind the cliff quarry to the beach. It now follows the back of the beach for some 1.5 miles/2.5km. This is possible even at high tide, and usually on firm sand. At Cotty's Point the tide often makes it necessary to take the path over the little headland. It descends back to the beach on the south side and then crosses the stream by the footbridge when nearly at Perranporth, where there are again all needed facilities.

Week 3 - Day 4

OS Maps: Landranger 200 (Perranporth); Landranger 203 (remainder); Explorer 104

	This Walk	Cumulative	This Walk	Cumulative	Grading	Timing
Ascent	2,250ft	42,076ft	686m	12,825m	Moderate then strenuous	5.75 hours
Distance	12.2mi	214.5mi	19.7km	345.4km		

For detailed directions see our Perranporth to Portreath Path Description booklet.

This Section is one in which Cornwall's coastal mining heritage is paramount. There is much evidence of former mining activity, this including somewhat stark areas of spoil and sometimes slightly sad building relics, but also some grand and imposing engine houses and chimneys. In some locations, the large-scale level of the activity is difficult to imagine now. Nevertheless, the scale and grandeur of the cliffs, the beaches and the surf mean that nature always re-asserts itself.

Directions

A summer bus service links Perranporth to Portreath, also passing St Agnes and Porthtowan along the way, giving numerous bus-walk options.

Perranporth is a busy holiday centre with all facilities. The Coast Path goes west from the main car park and follows the hill up Cliff Road. Keep left of the castellated building then along Tregundy Lane. Go half left at the entrance to the Youth Hostel and on to the cliffs, the path clinging to the cliff face out to Cligga Head. Here the path enters quarry and mine workings, but is well signposted. There is then a level stretch alongside Perranporth Aerodrome before the steep descent to Trevellas Porth, a valley marked by many relics of the mining industry. Go upstream to cross at the road bridge, then back to the cliffs and back down again into Trevaunance Cove, where there are toilets and refreshments. The bus stop at St Agnes is a little way inland.

On reaching the road at Trevaunance Cove go straight across passing the Driftwood Spars car park and a large tall house on the right. Follow the waymarked footpath immediately right along a metalled lane then fork right along a footpath. Soon the path climbs steeply to the cliff top. A long and scenic high-level path now goes around St Agnes Head, giving superb views ahead, then past the iconic engine house at Towanroath before descending to Chapel Porth, a small and attractive cove with toilets and seasonal refreshments. Refreshments are available at the Chapel Porth Beach Cafe daily in the holiday season and weather permitting during the winter. Phone 01872 552487 to check opening times. Follow the stream inland for 200 yards/185m then turn right and up to the cliffs, before it is back down again into Porthtowan. Again there are toilets and refreshments and a magnificent beach. There is a bus stop a little inland.

Iron & Arsenic colours

Follow the road inland then turn right up West Beach Road, then left up the narrow road to the cliff top. In the valley look out for signs taking the path back to the cliffs. More mine workings are passed, then the path runs alongside a prominent fence next to MOD land before reaching a road which descends into Portreath. This former industrial harbour town has all facilities.

Week 3 - Day 5

OS Maps: Landranger 203; Explorer 104 (eastern half); Explorer 102 (western half)

	This Walk	Cumulative	This Walk	Cumulative	Grading	Timing
Ascent	1,362ft	43,438ft	415m	13,240m	Moderate/ easy	5.5 hours
Distance	12.4mi	226.9mi	19.9km	365.3km		

For detailed directions see our Portreath to Hayle Path Description booklet.

There are two distinct characters to the coast of this Section. Between Portreath and Godrevy it is one of high, level cliffs, the sea far below. In contrast, between Godrevy and Hayle the walk focuses on sand, either dunes or beach, on the focal view of Godrevy lighthouse and on the great colourful sweep of St Ives Bay. This is never a lonely or remote length, but it is a scenic, fascinating and rewarding one.

Directions

A summer bus service links Portreath and Hayle, and also passes Godrevy, half-way between the two. This allows for bus-walk options over the whole Section or over either of the two distinct character lengths.

Portreath has all facilities and a nice beach. Leave the town crossing the bridge next to the car park then right, up Battery Hill. Continue ahead, meandering between properties at the end, turning right just beyond them up steps to the top of Western Hill, with its excellent views. After a couple of noticeable valleys the path then embarks on a long easy cliff-top walk along Reskajeague Downs, eventually arriving at Hell's Mouth, where there is a seasonal cafe. The path then narrows and turns right at an obvious T-junction. Cross a stile next to a gate and cross the seaward side of a field before continuing easily round Navax and Godrevy Points, the lighthouse becoming a focal point offshore. Keep seaward of the car park and access road and follow the signs along the low cliffs and over the dunes to another car park, at the Godrevy Cafe. Follow the boardwalk from the car park to cross the Red River. Turn left for 30 yards/29m then go right, following the large slate waymarks through the former quarry, now a nature reserve.

Keep ahead through the dunes, following the signposts. Note it is often possible to walk along the beach here but beware the incoming tide which can mean being cut off below the cliffs. If the tide is right, leave the beach at the lifeguard hut near the foot of Black Cliff. If coming through the dunes, keep ahead above the hut. Then, with either option, turn left up some steps just before two chalets. Turn right towards a house, leaving it on the right, and walk along a line of chalets on the left. The path is slightly overgrown but then opens out at a car park. Follow the access track parallel to the estuary of the River Hayle through the former harbour area, bear right to cross the old swing bridge to the road then turn right to reach the railway viaduct in the centre of Hayle.

Hayle

Week 3 - Day 6

OS Maps: **Landranger 203; Explorer 102**

	This Walk	Cumulative	This Walk	Cumulative	Grading	Timing
Ascent	617ft	44,055ft	188m	13,428m	Easy	2.5 hours
Distance	5.6mi	232.5mi	9.0km	374.3km		

For detailed directions see our Hayle to Pendeen Watch Path Description booklet.

This Section is never far from roads and houses, so often has a suburban air. However, this is outweighed by the views over the River Hayle estuary and, particularly, by the vistas over the great sweep of St Ives Bay with its vast sandy beaches and dunes, the iconic offshore Godrevy Lighthouse as a focal point and the fabulous sea colours, turquoises, greens and blues, whenever the sun shines on this length.

Directions

St Ives from Porth Kidney sands

A regular bus service links Hayle and St Ives, giving a bus-walk option. In addition, a branch-line railway plies between Lelant and St Ives, and this gives marvellous sea views. This makes for an unusual and especially scenic train-walk option.

Hayle has all facilities, including a railway station on the main line to Penzance. Walk to the viaduct and turn right on the path immediately before it. Go ahead to the road and immediately bear right, off the road, heading for the rear of Jewsons. Pass a metal gate then bear to the left, keeping left before the bridge on a narrow path which soon widens alongside a large lagoon. Keep on to the end then bear left to the road. Continue as the road passes alongside the River Hayle estuary on The Causeway, a birdwatchers' delight. Cross to the far side of the road then back to the riverside again before forking right at the Old Quay House - take care on the road here. Under the bridge turn right, signed to St Ives Park and Ride. At the car park attendant's kiosk turn left to a lane, then turn right here. Follow the lane next to the railway and estuary all the way to Lelant Church. Go along the path next to the church to pass under the railway. Just before the beach turn left along the seaward side of the railway through dunes. (NB this is also the route of the St Michael's Way, a cross-peninsula path from Lelant to Marazion - a guide leaflet is available at St Ives TIC.)

Follow the clear path parallel to the magnificent Porthkidney Beach. Approaching the headland of Carrack Gladden the path forks - keep right then continue ahead. Descend the road to Carbis Bay, where there are toilets and seasonal refreshments, walking inland of the cafe but seaward of the hotel. Climb over a railway bridge then continue as the path becomes a minor road. Pass the path taking St Michael's Way inland then at a little cross-roads go straight ahead, steeply downhill. (Turning right shortly after the St Michael's Way turning down a private, pedestrians only path gives a more scenic alternative to the official route, re-joining at the little cross-roads.) Cross the railway bridge and double back right then left to arrive at Porthminster Beach, just below St Ives railway station.

Week 4 - Day 1

OS Maps: **Landranger 203; Explorer 102**

	This Walk	Cumulative	This Walk	Cumulative	Grading	Timing
Ascent	3,428ft	47,483ft	1,045m	14,473m	Severe	7 hours
Distance	13.9mi	246.4mi	22.3km	396.6km		

For detailed directions see our Hayle to Pendeen Watch Path Description booklet.

There are no settlements on this Section and the character is lonely and remote. It is also tough going, with rocky scrambles and boggy lengths. But it can only be described as a magnificent length. Stark cliffs, rock pinnacles, tiny scenic coves with translucent water, rugged exposed headlands - all are here. Inland the view is often of empty moorland. This is the Coast Path at its most awe-inspiring. Prepare for its rigours, then enjoy the wonderful experience.

Directions

A regular summer bus service links St Ives and Pendeen village, a little inland of the Coast Path. It also passes through other inland settlements linked by footpath to the Coast Path, principally Zennor, Treen (Gurnard's Head) and Morvah, allowing for various bus-walks options.

A warning:- this is a tough and deserted length of the Coast Path. There are no settlements or refreshment facilities, though there are some path links inland to small settlements. The terrain is often rough and rocky and in places can be boggy. But a compensation:- this is a length of wonderfully dramatic coastal scenery.

From the path below St Ives railway station keep along as close as possible to the sea and harbour. The official route goes round the green St Ives Head, usually known as The Island. This is reached by following signs to the museum from the far end of the harbour and on through a small car park. From The Island go through the old "Downlong" quarter to Porthmeor Beach and the Tate. There are also short cuts direct to here - follow signs to the Tate.

Go along the rear of Porthmeor Beach then bear off right along the path next to the putting green. The Coast Path now leads out to the rugged Clodgy Point and then on round Hor Point to Pen Enys Point, where it cuts across the neck of the headland. Pass the trig point on Carn Naun, where there are extensive views forward and back, then descend to cross the stream at River Cove. Just beyond the path passes the offshore Carracks, where seals are regularly seen. Approaching Zennor Head the path forks - keep right to follow the seaward path round the headland. From Zennor Head the path heads inland - look out for the signed Coast Path descending steeply to the right. If in need of refreshments, or for the bus, continue along the path inland to Zennor, where there is a pub and seasonal cafe.

View from Bosigran

On the Coast Path, more ups and downs lead to the distinctive headland of Gurnard's Head. The path cuts across its neck, but a diversion onto the headland, an Iron Age fortified site, is worth the effort. There are also diversions inland here to Treen, where refreshments are available at the Gurnard's Head Inn and there is a bus stop.

The Coast Path continues, generally easy to follow if not always an easy walk. Approaching Bosigran, another Iron Age fortification, can be confusing. Aim for the high point of the rocky ridge ahead and follow the most obvious path towards it. It is likely to lead just inland of the summit - turn right to reach it then follow the clear path down the other side. Cross the stream on a small bridge near a ruined building then follow the path uphill, just seaward of an obvious stone wall. There is a diversion path inland here to a bus stop at Rosemergy.

Further on the Coast Path, look out for a path inland to Morvah for another bus stop if needed. Otherwise keep on the obvious Coast Path round the back of Portheras Cove and on to the lighthouse at Pendeen Watch. Pendeen village, with its pubs, cafe, shop, toilets and bus stop, is about 1 mile/1.5km inland.

28 • Pendeen Watch to Sennen Cove

Week 4 - Day 2

OS Maps: Landranger 203; Explorer 102

	This Walk	Cumulative	This Walk	Cumulative	Grading	Timing
Ascent	1,683ft	49,166ft	513m	14,986m	Moderate	4.25 hours
Distance	9.0mi	255.4mi	14.6km	411.2km		

For detailed directions see our Pendeen Watch to Porthcurno Path Description booklet.

This Section offers a wide range of walking experiences. Between Pendeen Watch and Botallack the overriding experience is of Cornwall's coastal mining heritage. This ranges from unattractive early 20th century industrial relics to romantic stone-built cliff-face engine houses, all this next to sheer cliffs and often wild seas. Beyond Botallack is a superb length of scenic exposed cliffs, highlighted by the magnificent headland of Cape Cornwall. This Section has all that is best on the Cornish coast - rugged cliffs, mining relics, translucent water, turquoise coves, purple heather, rocky scrambles, the view of a lighthouse. Then, approaching Sennen Cove, there is a sweep of broad sandy beaches backed by dunes, and the length ends with a scenic harbour and a lifeboat station. A wonderful length.

Sennen Cove

Directions

A regular summer bus service links Pendeen village, a little inland of the Coast Path, with Sennen Cove. It also serves St Just, inland of Cape Cornwall, which is used as the centre of various Coast Path-based circular walks. Bus-walks are also possible from Geevor and Botallack, reached by footpath from the coast.

Priest's Cove at Cape Cornwall

From Pendeen Watch the path goes along the road to the end of the row of cottages, then turns right at a granite marker. (The road continues into Pendeen village, with its range of facilities.) The Coast Path is clear and leads to the old mining area at Geevor. A diversion inland leads to refreshments and toilets at the mining museum, which is itself well worth a visit if possible. Follow the signed track beyond Geevor to the Levant Beam Engine House, open for steaming at certain times. From here the official path follows the clear track parallel to the coast, but a narrower path to seaward with better views leads from the far end of the car park. The two options come together as more mines are passed at Botallack. Look to seaward to see the famous Crowns Mine engine houses perched improbably on the cliff.

Beyond Botallack, as the mines give way, look for the signed path to the right which leads to the headland at Kenidjack Castle. A lot of the waymarking in this area uses granite stones, perfect for the landscape setting. From the old building on the headland descend to a track, go left then quickly right to another track. Go left here then turn right to cross the floor of the Kenidjack Valley. Climb to the top and turn right. Ahead now is the distinctive shape of Cape Cornwall, surmounted by its chimney. Turn right immediately before the road and then bear right across a field past the ruins of a chapel to a stone stile. Cross this, turn left and then climb right to reach the top of the headland. Savour the views, then join the path which descends over the seaward side of the Cape by zigzags and steps to reach the National Coastwatch Institution watchhouse. This recent addition to the Coast Path provides a superb experience. Go to the left of the watchhouse then down the steps and along a path past some stone buildings and through a gate to reach another set of granite steps descending to the right. In the nearby car park are seasonal refreshments and toilets. St Just is about 1 mile/1.5km up the road.

At the bottom of the steps go left then climb right to a road at the top. Bear off right at the sign and follow the clear path into the Cot Valley. Turn right at the road to the cove at Porth Nanven, and here cross the stream and climb onto the cliffs. There is a good clear cliff-face path to the beach at Gwynver, although with one awkward scramble. From Gwynver the path continues through the dunes behind the sandy beaches, which can be walked at low tide, to the car park at Sennen Cove. This is a popular family and surfing spot with all facilities.

Week 4 - Day 3 (half day)

OS Maps: **Landranger 203; Explorer 102**

	This Walk	Cumulative	This Walk	Cumulative	Grading	Timing
Ascent	1,542ft	50,708ft	470m	15,456m	Moderate	3.25 hours
Distance	6.6mi	262.0mi	10.6km	421.8km		

For detailed directions see our Pendeen Watch to Porthcurno Path description booklet.

This is the most westerly length of coast in England. Much of it has the character of moorland meeting the sea, with great granite headlands and massive rock outcrops interspersed with isolated coves with exquisite sea colours. Towards Porthcurno the moorland is replaced by a more pastoral landscape, but the cliffs and coves continue. Much of this Section has a quiet character, interrupted only by the visitor mecca of Land's End.

Porth Chapel

Directions

Sennen Cove and Porthcurno are linked by a regular bus service, which also goes to Land's End. This allows for a choice of bus-walks and there are also numerous circuits possible based on the Land's End area.

Sennen Cove has all facilities. Leave the village passing the Round House gallery into the car park. Turn left up steps then right, towards the lookout. From here a range of parallel paths all lead to Land's End. Bear right to the First and Last House, at England's most westerly point, then keep seaward of the main complex to the outpost at Greeb Cottage. The complex has toilets and refreshments if needed. The path goes behind Greeb Cottage; then again a choice of paths all lead towards the beautiful bay of Nanjizal. At the far end of the bay head inland up the track then turn right steeply uphill on a stepped path. After passing through a gate look out for the official, unsigned, path leaving the main track to go seaward over a little rocky scramble. The path descends then climbs to the Coastwatch station on Gwennap Head. The main track also leads here, but less scenically.

The official path is clear from Gwennap Head down into Porthgwarra. An alternative, in good conditions only and for the sure-footed only, is to leave the main path to the right some 150 yards/140m after the Coastwatch station, then pass the hole of Tol-Pedn-Penwith ("the holed headland of Penwith") before bearing left to re-join the main path.

Porthgwarra is a charming little hamlet with toilets and seasonal refreshments and unusual passages through the cliffs. Leave along a track next to some cottages, climbing again to the cliffs. The clear path descends to Porth Chapel, passing St Levan's Holy Well. Bear left above the beach, climbing again to arrive at the car park of the unique cliff-face Minack Theatre. Leave by the path next to the theatre entrance. The path drops very steeply, with deep steps, to Porthcurno Beach. If in doubt, because of the conditions or possible vertigo, follow the road. At the bottom of the steps keep left above the beach to Porthcurno's facilities.

Week 4 - Day 3 (half day)

OS Maps: **Landranger 203; Explorer 102**

	This Walk	Cumulative	This Walk	Cumulative	Grading	Timing
Ascent	1,381ft	52,089ft	421m	15,877m	Strenuous	3.25 hours
Distance	5.5mi	267.5mi	8.8km	430.6km		

For detailed directions see our Porthcurno to Penzance Path Description booklet.

This is a quiet, remote and very scenic Section of cliffs and headlands, punctuated by some picturesque coves and a lighthouse. The larger coves, at each end, Porthcurno and Lamorna, are particularly attractive and are the only access points for cars, so are more popular, Otherwise, the sound of the sea and seabirds are likely to be the only disturbances in this beautiful length.

Directions

A regular bus service goes to Porthcurno and passes about 1 mile/1.5km inland of Lamorna Cove, making a bus-walk feasible. Many undertake one of a variety of circular walks between Porthcurno and Treen using the Coast Path.

Porthcurno has all facilities in summer. The Coast Path leaves at the back of the beach, climbing a steep track to Percella Point before turning to run parallel to the sea. A seaward loop gives a good view of the beautiful Pednvounder Beach, but requires a little scramble to return to the official route. The path then reaches the neck of Treen Head, or Treryn Dinas, the site of an Iron Age fortification. A cul-de-sac diversion heads for the end and the Logan Rock.

Continue on the clear path over the cliff to descend into Penberth Cove, a superb little fishing hamlet with an old capstan. There are toilets but no refreshments. There is a necessary inland diversion loop for dog walkers here.

After climbing away from Penberth the path continues along the cliff top, with one steep descent and climb at Porthguarnon, then starts to head inland. After passing a seaward house look out for the signed path to the right which descends into the wooded valley of St Loy and on to the boulder beach. Keep along the top of the beach for 55 yards/50m before leaving up the path. This climbs to pass above the lighthouse of Tater-du. Approaching Lamorna Point the path crosses a length of tumbled rocks, making for slow going, until it suddenly descends to the car park at Lamorna Cove. Here are toilets and seasonal refreshments.

War memorial at Lamorna

Week 4 - Day 4

OS Maps: Landranger 203; Explorer 102

	This Walk	Cumulative	This Walk	Cumulative	Grading	Timing
Ascent	725ft	52,814ft	221m	16,098m	Strenuous then easy	3.5 hours
Distance	9.4mi	276.9mi	15.1km	445.7km		

For detailed directions see our Porthcurno to Penzance and Penzance to Porthleven Path Description booklets.

West of Mousehole this Section is one of lushly vegetated cliffs, but most of it is urban or semi-urban in character as it passes through Newlyn and Penzance. However, it is really defined by its views over the magnificent Mount's Bay, dominated by the iconic sight of St Michael's Mount and its castle, which give this coast a magical character.

Directions

A regular bus service passes about 1 mile/1.5km inland of Lamorna Cove and also serves Newlyn, Penzance and Marazion, giving a variety of possible bus-walk options.

Lamorna Cove has a seasonal cafe, toilets and, a little way inland, a pub. The Coast Path leaves the cove behind the harbour, bearing right to the cliffs. The well-marked path eventually leads to a road which descends into Mousehole. The road leads to the harbour; however, the official route turns right opposite "Lowena" then continues towards the sea, turning left along a terrace to a car park. It briefly passes along the harbour before turning left then right to reach the main harbour-side road. Mousehole has all facilities and is very picturesque.

At the far end of the harbour go through the car park, on along a concrete walkway then up some steps. Turn right along the road, then along a seaward track to arrive at Newlyn. Follow the road round the harbour and past the fish market, turning right just after the Seamen's Mission to cross a bridge. Bear right past the Tolcarne Inn then follow the promenade to Penzance. Pass the harbour then go right through the large car park to where a walkway leaves from its far right-hand end. Penzance has all facilities, is the end stop of the main-line railway and is the hub of local bus services. The train and bus stations are next to the car park.

The walkway follows the sea wall to the edge of Marazion. At the end of the roadside parking area either follow the road or cross the dunes to a large car park, cross this and continue behind the sea wall into Marazion.

Marazion is the centre for access to St Michael's Mount and is the southern end of the cross-peninsula St Michael's Way from Lelant. The little town of Marazion has all facilities.

Mousehole

Week 4 - Day 5

OS Maps: Landranger 203; Explorer 103 (Porthleven); Explorer 102 (remainder)

	This Walk	Cumulative	This Walk	Cumulative	Grading	Timing
Ascent	1,916ft	54,730ft	584m	16,682m	Moderate then strenuous	4.75 hours
Distance	10.6mi	287.5mi	17.1km	462.8km		

For detailed directions see our Penzance to Porthleven Path Description booklet.

Between Marazion and Cudden Point this Section is dominated by the sweep of Mount's Bay and its iconic focal point of St Michael's Mount. It is a charming length of low cliffs and small fields. East of Cudden Point the Mount is lost but the local landscape is bolder, with craggy headlands, long sandy beaches, inaccessible coves and picturesque cliff-top engine houses.

Directions

There are regular bus services which link Marazion and Porthleven and also serve Perranuthnoe and Praa Sands between the two, making a variety of bus-walks possible, Marazion is a pleasant little town with all facilities and the causeway to St Michael's Mount.

St Michael's Mount

The Coast Path leaves along the main road, following it for some way to the speed restriction sign. Turn right before the cemetery, then bear left on a concrete path down steps and follow the path to the beach. Cross the top of the beach to some metal steps, climb them and continue ahead. Just after Trenow Cove the path turns inland. Look out for the signed right turn after 275 yards/250m, which goes back to the low cliffs and on to Perranuthnoe. There are toilets and seasonal refreshments here.

Take the lane on the seaward side of the car park, bearing right and then left into a field. The well-marked path leads to Cudden Point, with magnificent views over Mount's Bay. It descends past Little Cudden to Bessy's Cove, where it joins a track. Go ahead, bearing right at some granite gate posts, then through Prussia Cove on a lane between large stone buildings. Keep ahead on the path which passes above Kenneggy Sand and then descends to Praa Sands, where there are toilets and seasonal refreshments. Go down the slipway to the beach then along in front of the shop, taking the steps up beside the cafe. Keep along the top of the grassy dunes, turning left when signed at the end then right into a housing estate. At the end bear right and climb to the cliffs. The path skirts behind Rinsey Head then through a car park and down to a restored engine house. It continues to Trewavas Head, inland of more restored engine houses. Beyond there have been numerous cliff falls - be sure to follow the signed path. This then enters Porthleven on a lane - fork right entering the town to pass alongside the harbour to its head. Porthleven has all facilities.

33 • Porthleven to Mullion Cove

Week 4 - Day 6 (half day)

OS Maps: Landranger 203; Explorer 103

	This Walk	Cumulative	This Walk	Cumulative	Grading	Timing
Ascent	1,109ft	55,839ft	338m	17,020m	Moderate	3.25 hours
Distance	7.1mi	294.6mi	11.4km	474.2km		

For detailed directions see our Porthleven to The Lizard Path Description booklet.

This is a Section mostly of low cliffs with cliff-face paths, long stretches being above extensive beaches. It harbours a couple of unexpected features, firstly in the shape of Loe Bar, a large strip of shingle barring the freshwater Loe Pool from the sea, and secondly in the unusual position of Gunwalloe Church, hidden away in the corner of a sandy cove. Add a cliff-top monument to Marconi, a couple of picturesque coves and the rocky and atmospheric harbour at Mullion Cove and it makes for a fascinating length.

Directions

Porthleven and Mullion village, which is some 0.5 mile/1km from the Coast Path, are both served by regular but separate bus routes, which meet at Helston. The Mullion bus also serves Poldhu Cove, 1.5 miles/2.5km along the coast from Mullion Cove, allowing various bus-walks.

Porthleven has all facilities. The Coast Path goes alongside the harbour towards the clock-tower at the end near the pier. Follow the road past this building, going right at the fork and keep on out of the town to a car park. Climb the steps and continue ahead on the track to Loe Bar. Cross the bar to the far side, forking right, downhill, shortly after the memorial. After passing renovated fishery buildings the path arrives at Gunwalloe Fishing Cove. Go ahead onto the National Trust's Baulk Head, then above Halzephron Cove to a road. Bear right to a small car park then go right again, away from the road, on the cliffs down to Gunwalloe Church Cove. There are toilets and seasonal refreshments here. The picturesque church is tucked away at the right-hand end of the cove.

Skirt the beach to a road, then take the signed path over a footbridge and over the rear of the beach to the path rising away. Immediately after the car park at the top turn right along the cliff top before returning to the road and dropping into Poldhu Cove, where there is a bus stop, toilets and refreshments. Cross the stream on the road and turn right up the driveway signed to the Marconi Centre, leaving this after 110 yards/100m for a path to the right. This passes the Marconi monument on the cliffs then drops into Polurrian Cove. Climb away past the Polurrian Hotel and along the slightly suburban path to the Mullion Cove Hotel. Keep to seaward and drop down to the harbour, where there are seasonal refreshments. There are toilets 110 yards/100m up the road.

The Marconi Monument

Week 4 - Day 6 (half day)

OS Maps: **Landranger 203; Explorer 103**

	This Walk	Cumulative	This Walk	Cumulative	Grading	Timing
Ascent	1,303ft	57,142ft	397m	17,417m	Moderate	3.25 hours
Distance	6.8mi	301.4mi	10.9km	485.1km		

For detailed directions see our Porthleven to The Lizard Path Description booklet.

This is an exposed Section of high, flat-topped cliffs and spectacular coves and bays. The coastal landscape is superb throughout, but punctuated by some real scenic gems, of which Kynance Cove is probably the pick. The combination of steep cliffs, unusual geology and flora, beautiful sea colours and long stretches of easy walking make this a rewarding length. And watch out for choughs, Cornwall's iconic bird now returned to re-colonise this coast.

Directions

A regular bus service links Mullion village with Lizard Town, each settlement about 0.5 mile/1km inland from its respective end, thus giving a possible bus-walk. In addition, there are many easy local circuits based on the Coast Path in the Lizard-Kynance area.

Mullion Cove has seasonal refreshments and there are toilets a little way inland. The Coast Path leaves the quay slightly inland to the right, up the hill just after the cafe. Climb to the cliffs, keeping to the right to hug the coastline. There is an information board on the unique flora and fauna of the area here.

The easy and clear path rounds Parc Bean Cove and Lower Predannack Cliff. Approaching Vellan Head, be sure to keep close to the coast for the official route - the more obvious track misses the views. After the deep valley at Gew Graze the path rounds Rill Point and descends to Kynance Cove. The steep descent leads to a footbridge by the seasonal cafe. There are also toilets here. If the sun is shining the sea is brilliant turquoise.

From the cafe either follow the main track up towards the car park or cross the little beach (at low tide) and climb a partly stepped path to the cliffs, leaving this at a sign pointing right. This passes adjacent to the car park, where the main track arrives, and the Coast Path then continues clearly and easily above Pentreath Beach at Caerthillian and round Old Lizard Head, and on to Lizard Point, England's most southerly point, where there are cafes, gift shops and toilets. The nearby lighthouse is open to visitors at certain times. A path leads inland to Lizard Town, which has all facilities including regular bus services.

Kynance Cove

Week 5 - Day 1

OS Maps: Landranger 203 (Lizard); Landranger 204 (remainder); Explorer 103

	This Walk	Cumulative	This Walk	Cumulative	Grading	Timing
Ascent	2,293ft	59,435ft	699m	18,116m	Moderate, strenuous in places	5.75 hours
Distance	10.6mi	312.0mi	17.1km	502.2km		

For detailed directions see our The Lizard to Coverack Path Description booklet.

This is a Section of cliffs and coves, punctuated by headlands giving excellent views along the coastline. Here and there are areas of sandy beach at the foot of the cliffs, but only at Kennack are they very extensive. This coast is largely sheltered from the worst of the prevailing south-westerly winds, and consequently has a lush, well-vegetated character. This being a relatively unfrequented stretch, substantial lengths are quiet and remote.

Poltesco Old Serpentine Factory & Pilchard Store

Directions

Lizard Town, about 0.5 mile/1km inland of the Coast Path, has a bus service which also passes a little inland of Cadgwith, about half-way along this length, which presents a bus-walk possibility. In addition, there are numerous easy circuits based on The Lizard using the Coast Path which are popular and attractive.

Lizard Point has cafes and toilets, while Lizard Town, inland, has all necessary facilities. Lizard Point has the distinction of being England's most southerly point and is a fine location. The Coast Path leaves the Point alongside the car parking area and on in front of the lighthouse. There is a Heritage Centre at the lighthouse and both lighthouse and Heritage Centre are open to the public at certain times (www.lizardlighthouse.co.uk). After passing the lighthouse descend to cross a footbridge then climb, passing in front of the Housel Bay Hotel and on past the Lloyds Signal Station, bearing right here. The route passes Bass Point National Coastwatch Institution lookout, the first in the country to be established. At Kilcobben Cove the path goes behind The Lizard lifeboat station with its new boathouse which was completed in 2011. It then arrives at Church Cove. Go left for a short distance then take the path through the gate on the right. There are some ups and downs to a path junction just after a stone stile at Polgwidden Cove; keep right here. A little further on the path skirts the dramatic collapsed cave of the Devil's Frying Pan. Follow the signed path past the cottages and down into the picturesque little fishing hamlet of Cadgwith.

Cadgwith has a pub, shop, refreshments and toilets. There is a superb little beach here where the fishing boats are hauled up. This is overlooked by a convenient grassy knoll with seats known as The Todn (Cornish for lawn). Walk through Cadgwith and up the hill, turning right on the signed path a little way up. The Path then descends to Poltesco, crossing a footbridge. There is a diversion to the right leading to the attractive and interesting cove, complete with old serpentine works, where the local colourful rock was made into useful items. Climbing out of Poltesco, the path then joins a road which leads to the beach at Kennack Sands. There are toilets here and seasonal refreshments.

Follow the path behind the beaches and on to the cliffs to reach the neck of the long promontory of Carrick Luz, the site of an Iron Age cliff fort. The path cuts across the neck and then negotiates the steep valley at Downas Cove. Another, shallower valley crossing leads to the end of Black Head and its lookout hut. The path now descends over the cliffs towards Chynhalls Point going amongst the natural rock outcrops which can be slippery in wet weather. Beyond the Point the path soon reaches Coverack.

An alternative inland path avoids the slippery Chynhalls Cliff. At the top of the Coast Path descent, the wide alternative path goes through gorse and passes a Sculpture Park, then the edge of a caravan park before arriving at a bungalow on a tarmac road. Turn right towards the hotel and then almost immediately bear left down a narrower path to rejoin the Coast Path at Chynhalls Point.

Reaching the road at Coverack, the path soon veers off right down some steps to arrive at a car park at the end of the village. Follow the road past the harbour. Coverack, a pretty place, has all facilities, including a regular bus service into Helston.

Week 5 - Day 2

OS Maps: Landranger 204; Explorer 103

	This Walk	Cumulative	This Walk	Cumulative	Grading	Timing
Ascent	2,192ft	61,627ft	668m	18,784m	Moderate	5.75 hours
Distance	13.1mi	325.1mi	21.1km	523.3km		

For detailed directions, see our Coverack to Helford Path Description booklet.

This is a sheltered Section of the Coast Path. It includes low cliffs facing away from the prevailing winds, but also lengths of pleasant rural field paths, a little inland, necessary to avoid inaccessible coastal working and former quarries. In addition this Section has substantial lengths which fringe a tidal creek and on wooded estuary-side paths passing pretty beaches where the Coast Path reaches the Helford River. While not as dramatic as some Sections, it is an attractive stretch with a quiet charm of its own.

Directions

Separate bus routes from Helston serve Coverack and Helford Passage, across the river via ferry (Good Friday or 1st April to October) from Helford, allowing a bus-walk based on Helston. There is an attractive local circuit using the Coast Path between Helford and Gillan Creek.

There are all necessary facilities at Coverack. The Coast Path follows the road away from the pub and past the harbour, continuing straight ahead on a narrow lane when the road goes left. Look out for the sign pointing right, just before the end of the lane. The path goes over sometimes boggy ground next to the coast to arrive at Lowland Point. Next, the old workings at Dean Quarry are passed on their seaward side. The well-signed path then arrives at the open area at Godrevy Cove. The next length of coast is inaccessible due to operating quarries, so the Coast Path heads across the open area inland to pick up a signed path going uphill between fields. This leads to the little hamlet of Rosenithon. At the T-junction, turn right on the lane, uphill, turning left into a field just after the right-hand bend. Cross three fields in the same direction, stone stiles between them, to emerge on a lane. Go left then, at a junction, right, which leads to Porthoustock, a coastal hamlet with public toilets.

The route of the next stretch, to another coastal hamlet, Porthallow, is also a rural inland walk. It leaves Porthoustock past the telephone box and up the hill. Where the road bears right go straight ahead on a narrower lane. Go past a row of thatched cottages and over a little grassy bank at the end next to a greenhouse to a kissing-gate. Just past the gate there is a fork in the path. Bear right and follow the path climbing to the far top corner of the field to cross a lifting-bar stile and a Cornish stile (a sort of stone cattle grid) into another field. Turn right in this field alongside the hedge, then bear away left at the top to cross another Cornish stile to a road. At the road go left, passing through the tiny hamlet of Trenance. Here the route follows the road round to the right to a T-junction. At the junction go slightly right and immediately left onto an enclosed path which leads to a track between buildings. At the road turn right to arrive at Porthallow.

Porthallow has a pub, toilets and seasonal refreshments. Look out for the marker indicating the half-way point of the Coast Path, equidistant (at 315 miles) from Minehead and Poole. Leave Porthallow along the back of the beach and up the steps. The path now follows the coastline, keeping close to the edge round Nare Point and then past a couple of pretty beaches. Moving into the mouth of the Helford River the path continues alongside its tidal tributary, Gillan Creek.

Near Helford

A seasonal ferry operates here when the tide is high enough (about three hours either side of high water) which cuts out the need to walk round the creek. Ferry operates most days, Easter and April to the end of October. If operating, there is a board to display a signal requesting the ferry. Telephone 01326 231357 or see page 18 for ferry details.

Otherwise, the route goes left from the creekside up the hill to a sharp left-hand bend. Here go straight ahead along the field edge, then bear right over two further fields to a road. Turn right to Carne, at the head of the creek, then right again along the north side of the creek to St Anthony Church. Past the church turn left uphill then shortly right on a farm track which leads into a field. Cross diagonally left to the top of the field to a kissing-gate.

For a short, direct route from here go through the gate and turn left. However, the Coast Path includes an optional extra of a circuit of Dennis Head. For this circuit do not pass through the gate but turn right then almost immediately left over a stile. At the next junction continue straight ahead to reach the end of the headland. The path circles around the headland, re-joining the outward route to the stile and then the kissing-gate.

Go through the gate and continue along the top of the field. The route now heads up the estuary side of the Helford River through woods and past coves. Towards the end the path reaches a track - follow to the road and go right here then quickly left. The path then emerges next to the main car park at Helford. Go down the hill into the village. Helford has a pub and shop and there are toilets and a seasonal cafe at the car park. The cafe will take telephone orders to be ready on arrival, so it is possible to phone from St Anthony and have your order ready when you reach Helford - call 01326 231893.

Week 5 - Day 3

OS Maps: Landranger 204; Explorer 103

	This Walk	Cumulative	This Walk	Cumulative	Grading	Timing
Ascent	1,397ft	63,024ft	426m	19,210m	Moderate	4.5 hours
Distance	10.0mi	335.1mi	16.1km	539.4km		

For detailed directions see our Helford to Falmouth Path Description booklet.

There are two contrasting parts to this Section. Between Helford and Rosemullion Head it is a sheltered walk alongside the mouth of the beautiful Helford River, with undulating, relatively low cliffs alternating with charming little beaches. Between Rosemullion Head and Falmouth the walk flanks the sweep of Falmouth Bay, with rather larger coves overlooked by the great headland of Pendennis Point at the Falmouth end, crowned by its castle. Over the bay is St Anthony Head lighthouse. None of this is a lonely or remote walk, and the Falmouth end is decidedly urban, but it is never uninteresting and always very scenic.

Directions

Helford Passage and Falmouth are linked by a regular bus service, which also serves two of the beach coves along the route, at Maenporth and Swanpool, giving numerous bus-walk options. The short circular walk round Pendennis Head in Falmouth is a great local favourite.

Helford has pub, shop and toilets; Helford Passage, over the river, has a pub and seasonal refreshments. There is a seasonal ferry link.

The ferry operates between Easter and 31st October, 9:30 to 17:30 daily on demand - telephone 01326 250770.

For ferry details see page 19.

It is possible to use local taxi services if the ferry is not operating - Autocabs, tel: 01326 573773 or Cove Cars tel. 07980 814058. Alternatively Sailaway St Anthony Ltd, tel: 01326 231357 may be able to help.

Walk around Helford River

If the ferry is not operating, a 13 mile/21km walk around the Helford River is possible. This will add another day to the itinerary. For this route, from Helford take the path up the hill in front of the Shipwright Arms to arrive at Penarvon Cove. Go round the back of the cove and turn inland up a track to a road. Turn right then left on a track to the permissive path along the atmospheric Frenchman's Creek. At the end take the path on the right signed to Withan past Frenchman's Pill Cottage, crossing a footbridge. Follow the path through the woods and aim for the far left corner of the field, taking the stile on the left. Follow the boundary on the left past Withan Farm, then head west over the fields to a lane. Here turn left to a crossroads, turning right here towards Mawgan. The lane joins a larger road; turn right past Gear then down and up into Mawgan-in-Meneage village. Turn right just after the church on the path towards Gwarth-an-drea then left behind a bungalow to a road.

Turn right and at the junction bear right and continue downhill to the bridge at Gweek. There is a shop and pub here. Take the road opposite the Gweek Inn and at Tolvan Cross turn right along a bridleway to a road junction. Go straight ahead, towards Porth Navas. After crossing the stream take the footpath on the left along the field edge to the road.

Maenporth

Follow the road ahead to Nancenoy and Polwheveral. At the crossroads after Polwheveral turn right then after 140 yards/128m take the path on the left along the field edge then across the field corner to a road junction. Take the Porth Navas road opposite through the village to Trenarth Bridge, then turn right towards Falmouth. At the junction at Trebah turn right, then right again into Bar Road. At the end turn left on a footpath which leads to the Helford River, turning left to the Ferryboat Inn at Helford Passage, the landing place for the ferry from Helford.

Ferry users start from here

Coast Path, Helford Passage - Falmouth

From the Ferryboat Inn, facing the pub, turn right along the river and up to a grassy hill. Keep on to a concrete track and follow this, passing behind Trebah Beach at Polgwidden Cove. Continue on the riverside to Durgan, turning sharp right to enter the little village. Go up the road, ignoring one path to the right, until the road turns left and the path continues straight ahead. Follow this path, arriving at Porth Saxon Beach behind a building and then through a field to Porthallack Beach. The path then climbs round Toll Point to arrive at a wooded area. At the fork keep right and follow the path onward to Rosemullion Head, leaving the Helford River behind.

Keep seaward round the headland then descend to go through a small wood and then on, the path becoming suburban now, to reach Maenporth where there are toilets and refreshments and a bus stop. Turn right behind the cafe and continue to Swanpool, with more toilets and refreshments and another bus stop. Take the path from the far end of the beach to arrive at Gyllyngvase, then keep along Falmouth's promenade to the far end. The official path goes around the magnificent Pendennis Point - keep to the seaward road all the way to the end then at the car park descend on the signed path up the river, parallel to the road above. The path emerges from woods and passes the Leisure Centre, descending above the docks to a T-junction. Turn right then go ahead under the railway bridge, passing the Maritime Museum and along Falmouth's main shopping street to arrive at the Prince of Wales Pier at the far end. Falmouth, of course, has all facilities, including a rail link to the main line at Truro.

Week 5 - Day 4 (half day)

OS Maps: **Landranger 204; Explorer 105**

	This Walk	Cumulative	This Walk	Cumulative	Grading	Timing
Ascent	974ft	63,998ft	297m	19,507m	Easy	2.75 hours
Distance	6.2mi	341.3mi	10.0km	549.4km		

For detailed directions see our Falmouth to Portloe Path Description booklet.

This Section includes a trip on the ferry across the mouth of the River Fal, a treat of scenery and interest in its own right. Beyond, the walk round St Anthony Head is one of superb estuarine and coastal views, followed by an easy but charming path on low cliffs, sheltered from the westerlies, while passing some fine sandy beaches and giving excellent views up the South Cornwall coast.

Directions

A regular bus route serves Portscatho and St Mawes from Truro, which is also linked to Falmouth by bus and train. There is also a very popular circular walk using the Coast Path in the St Anthony Head area and another from Portscatho.

Two ferries are required to cross between Falmouth and the Coast Path at Place, east of the large estuary. The first goes between Falmouth and St Mawes, across the mouth of the main Fal Estuary, sometimes referred to as Carrick Roads.

The ferry operates all year except winter Sundays, June-October inclusive 3 ferries per hour, fewer at other times - telephone 01326 313201. The ferries operate from Prince of Wales Pier year round and Custom House Quay summer only.

For ferry details see page 19.

The second leg of the crossing is the ferry between St Mawes and Place, crossing the mouth of the Fal's tributary, the Percuil River. This ferry operates Easter to 31st October, 10:00 to 16:45, every half hour; telephone 07791 283884.

For ferry details see page 19.

There is also Falmouth Water Taxi service which operates between Falmouth and St Mawes or Place, weather permitting, between Easter and September, 12:00 to 15:00. If needed, it is best to telephone a day in advance. Tel: 07970 242258, www.falmouthwatertaxi.co.uk.

Information is also available from the Fal River Visitor Information Centre at Prince of Wales Pier, or visit www.falriver.co.uk.

If arriving at St Mawes and wishing to proceed to Place when the Place ferry is not operating it is possible to take the regular bus service from St Mawes to Gerrans, walking from here to Place (2.5 miles/4km). For this option, go to Gerrans Church and pick up the walking route described below. In addition, a local taxi company, Roseland Taxis, will carry walkers around here and throughout the Roseland

St Mawes Ferry

Peninsula - tel: 01872 501001, M: 07817 447667, website www.roselandtaxis.co.uk

Walk between St Mawes and Place

St Just in Roseland

A walking route also exists between St Mawes and Place, via Gerrans. This adds 9 miles/14km to the overall route, effectively an extra day to the itinerary. Leaving the ferry point in St Mawes, turn left along the road. Approaching the castle, take the minor lane left, which leads to a footpath at the end. This becomes a scenic path alongside the Carrick Roads - the Fal Estuary. At a minor road go right then bear left in front of the boatyard and then on a bank above the shore. This leads to the churchyard of St Just in Roseland, a beautiful spot. Pass the church and keep to the path next to the shore. Follow the path as it bears right up the hill, signed St Just Lane, to emerge on a road. Turn left, ignoring the first footpath on the right, but take the second a little afterwards. Follow the path alongside field boundaries, first to the right, then to the left, then to the right again. Go down to the road at the end of the fourth field and turn right to the A3078 at Trethem Mill. Turn left and immediately right after the bridge up some steps and through a small wood. Out of the wood, cross the field diagonally right (bearing 110) then in the next field bear diagonally right again (bearing 140), leaving it by a wooded track. Cross the stile at the top and bear diagonally right again (bearing 137) to meet a hedge, which is followed to a road. Turn right on the road. At the next junction follow the road curving to the right past Polhendra Cottage then turn left through the second gate. Descend towards the bottom of the hedge visible on the opposite side of the valley (bearing 123). Cross the bridge and climb as close as possible with the hedge to the left. Cross the stone steps behind the gorse at the top and bear slightly left across the next two fields (bearing 125) to emerge on a road. Turn right to arrive at Gerrans Church. (Those who have taken the bus from St Mawes will join here - see above.)

At the church fork left into Treloan Lane, keeping ahead past the buildings. Go through the gate at the end of the lane, crossing an open field ahead into another enclosed track, which leads to Porth Farm. At the road turn right then go left at the sign indicating “Footpath to Place by Percuil River”. Follow this very scenic path which leads to the ferry landing point then on to Place itself.

Coast Path, Place - Portscatho

At Place, walk up the lane past the gates to the grand house. Turn right into the churchyard of St Anthony Church, passing behind the church and up into a wooded area. Turn right at the track then at the creek look for the sign on the left taking the path alongside the plantation. The path now gives superb views over Carrick Roads to Falmouth. Approaching St Anthony Head keep to the coastal path to the right until passing through the gate towards the lighthouse. Just after the gate climb the steps to the left to the car parking area. There are also toilets here. Leave the car park next to the coast and the superb and easy path then leads to Portscatho, which has a shop, toilets and pubs, as well as a bus service to St Mawes and Truro.

Week 5 - Day 4 (half day)

OS Maps: **Landranger 204: Explorer 105**

	This Walk	Cumulative	This Walk	Cumulative	Grading	Timing
Ascent	1,674ft	65,672ft	510m	20,017m	Strenuous	3.75 hours
Distance	7.5mi	348.8mi	12.0km	561.4km		

For detailed directions see our Falmouth to Portloe Path Description booklet.

This is a very quiet Section for the most part. Cliffs are relatively low at first, but increase in height as the great promontory of Nare Head, with its superb views, is approached. The long sandy beaches below the cliffs passed west of Nare Head are replaced by tiny isolated and inaccessible coves east of the headland. This length has a wonderfully remote atmosphere.

Directions

Portscatho and Portloe are both served by regular, but different, bus services, both linking with Truro. There are some local circular walks using the Coast Path around Nare Head, based on the inland village of Veryan.

Portscatho has a shop, pubs, toilets and bus service. The Coast Path leaves past the Harbour Club; keep right just after leaving the village at the footpath junction. The path goes round the back of Porthcurnick Beach, then up the road on the far side, turning right along the coastal edge. The path continues to undulate along the coast until it turns inland to reach a road. Turn right, past Pendower Court and down the road to its end at Pendower Beach. Cross the rear of the beach and head for the public toilets, going up the hill and turning right. The path soon diverts around the rear of the Nare Hotel to a road, descending to Carne Beach. Follow the road round the bend and up the hill for a short way, turning right to return to the cliffs. The path now heads for Nare Head, via a steep descent and ascent at Tregagle's Hole and past an old fisherman's cottage. A short diversion at the top of Nare Head reveals some stunning coastal views.

The path now goes round the seaward edge of Rosen Cliff and over the valley behind Kiberick Cove to Blouth Point. At the point enter a field and keep left for a short way before bearing right, downhill, towards some trees. The path zigzags upward to pass Broom Parc and then goes through a field to round Manare Point. After this it is downhill going over a short uneven section before joining a tarmac path which descends into Portloe. The village is very picturesque and has pubs and toilets as well as a bus service.

Portloe

Week 5 - Day 5

OS Maps: Landranger 204; Explorer 105

	This Walk	Cumulative	This Walk	Cumulative	Grading	Timing
Ascent	2,841ft	68,513ft	866m	20,883m	Strenuous then easy	5.75 hours
Distance	12.3mi	361.1mi	19.8km	581.2km		

For detailed directions see our Portloe to Mevagissey Path Description booklet.

This is a quiet Section of mostly high cliffs, often covered in lush vegetation. Towards Gorran Haven these cliffs reduce in height. The Section includes the great headland of Dodman Point, from where there are views to the Lizard in one direction and Devon in the other on a clear day. Below the cliffs are some sandy beaches, often all but inaccessible. This is a coastline for those preferring remoteness.

Directions

Gorran Haven and Mevagissey share the same regular bus service, making a bus-walk a good option at this end of the Section. There are also some excellent circular walks using the Coast Path at Dodman Point and linking to Gorran Haven, giving a further variety of options here.

Gorran Haven harbour

The scenic little harbour village of Portloe has toilets, pubs and a bus service. The Coast Path leaves behind the Lugger Hotel, leaving the road to reach a prominent converted chapel. Pass this then climb steeply to the cliffs. After a quite strenuous length the path arrives at West Portholland. Follow the road above the shore to a junction, then turn right to East Portholland. There are toilets here and a seasonal cafe and shop. Pass the cottages at the far end and climb behind them on a clear path to a field, turning right down the field edge. The path leads to a road which descends to Porthluney Cove. Here are toilets and seasonal refreshments and the picturesque setting is enhanced by the presence of Caerhayes Castle just inland. Walk behind the beach and turn right into parkland. Climb behind the field-edge trees then go to the right and follow the field edge to the woods. After crossing the rocky ridge at Greeb Point the path descends to a road behind Hemmick Beach. Cross the bridge and go right, climbing to the headland of Dodman Point ("The Dodman"), with its memorial cross and superb views. The path stays clear above the lovely sands of Bow or Vault Beach, then rounds the headland of Pen-a-maen to enter Gorran Haven. This little harbour village has a shop, pub and toilets and a regular bus service.

Leave Gorran Haven up Church Street, turning right into Cliff Road. Turn right near the top of the hill and a stile on the left leads to the cliffs. The clear path leads to Chapel Point, where it crosses the tarmac access road to follow the path along the coast into Portmellon. Follow the road uphill and go down through the park on the right on entering Mevagissey. Steps descend to the harbour. Mevagissey is the archetypal Cornish fishing village and has all facilities.

Week 5 - Day 6

OS Maps: Landranger 204; Explorer 105 (western half); Explorer 107 (eastern half)

	This Walk	Cumulative	This Walk	Cumulative	Grading	Timing
Ascent	2,434ft	70,947ft	742m	21,625m	Strenuous then easy	5 hours
Distance	10.5mi	371.6mi	17.1km	598.3km		

For detailed directions see our Mevagissey to Charlestown and Charlestown to Fowey Path Description booklets.

The western half of this Section has a relatively remote feel, enhanced by some quite strenuous climbs and some attractive cliffs and headlands. To the east the coastline is more urbanised but with beaches and the lovely Georgian docks of Charlestown found among the houses, golf courses and clay industry. The cliff-top path between Porthpean and Charlestown was reinstated in late 2011, avoiding two miles of road diversion.

Directions

There are bus routes from St Austell to Mevagissey, Charlestown and Par, one of these routes serving both the latter two locations, so that a range of bus-walks is possible.

The attractive fishing village of Mevagissey has all facilities. The Coast Path goes along the back of the harbour and then turns right along its eastern side before forking left steeply uphill. After crossing some playing fields, pass seaward of the houses then continue along the undulating cliffs to descend behind the ruined fish cellars at Portgiskey Cove. Continue uphill along the seaward and far field boundaries to a fenced path at the top. Turn right here, parallel to the road. At the entrance to Pentewan Sands Holiday Park follow the B3273 road pavement and turn first right before the petrol station, signposted to Pentewan. There are a few shops, toilets and a pub in the village. The official route then follows the road through Pentewan and up the hill for about 100 yards/90m, taking the first turn sharp right along The Terrace and along a narrow path at the end to arrive at the cliffs. A more interesting alternative turns right, away from the road into the harbour area just after the public toilets then, immediately after the last cottage, goes left steeply uphill, through gardens, to arrive at the official route on the cliffs.

After some 1.25 miles/2km the path descends through a wood and reaches a track. Turn right here to arrive at another track just behind the remote Hallane Mill Beach. Turn left here then quickly right, climbing back up the cliffs to arrive at Black Head. A diversion from the memorial stone goes to the tip of this atmospheric location. Continuing from Black Head the path enters Ropehaven Woods with some confusing paths - it is important to follow the waymarking. Entering the wood turn right down a rocky and sometimes slippery path, then left. Go left again onto a walled path, ignoring descending paths on the right, to arrive beside a cottage and emerge onto a track. Go right here then leave the road to the right just after a parking area and follow the cliff-top path down, up and down again to Porthpean. Walk along the promenade to the far end and climb the steps to rejoin the newly reinstated cliff-top path all the way to Charlestown.

Charlestown harbour

Charlestown has a fascinating Georgian harbour, the home of a group of tall ships, and has refreshments, toilets, pubs and buses. Note that the official Coast Path does not cross the dock gate at the mouth of the harbour, though many people use that route. On the east side climb past the public toilets and on to reach a suburban road for a short way, soon forking off right over a long grassy area. Arriving at a large car park above Carlyon Bay Beach keep to seaward then cross the beach access road where a new resort is being developed and continue ahead on the low cliffs. Keep seaward of the golf course to approach the old china clay works at Par Docks. At the little beach at Spit Point turn inland and follow the narrow path past the works and then alongside a railway line to emerge on a road. Turn right along the pavement past the docks entrance and under a railway bridge. Turn right at the junction, signposted to Fowey, over a level crossing and then under another railway bridge before forking right on the road, Par Green.

To continue beyond Par on the Coast Path, walk along Par Green, looking for house no.52 and follow the path signed on the right.

Par has all facilities, including a mainline railway station; for the station turn left at the far end of Par Green along Eastcliffe Road.

Mevagissey harbour

Week 6 - Day 1 (half day)

OS Maps: Landranger 200 or 204; Explorer 107

	This Walk	Cumulative	This Walk	Cumulative	Grading	Timing
Ascent	1,132ft	72,079ft	345m	21,970m	Moderate	3 hours
Distance	7.0mi	378.6mi	11.1km	609.4km		

For detailed directions see our Charlestown to Fowey Path Description booklet.

This Section goes out to the prominent Gribbin Head. The west side of the headland is relatively exposed, mostly on high cliffs, with views west over St Austell Bay. The east side is more indented and sheltered, the cliffs lower, and the path passes numerous scenic little sandy coves. At its eastern end the path enters the lovely part-wooded estuary of the River Fowey, culminating in the atmospheric little town of Fowey.

Directions

Par and Fowey are linked by a bus service, making this a bus-walk option. In addition, a popular local circular walk from Fowey takes in most of Gribbin Head, using the waymarked Saints' Way path with the Coast Path.

Par has all facilities, including a mainline railway station. For the Coast Path walk along the road called Par Green and follow the path which leaves the road next to no.52. After crossing the private clay haul road, fork right along a grassy path immediately before the chalet park. Follow this path before turning left then quickly right along the road to a small car park at the western end of the sands of Par Beach. Walk along the back of the beach to another car park at the far, eastern end. This is Polmear; a pub and buses are to be found on the road outside the car park.

The Coast Path crosses the car park to a footbridge and then up the cliffs and continues on to the little harbour village of Polkerris. Here are a pub, toilets and restaurant. The path continues from the back of the beach, up a ramp to join a zigzag path through woods to the top. The path now continues to the Daymark on Gribbin Head (or "The Gribbin"). The tower is open to visitors on some summer Sundays. From the Daymark follow the path downhill to the scenic cove at Polridmouth ("Pridmouth"), said to have inspired the setting for Daphne du Maurier's "Rebecca". Cross behind the beach and go up into the woods, then on over cliff-top fields and past a couple of small coves to arrive at another woodland. Look out for the path on the right, which goes past St Catherine's Castle and gives superb views upriver to Fowey. Now follow the path down a rocky track and behind Readymoney Cove before following the lane into Fowey.

Note that it is possible to walk Coast to Coast across Cornwall between Fowey and Padstow on the north coast using the Saints' Way. A guidebook is available from Fowey TIC.

Gribbin Tower

Week 6 - Day 1 (half day)

OS Maps: Landranger 200 or 204 (Fowey); Landranger 201 (remainder); Explorer 107

	This Walk	Cumulative	This Walk	Cumulative	Grading	Timing
Ascent	1,939ft	74,018ft	591m	22,561m	Strenuous	3.5 hours
Distance	7.1mi	385.7mi	11.5km	620.9km		

For detailed directions see our Fowey to Polperro Path Description booklet.

This is a connoisseur's Section - it is quiet and remote; it is scenic, with beautiful large sandy bays and smaller coves plus impressive headlands; it is started and finished at superbly picturesque locations, the Fowey estuary at one end and Polperro at the other; and it is quite hard work, emphasising that nothing this good should come too easily.

Directions

Polruan and Polperro are linked by a bus service, giving a bus-walk option, though unfortunately it does not operate at weekends. There is a popular scenic circular walk taking in Fowey and Polruan and using two ferries, an estuary tributary valley and the Coast Path.

Polperro

Fowey is a charming little town, well worth exploring, with all facilities.
The crossing of the river to Polruan on the opposite bank is by foot ferry. In summer it usually operates from Whitehouse Quay, along the Esplanade, and in winter from the Town Quay.

The ferry operates all year except Christmas Day at 5-10 minute intervals, 07:15 to 23:00 1st May-30th September (Saturdays 07:30 start, Sundays 09:00 start) and 07:15 to 19:00 1st October - 30th April (Saturdays 07:30 start, Sundays 10:00 to 17:00) - telephone 01726 870232.

For ferry details see page 19.

At Polruan, a picturesque little place, go up the steps next to The Lugger. Turn right at the top in West Street then turn left up Battery Lane. At the grassy area keep left by the wall then through the car park parallel to the coast to a signed path on the right. After around 2 miles/3km the path passes above and behind the impressive Lantic Bay, climbing steeply at the far end. There is a higher path here, going to the top of the hill and turning right, or a lower one, turning off right 30 yards/28m before the top, dropping then climbing again to meet the higher path (ignore beach turnings to the right). The path goes out around Pencarrow Head then behind an old watch house to descend and pass behind two charming and remote coves at Lansallos West and East Coombes. After climbing past a marker warning shipping of an offshore rock more ups and downs follow until the path approaches the almost hidden inlet of Polperro. Follow the waymarked path to arrive at a rocky outlook point - go left here then fork right to descend to the harbour. Polperro, an impossibly picturesque harbour village, figures justifiably in most picture books and calendars of Cornwall. It has all facilities.

Week 6 - Day 2 (half day)

OS Maps: **Landranger 201; Explorer 107**

	This Walk	Cumulative	This Walk	Cumulative	Grading	Timing
Ascent	774ft	74,792ft	236m	22,797m	Moderate	2.25 hours
Distance	5.0mi	390.7mi	8.0km	628.9km		

For detailed directions see our Polperro to Looe Path Description booklet.

The cliffs on this Section, never really lofty, tend to decrease in height towards the east. This is a relatively sheltered length passing around lush bays, while offshore, Looe Island is a seaward focal point from the eastern end. Here, also, extensive rocky platforms are exposed at low tide. These factors, and the popularity of Polperro and Looe, have made this a justifiably popular length of coast.

Directions

There is a bus route between Polperro and Looe, making a bus-walk a popular option here.

Looe Pier

Polperro is a popular visitors' destination with all facilities. The Coast Path crosses the stone bridge behind the harbour then turns right along The Warren. Climb out of the village, keeping left at the first fork and right at the second, which leads to the War Memorial on its headland. The path turns left here to descend towards Talland Bay, turning right near the bottom down a steep track towards the beach. There are toilets and seasonal refreshments here. Pass behind the beach, going left then right by the public toilets and behind a second beach to a small car parking area. The path climbs back to the cliffs from here - keep well back from the crumbling edge. It then continues very clearly (ignore all turnings towards the beach) eventually arriving at the end of a suburban road at Hannafore, the western end of Looe. Continue along the road, or the lower promenade; there are toilets and seasonal refreshments along here. At the end a short stretch of road with no pavement turns alongside the mouth of the Looe River. Take steps down on the right to the riverside of West Looe. There is a seasonal and tidal ferry from here to East Looe, the main part of the town, as an option. Otherwise continue along the West Looe riverside and over the bridge, turning right into East Looe's main street. Looe has buses to Plymouth and a branch to the mainline railway at Liskeard - for the station turn left after the bridge. Between them, East and West Looe have all necessary facilities.

Week 6 - Day 2 (half day)

OS Maps: **Landranger 201; Explorer 107 (western half); Explorer 108 (eastern half)**

	This Walk	Cumulative	This Walk	Cumulative	Grading	Timing
Ascent	1,965ft	76,757ft	599m	23,396m	Strenuous, moderate in places	4.5 hours
Distance	7.6mi	398.3mi	12.2km	641.1km		

For detailed directions see our Looe to Portwrinkle Path Description booklet.

Quiet and relatively remote cliff lengths in the western and eastern parts of this Section are separated by a low-level, suburban length, or by an optional route via sea wall and beach between Seaton and Downderry. The western cliffs are covered in lush vegetation, scrub and woodland, and there are stretches where the sea is only glimpsed through the trees. The eastern cliffs are more open and give some superb views along the coast in both directions, with the distinctive Rame Head a focal point.

Directions

A bus service connects Seaton, Downderry and Portwrinkle, making a bus-walk option possible over the eastern end of this section. Further bus-walk options may be possible with a change of bus from Looe at Hessenford (inland from Looe).

From East Looe's town centre, turn up Castle Street and keep climbing until it becomes a footpath above the sea. Continue, then at a road turn right, passing Plaidy Beach, and continue until just after the road veers left inland. Here go right, up a steep tarmac path then ahead at the top until the road turns left. The Coast Path descends steps between houses to Millendreath Beach. On the far side go up the cul-de-sac road and climb the sunken lane to reach another road. Shortly, go right at the signed footpath, passing left of a picnic area to the cliff path. Follow this, partly through woodland, until it emerges on a road. Turn right to descend to Seaton Beach. Turn right and along the road behind the beach, where there are toilets and seasonal refreshments.

Although the official path follows the narrow and busy road up the hill to Downderry, if the tide is not high it is preferable to walk along the top of the sea wall from Seaton and then the beach, taking one of the choice of footpath links into Downderry, where there are pubs, shops, toilets and seasonal refreshments. The last link path goes up steps beside the village school. Follow the road to the eastern end of Downderry, where it turns inland, and take the signed path right, which zigzags steeply upward. A superbly scenic cliff-top path, with several ups and downs, continues until it arrives at a road just above Portwrinkle. Turn right to descend to the village and the quiet sea-front road. There are toilets at Portwrinkle but other facilities and buses are at Crafthole, a 10 minute walk uphill inland.

Portwrinkle

Week 6 - Day 3

OS Maps: **Landranger 201; Explorer 108**

	This Walk	Cumulative	This Walk	Cumulative	Grading	Timing
Ascent	2,169ft	78,926ft	661m	24,057m	Moderate	5.75 hours
Distance	13.3mi	411.6mi	21.4km	662.5km		

For detailed directions see our Portwrinkle to Plymouth Path Description booklet.

This is a Section of great interest rather than spectacular drama. There is a golf course, a gunnery range, a cliff face of wooden chalets and an historic Country Park. It also includes the magnificent and atmospheric Rame Head, which is a significant landmark for many miles along the coast in both directions, the charming twin villages of Cawsand and Kingsand and some superb views, including Plymouth Sound and, indeed, the city itself.

Directions

A bus route links Cremyll to Cawsand, part-way along the section, and also runs along the coast road adjacent to the Coast Path between Rame Head and Tregantle, giving various bus-walk options. There are a number of popular circular walks using the Coast Path based on Mount Edgcumbe Country Park, next to Cremyll, and also around Rame Head.

From Portwrinkle walk up the road, past the first footpath, which is a cul-de-sac, then turn right on the signed path opposite the golf club. After climbing, the path goes along the seaward side of the golf course. After leaving the golf course the path begins to rise towards the Tregantle Firing Ranges. When firing is not taking place it is possible to walk an excellent, well-signed permissive path through the ranges. In 2013 non-firing weekends (Friday to Sunday inclusive) will normally alternate throughout the year starting with 4th, 5th and 6th January. But please note that live firing may still take place on these weekends if operational requirements demand. In addition there is no live firing on Bank Holiday weekends nor on any day in August. Other non-firing days are known up to two weeks in advance - telephone Range Control on 01752 822516 during office hours to check. If live firing is in progress red flags will be raised and the access gates locked - do not proceed into the range. If open, keep closely to the marked path and, at the far end of the range path, emerge through another security gate onto the National Trust's cliff-top path.

If the range path is closed, continue on the official Coast Path through a field to a road, where the path initially continues inside the hedge before joining the road further along. The road is usually quite busy so take care. There is the compensation of a magnificent view up the Tamar to Plymouth from the car parking area here, where there is often a refreshment van. Follow the road then turn right at the first road junction and continue along the road (past Tregantle Fort entrance) to the cliffs, near where the range path emerges.

Cawsand

The Coast Path is then off-road, along National Trust land, before it rejoins the road for about 1.25 miles/2km. The signed path then leaves the road again to descend onto the sloping cliff face. There is a cafe just off the path down the cliff at this point. The path undulates quite steeply and meanders unexpectedly among chalets and gardens - keep alert for the waymarking - climbing at one point back to the road before descending gently across the cliff slope to Polhawn Cove at the base of Rame Head. After crossing a private access road for Polhawn Fort the path climbs to reach the headland. The official path omits the very end, with its medieval chapel, but the easy climb is worthwhile for the views and the atmosphere.

A good cliff path then goes to Penlee Point, where there are the first views of Plymouth Sound. Bear left to reach a road then fork off to the right on the signed path through woods to descend to the charming little village of Cawsand, with pubs, toilets, shops and refreshments. Go through the village square to Garrett Street and continue, turning right in front of the Post Office having, imperceptibly, crossed into Kingsand. At The Cleave turn left then first right up Heavitree Road, which leads to a gate on the right into Mount Edgcumbe Country Park. Continue through the park to a road, turning right then almost immediately left, forking uphill through woods. After a woodland drive there is a waymarked diversion to avoid a cliff fall, the route climbing left to a higher level path before continuing parallel to the coast. Once around the fallen cliff the path descends to the foreshore of Plymouth Sound. Keep on the signed path up and through a deer gate then back down towards the shore to follow into an Italianate garden, past the Orangery of Mount Edgcumbe House (refreshments), and out through the park gates to the ferry point. Cremyll has a pub and toilets, but most will use it as the staging point for the ferry across the Tamar to Plymouth, an interesting excursion in its own right.

Week 6 - Day 4 (half day)

OS Maps: **Landranger 201; Explorer 108**

	This Walk	Cumulative	This Walk	Cumulative	Grading	Timing
Ascent	463ft	79,389ft	141m	24,198m	Easy	3.5 hours
Distance	7.5mi	419.1mi	12.0km	674.5km		

For detailed directions see our Plymouth to Wembury Path Description booklet.

This is an urban walk along the waterfront of one of the country's prime historical maritime cities. It is therefore quite different to the vast majority of the Coast Path, but is nevertheless well worth doing. The view over the Sound, flanked on both sides by cliffs, is inspiring, and often referred to as the finest urban vista in the country. Elsewhere are lengths of waterside industry, historic quays and modern marinas, making this a fascinating excursion.

Directions

A range of urban bus services runs throughout Plymouth, including to and from Admiral's Hard, the ferry point for Cremyll, and Mount Batten. Though not on the same route, they link in the city centre. There is also a ferry link across the mouth of the River Plym between the historic Sutton Harbour and Mount Batten. These links make a range of public transport-walks possible.

The Coast Path from Cremyll uses the ferry across the Tamar.

The ferry operates all year, weather, tide and other circumstances permitting, generally at 30 minute intervals. Summer service, 1st April-30th September 06:45 to 20:30, Saturdays 08:00 to 20:45, Sundays 09:00 to 21:00; winter service 1st October-31st March 06:45 to 18:00, Saturdays 08:00 to 18:30, Sundays 09:00 to 18:00; closed Christmas, Boxing and New Year's Days; telephone 01752 822105.

For ferry details see page 19.

Plymouth's Waterfront Walk is enhanced by a variety of information plaques and pieces of artwork relating to the city's history. A companion guidebook "Plymouth's Waterfront Walkway" is available from Plymouth TIC free of charge.

Most of the route is waymarked by white bands on lamp-posts, red metal marker signs and pavement signs.

From the ferry walk up the road and turn right, going round the car park into Cremyll Street and on to the gates of the Royal William Yard. Go ahead to the left of the gates to the shore at Firestone Bay. At the sea wall bear left inland into Durnford Street and continue past the Royal Marines Barracks, turning right immediately after them. Continue along Millbay Road then, after the entrance to Millbay Docks, turn right into West Hoe Road. Fork right off here into Great Western Road, then bear off right down a narrow path along the shoreline. The path returns to the road; here turn right to walk along the Hoe promenade all the way to The Barbican and Sutton Harbour, Plymouth's original harbour. Above on the left, away from the path but worth a visit, are the lighthouse of Smeaton's Tower and the Drake statue.

At The Barbican on the right are the Mayflower Steps, the site of the Pilgrim Fathers' embarkation. Adjacent is the ferry point for Mount Batten, an unofficial short cut direct to the end of the section.

The ferry operates all year, at 15 and 45 minutes past the hour from The Barbican and 00 and 30 minutes past the hour from Mount Batten. The first ferry from The Barbican is 07:45 weekdays, 09:00 weekends; last ferry from Mount Batten 22:30 in summer, 18:15 in winter - telephone 07930 838614.

For ferry details see page 19.

Continuing on the Coast Path Waterfront Walk, walk across the lock gates at the entrance to Sutton Harbour, past the Marine Aquarium and then along Teat's Hill Road. At Breakwater Road turn right up a narrow hill and down to the industrial Cattedown Wharf area. Continue past warehouses, over an old railway and right into Maxwell Road then Finnigan Road to Laira Bridge. Turn right to cross the River Plym then, at the first roundabout, turn right (at the rhinoceros!) Go right, into Breakwater Road, and continue for about 500 yards/450m then turn left, still in Breakwater Road, to a dead-end. To the left of a steel fence is a path which is followed to Oreston Quay. At the quay walk past the grassy area into Marine Road then left into Park Road. Turn left at the top of the hill, and this path descends to Radford Lake. From here a Coast-to-Coast walk goes to Lynmouth on the north coast, following the Erme-Plym Trail and the Two Moors Way. Guidebooks are available at Ivybridge TIC.

Go across the causeway and turn right. Follow the path left and at a junction turn right down Hexton Hill Road to Hooe Lake. Keep to the shore, going along Barton Road and then turn left on a path to Turnchapel. Go through the village, up the hill then turn right to the marina and over the slipway and along the shoreline to Mount Batten and the Sutton Harbour ferry. There are toilets, refreshments and a pub here.

Plymouth Sound

Week 6 - Day 4 (half day)

OS Maps: **Landranger 201; Explorer OL20**

	This Walk	Cumulative	This Walk	Cumulative	Grading	Timing
Ascent	1,260ft	80,649ft	384m	24,582m	Easy	3 hours
Distance	7.3mi	426.4mi	11.8km	686.3km		

For detailed directions see our Plymouth to Wembury Path Description booklet.

This is a Section of low cliffs, much of it overlooking Plymouth Sound. Below the cliffs are extensive areas of rock platform and offshore the Great Mew Stone becomes a focal point. Caravan and chalet sites and suburban villages are never far away and this is never a lonely Section. Towards its eastern end, as the cliffs rise somewhat, is the picturesque mouth of the River Yealm, forming a dramatic wooded gap in the cliffs.

Directions

Separate bus routes serve Mount Batten and Wembury village, and also Heybrook Bay, midway along this section, all from Plymouth city centre, allowing bus-walk options. There is a popular circular walk using the Coast Path between Wembury and Warren Point and a longer, full-day circular using the waymarked Erme-Plym Trail between Wembury and Mount Batten plus the Coast Path.

Mount Batten has toilets and refreshments, as well as a direct ferry link to and from Plymouth's Sutton Harbour. From Mount Batten the Coast Path heads over the little hill and past the old fort tower to the grassy area at Jennycliff, where there are more toilets and refreshments. Keep close above the shore and at the end of the grass enter woodland. There has been a landslip here, so for the time being follow diversion signs up to the road, turn right for a short way along the road then turn back into the woods. The path then undulates and emerges above Fort Bovisand. Descend steeply to a road and turn left; there are seasonal refreshments here. Follow round to the right and up to pass seaward of the chalets, past a cafe and toilets and on round the point and so to Heybrook Bay. There is a pub a little way up the road here, as well as a bus stop. Keep right and follow the path above the shore around Wembury Point and on to Wembury Beach. Yet more toilets and refreshments await here and the bus stop, together with pub and shop, are in the village a little way inland.

From Wembury Beach a Coast-to-Coast walk goes to Lynmouth on the north coast, following the Erme-Plym Trail and the Two Moors Way. Guidebooks are available from Ivybridge TIC.

Continuing on the Coast Path, climb seaward of the church and along the now higher cliffs to a junction of paths at the Rocket House. The path going inland from here leads to Wembury village and its facilities. For the Coast Path, bear right, downhill, to reach the ferry point. Note that operating times on this ferry can be limited - see page 19 and Walk 49.

Above Mountbatten

Week 6 - Day 5

OS Maps: Landranger 201 (western end); Landranger 202 (remainder); Explorer OL20

	This Walk	Cumulative	This Walk	Cumulative	Grading	Timing
Ascent	2,450ft	83,099ft	747m	25,329m	Easy then strenuous	5.75 hours
Distance	13.5mi	439.9mi	21.8km	708.1km		

For detailed directions see our Wembury (Warren Point) to Bigbury-on-Sea Path Description booklet.

This is a fine Section of high-level coastal cliffs, cut mid-way by the substantial and extremely picturesque estuary of the River Erme. The western end is a particularly good length, since the superb cliff coastline is easily accessed by a scenic former carriage route. Beyond that a series of descents and ascents, some quite steep, accentuate the dramatic landscape of the coastline. At the eastern extremity is the tidally insular Burgh Island, a focal point on this part of the coast. Because of its remoteness and strenuous nature, much of this section has a quiet character which will specially appeal to those in search of a lonely coastline.

Directions

This remote length of coast only has public transport at its western end, so no bus-walks are feasible. There is a very popular local walk using the Coast Path on the carriage drive from Noss Mayo.

The ferry at Wembury's Warren Point operates three ways over the River Yealm and its tributary Newton Creek. Warren Point is thus linked with both Newton Ferrers and Noss Mayo, and these two points with each other. For the Coast Path the link between Warren Point and Noss Mayo is needed.

The ferry operates 2nd April - 30th September on demand, 10:00 to 12:00 and 15:00 to 16:00. During fine weather, weekends and school holidays the ferry will operate 10:00 to 16:00 daily, but telephone first to confirm - telephone 01752 880079.

For ferry details see page 19.

There is a signal board to summon the ferryman by the steps at Warren Point or the slipway at Noss Mayo. Alternatively, telephone beforehand.

Because of the somewhat limited nature of the ferry it may be necessary to make alternative arrangements to reach Noss Mayo. Both Wembury and Noss Mayo have a regular bus service to and from Plymouth, so it is possible to use these services as a link, perhaps combining with an overnight stop in Plymouth. Alternatively, local taxi companies are available:-

Eco-Taxi, based in Kingsbridge, will carry walkers between Plymouth and Dartmouth and from all estuaries in South Devon; telephone 01548 856347 or 07811 385275. Ivy Cabs, telephone 01752 696969, will also carry walkers round the South Devon estuaries.

Week 6 - Day 5

Paddling the Erme

It is also possible to walk round the Yealm Estuary from ferry point to ferry point. This is a distance of some 9 miles/14.5km, effectively adding an extra day or half day to the itinerary.

Walk around the Yealm Estuary

Walk uphill inland from the ferry steps to the house at the top, the Rocket House. Continue inland along the track, which in turn becomes a road. Where the road bears sharp right go ahead along a public footpath into a field, then keep ahead alongside a high wall. At the end of the wall, after two gates, bear left (bearing 330) across fields, then go down a few steps. The now enclosed path goes left then right to arrive at a road. This is Knighton, on the outskirts of Wembury. The bus stop for Plymouth is a little way to the left, just before the pub.

To continue the walking route around the estuary cross the road at Knighton to a minor lane, following it left to another junction. Turn right here and continue until the road meets another, more major, road. Cross this road, going ahead and left for a short way then turn right on a signed footpath. This is part of a waymarked route, the Erme-Plym Trail, and is shown on the OS Explorer OL20 map. Follow the waymarked route across fields, over Cofflete Creek, next to a lane and on to the village of Brixton. Turn right and follow the road through the village to Brixton Church then back on the Erme-Plym Trail up Old Road, along a suburban road, over fields, along a minor lane then over more fields to arrive at another village, Yealmpton. On reaching the A379 road at Yealmpton the Erme-Plym Trail is now abandoned. Here, turn right along the A379 then quickly left, into Stray Park. At the bottom bear right along a tarmac path then, when it arrives at a road, turn left along a stony track. At the footpath sign continue ahead, eventually emerging at a road by a car park. Turn left along the road to cross Puslinch Bridge then follow the road up the hill. Take the footpath on the right near the top of the hill, crossing a couple of fields to a road. Turn right and continue to meet a more major road, which is followed ahead to Newton Ferrers. At the edge of the village turn left down the road signed to Bridgend and Noss Mayo, and at the junction at the head of the creek keep to the right. Follow the riverside road, forking right into Noss Mayo. Keep on the road round Noss Creek and continue on the creekside road out of the village until this becomes a track. A signed path on the right leaves the track for the ferry point.

Coast Path, Noss Mayo-River Erme

From the ferry point, follow the path westward through the woods as it climbs to meet a track, an old carriage drive. The drive continues through woods, past a row of former coastguard cottages, into more woods, then on a superb cliff-face shelf round Mouthstone Point. Further on keep right where the more obvious path bears left inland to a car park, the drive continuing round Stoke Point and on to Beacon Hill. A series of ups and downs now ensues as the path approaches the estuary of the River Erme, which has been fairly described as England's most unspoiled river estuary, and is possibly the most attractive. The path crosses the top of a small beach then passes through a short woodland stretch to arrive at Mothecombe slipway on the Erme. There are seasonal refreshments a little way inland.

There is no ferry at the River Erme. It is usually possible to wade the river 1 hour either side of low water along the old ford and, under normal conditions, at low tide the water is about knee deep and the river bed is of sand with pebbles. The crossing is between grid references 614 476 and 620 478, ie the road by the row of coastguard cottages at Mothecombe and the end of the inland road to Wonwell Beach. However, great care should be taken as heavy rains or high seas can make conditions dangerous. Low water is approximately at the same time as at Devonport; see tide tables on pages 21-23.

If timing makes wading impossible there are local taxi companies, ie John Edwards, telephone 01548 830859, mobile 07967 374502, or Wembury Cabs - John Pitcher, telephone 01752 863710, or Eco-Taxi, telephone 01548 856347 or 07811 385275, or Ivy Cabs, telephone 01752 696969.

Alternatively, it is possible to walk round the estuary. There are no riverside rights of way and for the most part minor roads must be used. The distance is approximately 8 miles/13km, adding an extra half day to the itinerary.

Walk round the Erme Estuary

From the slipway follow the road inland, following signs to Holbeton. Go through the village and leave on the minor lane to Ford and then Hole Farm. At the sharp bend after this farm follow the waymarked Erme-Plym Trail to the A379 and across the River Erme at Sequer's Bridge. Then leave the waymarked trail, continuing very carefully along the A379 for a couple of hundred yards/metres, before turning right on the lane signed to Orcheton. Follow this for about 2 miles/3km then turn right, following signs for Wonwell Beach. Follow the lane downhill to arrive at the estuary.

Coast Path, River Erme-Bigbury-on-Sea

Just inland of the Wonwell slipway a path leaves the lane into the woods then continues above the shore, emerging on cliffs which rollercoaster up and down to the holiday park at Challaborough. Here are toilets and seasonal refreshments, and the path then soon reaches Bigbury-on-Sea. Here also are toilets and seasonal refreshments; the Bay View Cafe and Bistro will also supply packed lunches. On Burgh Island offshore, reached by walking across the sands or by unusual sea tractor, is a pub.

Week 6 - Day 6 (half day)

OS Maps: **Landranger 202; Explorer OL20**

	This Walk	Cumulative	This Walk	Cumulative	Grading	Timing
Ascent	876ft	83,975ft	267m	25,596m	Moderate	2.75 hours
Distance	5.7mi	445.6mi	9.2km	717.3km		

For detailed directions see our Bigbury-on-Sea to Salcombe Path Description booklet.

This is a well-used and popular Section, never far from residential and holiday accommodation. It is a length of low cliffs and sandy beaches, the coastline providing some interesting seascapes. These include views of the tidal Burgh Island, the estuary of the River Avon, the distinctive holed Thurlestone Rock and the headland of Bolt Tail. At the end of the Section, Hope Cove is a charming little settlement with a picturesque harbour and an old centre of historic cottages.

Directions

A regular, if infrequent, bus service links Thurlestone and Hope Cove, making a bus-walk option possible. There is a popular short circular walk using the Coast Path between Bantham and Thurlestone.

From the main facilities at Bigbury-on-Sea the Coast Path goes along the road, turning right immediately after the car park entrance to follow a short cliff-top length which re-joins the road further up. Cross the road and follow the path along the field edge next to the road. Leave the field where signed and cross the road, passing through Folly Farm and down the cliffs to the flat open area of Cockleridge Ham. At the edge is the ferry point for the crossing of the mouth of the River Avon.

The ferry operates 29th April - 28th September, daily except Sundays 10.00-11.00 and 15.00-16.00 - telephone 01548 561196.

For ferry details see page 20.

The ferryman is alerted by waving. It must be noted that if the ferry is not operating on arrival the river should NOT be forded, despite its sometimes benign appearance. There are local taxi services, ie:- Arrow Cars - Mr Kemp, telephone 01548 856120; John Edwards, telephone 01548 830859, mobile 07967 374502; Eco-Taxi, telephone 01548 856347 or 07811 385275; or Ivy Cabs, telephone 01752 696969.

Alternatively, there is a waymarked walk round the estuary between Bigbury-on-Sea and Bantham on the opposite bank. This route, the Avon Estuary Walk, is signed with blue waymarks and adds about 8 miles/13km to the route, or another half day to the itinerary. The route is shown on OS Explorer map OL20.

Avon Estuary Walk

The route is accessed by continuing up the road, without turning into Folly Farm, for a further 60 yards/55m and then turning right. The path reaches the golf course, turning left on a track then off this to the right, down another track past Hexdown Farm. Follow this track to the bottom then go left along a drive which eventually arrives at a road. There is a permissive path alongside the road and at the end of this a path goes right over a field, through the top of a wood then downhill over another field to a road alongside the estuary. This tidal road is then followed to Aveton Gifford on the A379. At high tide there is a waymarked diversion which crosses the tidal road on arriving at it and re-joins it next to the village. From Aveton Gifford cross the Avon on the A379 then take the first lane on the right, which becomes a track and continues to Stadbury Farm. Bear left approaching the farm onto a footpath, following field edges towards the valley bottom to cross Stiddicombe Creek. Enter the wood on the right and climb to leave at the far top corner. Follow the top edge of fields then cross a farm track and a stream to a junction of paths. Turn right and continue to Bantham village, where there is a pub, shop, toilets and seasonal refreshments as well as the ferry point.

Coast Path, Bantham-Hope Cove

From the ferry point go through the car park and round the edge of the dunes of Bantham Ham. Follow the shore, leaving the dunes and climbing past the edge of Thurlestone Golf Club to descend to Thurlestone Sands. Cross a long footbridge at an inland lagoon (South Milton Ley), pass public toilets and seasonal refreshments then join a road for a short stretch before turning back to the shoreline and over low cliffs to Outer Hope, where there are all facilities in season. Follow the path behind the little harbour and down to the old lifeboat station at Inner Hope, where the bus stop is situated. Buses to Kingsbridge leave from here. A little inland is the old village centre of Inner Hope, at The Square, a picture-postcard location worth seeing before leaving.

Hope Cove

Week 6 - Day 6 (half day)

OS Maps: **Landranger 202; Explorer OL20**

	This Walk	Cumulative	This Walk	Cumulative	Grading	Timing
Ascent	1,506ft	85,481ft	459m	26,055m	Strenuous	4 hours
Distance	8.0mi	453.6mi	12.9km	730.2km		

For detailed directions see our Bigbury-on-Sea to Salcombe Path Description booklet.

This is a very scenic Section of the coast, largely comprising quite spectacular high cliffs soaring above tiny, mostly inaccessible coves. Near both ends are dramatic headlands, Bolt Tail in the west and Bolt Head in the east, offering superb coastal views in their respective directions. At the eastern end this Section turns into the mouth of the estuary of Salcombe Harbour, and there is the contrast of softer, sandy bays. This is a length which is never really remote, but never really busy.

Directions

Separate bus routes serve Hope Cove and Salcombe from Kingsbridge, a few miles inland, making a bus-walk feasible from there. However, there are numerous popular local circuits using the Coast Path which are based on Hope Cove and Salcombe.

Leave Hope Cove from the old lifeboat station at Inner hope up the signed Coast Path and out to the magnificent viewpoint of Bolt Tail, where the ramparts of an Iron Age cliff fort are crossed to reach the end. The path doubles back along the cliff top over Bolberry Down and then down to the splendid little Soar Mill Cove. Climbing from the cove a long level stretch of easy walking follows. Keep along the cliff top and as the path approaches Bolt Head pass through a couple of gates, staying on the closest path to the cliff top as possible. A steep descent will then lead to the headland, where a sharp turn leads to the cliff-face path round Starehole Bay and then on to the Courtenay Walk below rocky pinnacles. Passing into woodland at the National Trust's Overbecks property the path joins a road which is followed past South Sands and North Sands - toilets and seasonal refreshments at both - and then on into Salcombe town centre. For a variation, there is a summer ferry service between South Sands and Salcombe. The town is a renowned yachting centre and has all facilities.

South Sands ferry steps

Week 6 - Day 7

OS Maps: Landranger 202; Explorer OL20

	This Walk	Cumulative	This Walk	Cumulative	Grading	Timing
Ascent	2,251ft	87,732ft	686m	26,741m	Strenuous	6.75 hours
Distance	12.9mi	466.5mi	20.8km	751.0km		

For detailed directions see our Salcombe to Torcross Path Description booklet.

This is a superb Section of walking. Part of it is on exposed cliff faces, the sometimes stark cliffs contrasting with numerous tiny sandy coves below. A significant length in the middle is on an old "raised beach", a low shelf a little above the sea giving an easy passage here. In the east the path crosses the rocky spine of Start Point, behind its lighthouse, a dramatic stretch, before following a lush, sheltered length into Torcross.

Directions

Salcombe and Torcross are both on regular bus routes to and from Kingsbridge, a little inland, making a bus-walk possible from that town. There is also a popular local circuit using the Coast Path from the Salcombe Ferry.

Salcombe has all necessary facilities. The ferry across the estuary leaves from steps next to the Ferry Hotel, a little way downstream from the town centre.

The ferry operates all year; July and August continuous service 08:00 to 19:00; September-June half-hourly service 08:00 to 17:30; weekends and Bank Holidays service starts 08:30 - telephone 01548 842061 or 01548 560558.

For ferry details see page 20.

From the ferry point on the eastern side, where there are toilets and refreshments, the Coast Path follows the road down the estuary side then, after crossing the rear of the beach at Mill Bay (toilets), follows a clear cliff path to Prawle Point. The path goes to the Coastwatch lookout at the very end, then descends to follow the "raised beach" shelf just above the waves before a rocky stretch leads to Lannacombe Beach. Beyond here a dramatic length goes along and up to the rocky ridge leading to Start Point, the path dropping to the lighthouse access road. From the car park at the top the path bears off right down the cliff face to Hallsands, passing above the old ruined village. A short diversion to the viewpoint is both instructive and interesting. The path continues over low cliffs to Beesands, where there is a pub, toilets and seasonal refreshments. Continue along the shingle ridge then behind an old quarry to descend into Torcross, with a panoramic view of Slapton Ley ahead on the descent. Torcross has all facilities, and buses to Plymouth, Kingsbridge and Dartmouth.

Gara Rock Lookout

Week 7 - Day 1

OS Maps: Landranger 202; Explorer OL20

	This Walk	Cumulative	This Walk	Cumulative	Grading	Timing
Ascent	1,493ft	89,225ft	455m	27,196m	Easy then strenuous	4.75 hours
Distance	10.2mi	476.7mi	16.4km	767.4km		

For detailed directions see our Torcross to Dartmouth Path Description booklet.

Something like a quarter of this Section consists of the low shingle ridge known locally as the Slapton Line, cutting off the freshwater lake of Slapton Ley from the sea. Most of the remainder of the Section is cliffs and coves, partly looking to the sea and partly to the outer reaches of the picturesque wooded Dart Estuary. This Section has some lengths a little more inland than is usual and some road lengths, one of which is frankly unpleasant, but in compensation there are also some splendid stretches.

Directions

A regular bus service runs along the coast road which is, for much of the Section, adjacent to the Coast Path. With stops at most obvious locations this gives numerous bus-walk options. There is also a very popular and scenic circular walk using the Coast Path between Dartmouth and the mouth of the Dart Estuary.

Blackpool Sands

From Torcross, with all facilities, the Coast Path runs along the shingle ridge. The official route is on the landward side but it is possible, if more tiring, to walk along the seaward side. At the end, Strete Gate, follow the narrow lane uphill to reach the A379 road. It is now necessary to walk along this and for the next 400 yards/365m **THE NEED FOR CAUTION ON THIS BUSY, NARROW AND DANGEROUS ROAD CANNOT BE OVERESTIMATED.**

Follow the main road through Strete village (pub and shop) then, just after the village end, take the path to the right which passes over fields and a footbridge to reach a high point above the sea. Continuing parallel to the coast for a while it then heads inland over a deep valley, crossing the main road and over more fields to a lane. Descend the lane then leave it across more fields until, after crossing the main road again, the picturesque cove of Blackpool Sands is reached. There are toilets and seasonal refreshments. Follow the path uphill through the woods then the route enters and meanders along various paths in the village of Stoke Fleming (pub, shop and toilets), arriving at the village hall. Cross the main road again and follow a lane to a National Trust car park. From here a scenic cliff path proceeds, latterly through woods, to reach the Dart Estuary and arrive at Dartmouth Castle. An estuary-side path passes the adjacent church and joins the road which is followed into the town. Look out for some steps on the right just after the public toilets before reaching the centre; the steps lead down to Bayards Cove through its little castle and on to the Embankment at the town centre. Dartmouth, of course, has all facilities.

Week 7 - Day 2

OS Maps: Landranger 202; Explorer OL20

	This Walk	Cumulative	This Walk	Cumulative	Grading	Timing
Ascent	2,992ft	92,217ft	912m	28,108m	Strenuous	5.75 hours
Distance	10.8mi	487.5mi	17.3km	784.7km		

For detailed directions see our Dartmouth to Brixham Path Description booklet.

This is a Section of superb cliff scenery, tough going in places and often quite lonely. In the west, near the mouth of the Dart, are substantial wooded areas but further along the cliffs become higher and more open. This makes for a dramatic, steeply undulating landscape ending at the sea in steep cliff faces.

Directions

A regular bus service links Brixham and Kingswear, on the east side of the Dartmouth Ferry, making a bus-walk possible. There is also a popular circuit using the Coast Path based on Kingswear.

Walkers have two ferry options from Dartmouth town centre to cross the river, the Lower Car Ferry, which also carries foot passengers, and the Dartmouth Passenger Ferry.

The Lower Car Ferry operates all year on a continuous service 07:00 to 22:45, on Sundays 09:00 to 22:45; telephone 01803 752342.

The Dartmouth Passenger Ferry also operates all year on a continuous service 07:00 to 23:00, Sundays 09:00 to 23:00 - telephone 01803 555872.

For ferry details see page 20.

From either ferry landing point in Kingswear cross the road and pass through an arch to ascend Alma Steps. Turn right along Beacon Road and continue out of the village. After some 1.25 miles/2km turn right down steps and undulate sometimes steeply into and through woodland to the old Battery buildings at Froward Point. Here the path descends steeply to the right from the corner of an old lookout building, passing World War II searchlight and gun positions before continuing along the cliffs. Pass Pudcombe Cove, by the National Trust Coleton Fishacre Gardens, and then on over Scabbacombe Head and past Scabbacombe Sands and Man Sands and over Southdown Cliff to Sharkham Point - this is a particularly strenuous length. Passing holiday accommodation the path arrives at Berry Head, a Napoleonic fortified area. Divert to the end of the headland to see the unusually squat lighthouse. Berry Head has toilets and seasonal refreshments. From here descend past an old quarry to a road, turn right then go right again through the Shoalstone Car Park and along above the shoreline, returning to the road before descending steps to Brixham Breakwater. Follow the promenade to the harbour. Brixham has all facilities.

55 • Brixham to Torquay to Babbacombe

Week 7 - Day 3

OS Maps: Landranger 202: Explorer OL20 (western half); Explorer 110 (eastern half)

	This Walk	Cumulative	This Walk	Cumulative	Grading	Timing
Ascent	1,972ft	94,189ft	601m	28,709m	Moderate	6 hours
Distance	12.8mi	500.3mi	20.5km	805.2km		

For detailed directions see our Brixham to Torquay and Torquay to Shaldon Path Description booklets.

This is mostly an urban Section, passing along the shoreline of the "English Riviera", or Tor Bay. There is a mixture of grand terraces, open green parkland, amusement parks and the elegant white buildings overlooking the sea at Torquay. At the western end there is also the old fishing town of Brixham and at the other end the almost rural wooded cliffs around Babbacombe. All in all, this is a surprisingly diverse Section.

Directions

A range of bus routes runs throughout the Torbay area, including one which follows the coast road between Brixham and Torquay, and another linking Torquay to Babbacombe. As a result, a wide variety of bus-walks is possible.

Leaving Brixham by the fish market, the Coast Path initially passes a car park and gardens before passing two small coves and climbing into woodland which takes the path to Elberry Cove. From here it passes behind the sweep of Broadsands, climbing by the railway viaduct at the far end to proceed alongside the steam railway line to the promenade at Goodrington. At the far end climb through ornamental gardens and go down a road to Paignton Harbour and so along the promenade. Paignton's railway station is inland of the pier. Turn inland at Hollicombe, at the far end of Preston Sands, going through a park to the main sea-front road which is followed to Torquay Harbour. Torquay Station is inland a little before the harbour.

Cross the pedestrian bridge across the harbour and climb the hill, turning right at the Imperial Hotel on the signed path which leads to the open area at Daddyhole Plain. Descend to the sea-front road at Meadfoot Beach, climbing again at Ilsham Marine Drive. Take the cliff path round Thatcher Point to Hope's Nose. A cul-de-sac path goes to the end of this low headland.

From Hope's Nose follow the path inland of the road, crossing the road to the Bishop's Walk, which in turn arrives at a car park above Anstey's Cove. The path now goes round the edge of the grassy downs on Walls Hill, bearing off right to descend to Babbacombe Beach. Cross a wooden footbridge to Oddicombe Beach then climb by the cliff railway to reach Babbacombe's facilities at the top.

Dartmouth Steam Railway, Goodrington

Week 7 - Day 4 (half day)

OS Maps: **Landranger 202; Explorer 110**

	This Walk	Cumulative	This Walk	Cumulative	Grading	Timing
Ascent	2,090ft	96,279ft	637m	29,346m	Strenuous	3.75 hours
Distance	6.4mi	506.7mi	10.3km	815.5km		

For detailed directions see our Torquay to Shaldon Path Description booklet.

This is a tough Section of almost constant ups and downs. The characteristic red cliffs of this part of Devon are often quite high and quite sheer, though unfortunately the terrain is such that sea and cliff views are perhaps less frequent than would be wished. Its strenuous nature makes it a relatively quiet Section, except for the two ends, although it is never far from roads or housing.

Directions

A regular bus service links Babbacombe and Teignmouth, making a bus-walk an option.

From Babbacombe, a pleasant suburb of Torquay with all facilities, the Coast Path descends next to the cliff railway and then soon climbs again to avoid a cliff fall. This diversion takes the path up a grassy area to a main road where it turns right, then right again into Petitor Road.

Oddicombe Cliff Railway

At the bottom turn left on the Coast Path again, which soon descends onto a cliff face before reaching the wooded valley at Watcombe. Cross the track running down the valley and on through a wooded length to a short rocky stretch, turning right at a junction before reaching the car park at Maidencombe. There is a pub and toilets here. Turn right after the car park and keep on the rollercoaster path which eventually climbs to go alongside the coast road, then quickly leaves it to pass alongside fields to a track. Turn right and go round the wooded Ness headland, with super views ahead, descending to the promenade at Shaldon, on the estuary of the River Teign.

The ferry service across the River Teign operates April-mid July 08:00 to 18:00; mid July-end of August 08:00 to dusk; September-October 08:00 to 18:00; November-January 08:00 to 16:30 (weekends 10:00 to 16:00); February-March 08:00 to 17:00 (weekends 10:00 to 17:00); telephone 01626 215617; ferry mobile 07896 711822.

For ferry details see page 20.

Walk, Shaldon-Teignmouth

If the ferry is not operating, continue inland along the riverside roads to Shaldon Bridge and cross the Teign. On the Teignmouth side turn right into Milford Park, through Bitton Sports Ground into Park Hill, cross into Bitton Avenue then into Clay Lane and right into Willow Street. At the end bear left then right into Quay Road, then right to go along the Strand and right to the Harbour Beach and the ferry point. Teignmouth has all facilities, including a mainline rail station and buses to Exeter.

Week 7 - Day 4 (half day)

OS Maps: **Landranger 192; Explorer 110**

	This Walk	Cumulative	This Walk	Cumulative	Grading	Timing
Ascent	488ft	96,767ft	149m	29,495m	Easy	3 hours
Distance	7.9mi	514.6mi	12.7km	828.2km		

For detailed directions see our Shaldon to Exmouth Path Description booklet.

This Section primarily comprises two fairly large seaside towns, flanked by a coastline of high red cliffs at one end and marshes and a sand bar at the other. Running through it, often next to the Coast Path, is possibly the most scenic part of Brunel's GWR railway line, the embankment of which forms the sea wall for much of this length. This is a busy, largely urban and much used Section with an historic importance to the tourist trade.

Directions

A regular bus service links Teignmouth and Starcross, the ferry point for Exmouth, and also passes through Dawlish and Dawlish Warren. As there are also stations on the railway line at these places, bus or train-walks are options here.

From the ferry point at Teignmouth, or from the town centre, go to the car park at The Point, jutting out into the Teign Estuary, and begin by walking along the promenade. Leaving the town the Coast Path continues between railway and sea below the red cliffs to the end, where it descends steps to pass under the railway and then up Smugglers Lane to the A379 road at the top.

High water route, Teignmouth-Smugglers Lane

With a high sea and an onshore wind the far end of the promenade can become very wet, and for about an hour either side of high tide the steps at Smugglers Lane become impassable. In these cases, immediately after leaving the town fork left and cross the railway on a footbridge on Eastcliff Walk, and this path eventually reaches the A379 which is then followed ahead to meet the official path at the top of Smugglers Lane.

Coast Path, Smugglers Lane-Dawlish Warren

Use the footway on the inland side of the A379 and walk for about 150 yards/135m before turning right into Windward Lane, going immediately left on a path which skirts fields before returning to the A379. Bear right into Old Teignmouth Road, which in turn returns to the A379 then, very soon, turn right by some railings on a path which zigzags down to the shoreline. Follow the sea wall through Dawlish, past the station - all facilities are found beyond the railway here. The best route is then to continue on the sea wall between railway and sea, again below the red cliffs, to Dawlish Warren. Just before the amusement area cross the obvious railway footbridge to a car park, turn right and follow to the main road.

High water route, Dawlish-Dawlish Warren

At high tides the sea wall becomes impassable between Dawlish and Dawlish Warren. In this case, go under the railway at Dawlish station to the station forecourt, turning left here up a narrow path then through an arch and up some steps. Continue past a housing area then through more arches to arrive at the A379. Continue ahead then right on the road signed to Dawlish Warren then immediately right again along a signed footpath which leads to Dawlish Warren and to join the more coastal path here.

Coast Path, Dawlish Warren-Starcross

The Coast Path does not go around the large sand spit at Dawlish Warren itself, jutting out into the mouth of the River Exe, or the marshes behind it, but if there is time this can be an exhilarating experience. Otherwise continue along Warren Road on the pavement, then opposite the entrance to Dawlish Warren Sandy Park join the cycleway and footpath to Cockwood Harbour. After following the road around the harbour join the A379. Cross the road and follow the footpath and cycleway to Starcross, and the ferry point to Exmouth. Starcross has all facilities.

The ferry operates mid-April - end October, hourly, 7 days a week; from Starcross, on the hour between 10:10 and 16:10 (Easter and October); until 17:10 (mid-May, and June - September); until 18:00 (August). From Exmouth, on the half hour between 10:40 and 16:40 (Easter and October); until 17:40 (mid-May and June - September); until 18:15 (August) - telephone 01626 862452 or 07974 022536.

For ferry details see page 20.

If there is no ferry operating on arrival at Starcross, there are several options to reach Exmouth.

Option 1: Explorer Water Taxi - this runs daily 1st April until 4th September, 08.45-18.00, weather permitting; will also pick up passengers from the end of Warren Point. Tel: 07970 918418; phone before relying on this service.

Option 2: Bus or train from Starcross to Exeter, bus or train from Exeter to Exmouth.

Option 3: Walk from Starcross to Turf Lock following the waymarked Exe Valley Way on the riverside road and footpath (3 miles/5km), then ferry Turf Lock-Topsham and bus or train from Topsham to Exmouth.

Ferry operates 7 days a week, Easter holiday, mid-May - mid September and weekends April - October; from Turf 11:45 to 16:00 and from Topsham 11:30 to 15:15 - telephone 07778 370582.

For ferry details see page 20.

Option 4: Walk from Starcross to Topsham Lock following the waymarked Exe Valley Way on the riverside road and footpath and Exeter Canal towpath (4.5 miles/7km), then ferry Topsham Lock-Topsham and bus or train from Topsham to Exmouth.

Ferry operates Easter - September daily except Tuesdays, 11:00 to 17:00; in October - March on Saturdays, Sundays and Bank Holidays 11:00 to 17:00 or sunset. Wave or phone for service. Between April and September the ferry may be available outside these hours, weather and tides permitting - telephone 01392 274306 (office) or 07801 203338 (ferryman).

For ferry details see page 20.

Near Dawlish

Week 7 - Day 5 (half day)

OS Maps: Landranger 192; Explorer 115

	This Walk	Cumulative	This Walk	Cumulative	Grading	Timing
Ascent	722ft	97,489ft	220m	29,715m	Moderate	3 hours
Distance	6.2mi	520.8mi	9.9km	838.1km		

For detailed directions see our Exmouth to Sidmouth Path Description booklet.

This is a well-used and popular Section, never far from houses and passing a large caravan site and a golf course on the way. Most of this length is on relatively low cliffs, and in the west these give excellent views over the mouth of the Exe and the great sandy bar of Dawlish Warren. Further east, the high point of West Down Beacon gives exceptionally fine panoramic views, while beyond the Beacon the path becomes more enclosed. It is an easy-going Section of some variety, ideal for those not wishing to explore remote or strenuous lengths.

Directions

A regular bus service links Exmouth and Budleigh Salterton, making this a good bus-walk option. In addition, a summer service links Exmouth with Sandy Bay, approximately mid-way along the section, giving another, shorter bus-walk.

Exmouth has all facilities, including a railway station on a branch line from Exeter. The obvious route for the Coast Path is to walk along the promenade from the former, now redeveloped, docks area at the mouth of the Exe, which is also the ferry landing point. Continue to the cliffs at Orcombe Point then climb the steps and continue on the cliff top, passing the Jurassic Coast marker and on to the Devon Cliffs Caravan Site at Sandy Bay. Follow the fence line inland of the Straight Point rifle range then climb to the high point at West Down Beacon. The path then descends steadily, seaward of the golf course though offering relatively few sea views on this stretch. Approaching Budleigh Salterton, a charming and traditional small town, the path turns inland then almost immediately, at a junction, goes right to descend to the end of the promenade. The shops, pubs and other facilities are immediately inland of the path, which continues towards the distinctive line of pine trees to the east of the town.

The Gate to the Jurassic Coast

Week 7 - Day 5 (half day)

OS Maps: Landranger 192; Explorer 115

	This Walk	Cumulative	This Walk	Cumulative	Grading	Timing
Ascent	1,037ft	98,526ft	316m	30,031m	Moderate then strenuous	3.5 hours
Distance	6.9mi	527.7mi	11.1km	849.2km		

For detailed directions see our Exmouth to Sidmouth Path Description booklet.

This pleasant Section is mostly on relatively low red cliffs with attractive views inland over an undulating pastoral countryside as well as to seaward. However, there are contrasts at both ends. The western end skirts the narrow, marsh-fringed estuary of the River Otter while the eastern end includes a wooded cliff top and high cliffs on the appropriately named High Peak and Peak Hill. This is a pleasant and quietly popular Section.

Directions

A regular bus service links Budleigh Salterton and Sidmouth, making a bus-walk a possibility.

Budleigh Salterton, a town with something of an olde-world air, has all facilities. The Coast Path goes along the promenade to the car park at the eastern end. Progress east seems tantalisingly close, but the River Otter, with no bridge at its mouth, bars the way. The path therefore passes through a gate at the rear riverside corner of the car park and follows the riverside path until it meets a road. Turn right and cross the River Otter on the road bridge, then bear right to follow the path back downriver to the sea, bearing round to the left on reaching the cliffs.

The path is clear to the caravan site at Ladram Bay, where there are toilets and seasonal refreshments. Here, descend across a field to the beach access track, going left then immediately right, past a pub and on to climb into woodland at High Peak. Here, the path goes behind the very top, emerging on a track. Turn right and climb again to the open land at Peak Hill. Follow the path down the cliff through woodland to a road, turn right then keep right along an old road length then onto a large grassy area down to a zigzag path next to the white Jacob's Ladder. At the bottom follow the seafront path to reach the main esplanade. Sidmouth is an elegant Regency town and has all facilities.

Sidmouth

Week 7 - Day 6

OS Maps: **Landranger 192; Explorer 115 (most); Explorer 116 (eastern end)**

	This Walk	Cumulative	This Walk	Cumulative	Grading	Timing
Ascent	2,408ft	100,934ft	734m	30,765m	Severe then strenuous	5.5 hours
Distance	10.4mi	538.1mi	16.7km	865.9km		

For detailed directions see our Sidmouth to Lyme Regis Path Description booklet.

This is a Section of lofty cliffs cut by deep and narrow valleys, making for a magnificent coastal landscape but a testing one to walk. In the west the cliffs are characteristically red, but this changes quite abruptly along the length as the Section reaches the most westerly chalk cliffs in England, appropriately bright white. Add an elegant Regency town, a charming picture-postcard village and a picturesque fishing town and the result is a length of great attraction.

Directions

A regular bus service links Sidmouth with Seaton, making a bus-walk an option. There are also regular, if less frequent, bus links to Branscombe and Beer, along the length, giving further options.

The Coast Path passes along the elegant esplanade at Sidmouth to the footbridge over the mouth of the River Sid at the eastern end. Some dramatic cliff falls have occurred just east of Sidmouth and a well-signed diversion is necessary past housing until, at the top of Laskeys Lane, it turns back to the cliff top. A steep climb up Salcombe Hill is soon followed by an equally steep descent and climb through the Salcombe Regis valley. The path skirts behind the hollow of Lincombe then descends to the beach at Weston Mouth. A short way along the beach the path leaves to climb steeply back to the cliffs and a good level stretch which eventually turns inland to meet a track. This descends to Branscombe Mouth, where there are refreshments and toilets. Beyond Branscombe the official path passes among some holiday chalets then along an undercliff path, with the cliffs rearing massively above, before climbing to the cliff top at Beer Head. These are the most westerly chalk cliffs in England. An alternative route from Branscombe Mouth climbs up the valley side and proceeds directly along the cliff top to Beer Head.

Follow the signed path from Beer Head, past a caravan site and into the village behind the beach. Beer, an attractive fishing village, has all facilities. Climb the path on the east side of the beach to the cliff top, descending to a road and down to Seaton Hole. If the tide is low, walk along the beach to the end of the promenade at Seaton. If not, an inland diversion must now be taken. A cliff fall caused by the extreme wet weather in 2012 has created a very large hole in Old Beer Road, necessitating permanent closure of the previous Coast Path route. At Seaton Hole one must now turn left on to Old Beer Road and walk approximately 330 yards/300m inland towards Beer. At the junction with the B3172 Beer Road, turn right towards Seaton. After approximately 1,100yards/1km, leave the Beer Road and take the path on the right through the chine and on to the promenade and so into Seaton, which has all facilities, including bus services to Exeter, Weymouth and Poole.

Week 8 - Day 1 (half day)

OS Maps: Landranger 193; Explorer 116

	This Walk	Cumulative	This Walk	Cumulative	Grading	Timing
Ascent	1,401ft	102,335ft	427m	31,192m	Moderate	3.5 hours
Distance	6.8mi	544.9mi	11.0km	876.9km		

For detailed directions see our Sidmouth to Lyme Regis Path Description booklet.

Most of this Section is unlike any other on the Coast Path. The western end crosses a golf course and there is a short length of cliff, but the majority of the Section passes through the National Nature Reserve of the Axmouth-Lyme Regis Undercliffs. Except for the path, this area has been undisturbed since the massive cliff fall which formed it in 1839. It is effectively a wilderness area of virtually virgin woodland and dense scrub, with an almost eerie character. For most of this length the sea will not be visible. It is an odd and impressive experience, delighting some but frustrating others.

Directions

A regular bus service links Seaton and Lyme Regis, making a bus-walk possible.

Seaton has all facilities, and has links to the railway network at Exeter and Weymouth. Leave Seaton at the east end, using the old concrete bridge to cross the River Axe. Turn inland along the road then turn right up the golf course access road, past the club house then due east over the fairway to the end of a lane. Turn right off the lane to reach the cliffs, and the path then enters the strange world of the Undercliffs.

This old landslip is a National Nature Reserve, being an area of virtual wildlife wilderness. The path through the Undercliff rarely offers sea views and can feel claustrophobic in places. There are no escape routes to the coast road inland nor safe paths to the sea shore. However, the route is well waymarked and the maps on the Natural England display boards show walkers their exact location: no one should ever feel lost. Eventually the path emerges on cliffs and is then waymarked down through woods to arrive adjacent to Lyme Regis's scenic harbour, The Cobb. Lyme Regis is a charming and attractive town and has all facilities.

Axmouth Harbour

Week 8 - Day 1 (half day)

OS Maps: **Landranger 193; Explorer 116**

	This Walk	Cumulative	This Walk	Cumulative	Grading	Timing
Ascent	1,883ft	104,218ft	574m	31,766m	Moderate then strenuous	3 hours
Distance	6.7mi	551.6mi	10.9km	887.8km		

For detailed directions see our Lyme Regis to West Bay Path Description booklet.

A major feature of this Section is the large number of cliff slippages caused by a combination of wet weather and geology. This means that as things currently stand there is effectively no proper coastal path between Lyme Regis and Charmouth (approximately 3 miles/4.5km), nor, indeed, immediately east of Charmouth. However, the remainder of this Section is a superb coastal experience, climbing as it does over the top of Golden Cap, the highest point on the entire south coast of England, with views to match as well as an energy requirement of a high level!

Directions

A regular bus service which could be used as a basis for a bus-walk links Lyme Regis, Charmouth and Chideock, which is about 0.75 mile/1.25km inland of Seatown.

Major diversions have had to be put in place in this Section, especially between Lyme Regis and Charmouth, to avoid the considerable cliff falls that have occurred. It looks likely that these diversions will remain in place for 2013. However, for up-to-date details check the Association's website (www.swcp.org.uk).

Lyme Regis is a charming and attractive town with all facilities. From the town centre the Coast Path follows Church Street and Charmouth Road (A3052) as far as Lyme Regis Football Club on the right, beyond which there is a gate at the corner of a lane to a footpath across fields to a lane where the route turns left for 100 yards/90m. Turn right at a sign up through woods and near the top is a path junction.

Official Coastal Route, Lyme Regis-Charmouth

If an official route is in place, and this is highly unlikely for 2013, turn right onto a path that runs between the cliff edge and the golf course. Take the track downhill to Charmouth and at the first junction (with Old Lyme Hill) turn sharp right to follow the signposted route back to the cliff edge. The old alternative route along the beach is also closed following a landslide.

Official Diversion, Lyme Regis-Charmouth

Dorset County Council have installed and waymarked their official diversion. At the path junction in the wood (at GR 3456 9330) turn left for 130 yards/120m to meet Timber Hill. Turn right here to join in some 440 yards/400m the A3052 road and continue on this for 110 yards/100m. Turn eastwards on a public footpath signposted to Fern Hill, crossing the golf course then north-east through woods to re-join the A3052. Turn right to the roundabout with the A35 and fork right, signposted to Charmouth, following the road into the village for 760 yards/700m. At the second road junction turn right into Higher Sea Lane. When the road bends right take a footpath south-east and continue for about 650 yards/600m to re-join the official Coast Path at GR3640 9305.

Official Diversion, Charmouth West

If the official route from Lyme Regis to the edge of Charmouth is in place, there may still be the necessity for a diversion at the western end of Charmouth. This will take the route from the west end of Old Lyme Hill north-eastwards to the main road through the village. It then turns right and, after 110 yards/100m right again into Higher Sea Lane as above.

Preferred Diversion, Lyme Regis-Charmouth

The Association recommends a preferable alternative to the official diversion above, which deviates from it at the A3052/A35 roundabout. Take the road signposted to Charmouth and shortly after the junction take steps on the right to a stile and public footpath. Follow the waymarked direction up the field to the former Lily Farm, now holiday accommodation. Cross a stile and pass between the buildings and the Dutch barn on the left and after the buildings cross a field to arrive at a tarmac lane (Old Lyme Hill). Turn right and after 90 yards/80m turn left to arrive at Old Lyme Road.

Preferred Diversion, Charmouth West

Go left along Old Lyme Road and after 80 yards/70m turn right into a private road, Westcliffe Road. Descend steeply for 330 yards/300m to a junction with Five Acres. Bear right here and at the end of the cul-de-sac take a footpath going forward into a narrow lane. Shortly it reaches a wider road (Higher Sea Lane). Turn right and continue ahead, ignoring various signs pointing off the lane, continuing round the bend to the west in the lane that rises for some 130 yards/120m to an oak signpost on the left. Here leave the lane through a metal gate to re-join the Coast Path, descending over grassy slopes to Charmouth Beach, with its toilets and refreshments.

Official Route, Charmouth East

The official route crosses a footbridge and climbs the obvious green path ahead. This is unlikely to be available for 2013.

Diversion, Charmouth East

From the approach to the footbridge go north-east along a tarmac lane (River Way) and at the end continue along a gravel path to Bridge Road. Continue to the main village road (The Street) then turn right, cross the bridge and fork right into Stonebarrow Lane. Continue up this narrow lane for nearly 0.75 mile/1.25km. At the car park at the top turn sharp right to a signpost then take a grassy track as signed south-westward to re-join the Coast Path.

Coast Path, Charmouth East-Seatown (Chideock)

There is a hefty climb to Golden Cap, the highest point on England's south coast, but the views from the top are spectacular. At the top go slightly left to the trig point which then leads to the long and steep descent. There is a minor diversion on the approach to Seatown, taking the Coast Path slightly inland then back to the coast along the access road. Seatown has toilets and refreshments. Other facilities are at Chideock, 0.75 mile/1.25km inland.

Towards Golden Cap

Week 8 - Day 2

OS Maps: **Landranger 193 (western half); Explorer 116 (western half)**
Landranger 194 (eastern half); Explorer OL15 (eastern half)

	This Walk	Cumulative	This Walk	Cumulative	Grading	Timing
Ascent	1,489ft	105,707ft	454m	32,220m	Strenuous then moderate	6.25 hours
Distance	12.4mi	564.0mi	19.9km	907.7km		

For detailed directions see our Lyme Regis to West Bay and West Bay to Abbotsbury Path Description booklets.

This is a Section of two contrasting halves. West of West Bay is a rollercoaster of steep and high cliffs, giving far-reaching views along the coast and also inland, over the deeply dissected pastoral countryside. East of West Bay a sheer red sandstone cliff rises from the sea, looking almost artificial in its straight lines, and then the coastline subsides to a low level and the Coast Path loses its ups and downs, though not its hard work, as the shingle of what is the far western end of Chesil Beach tests the legs.

Directions

A regular bus service links Chideock, which is 0.75 mile/1.25km inland of Seatown, with Abbotsbury, and also calls at West Bay and Burton Bradstock which are along the length of this Section, giving various bus-walk options. A popular circular walk based on Abbotsbury uses the Coast Path as well as the South Dorset Ridgeway.

From the pub and toilets at Seatown the Coast Path climbs the cliff slope on its way to the high point of Thorncombe Beacon. There is a descent to the little beach at Eype then a further climb and descent to the harbour at West Bay, which has most facilities. Go round the back of the harbour, pass to the right of the church and ahead to the West Bay public house, opposite which is the Coast Path sign pointing to the surprisingly steep cliff. Arriving at Burton Freshwater the path runs between the caravan park and the beach and is well signed. Following major cliff falls in the summer of 2012 at Burton Cliff the Coast Path was closed from Burton Freshwater to Burton Beach and the signed alternative on more inland paths should be followed. The Coast Path is likely to be permanently diverted at Burton Hive. This leads to Burton Beach, where there are refreshments and toilets. Further on, the path passes inland of Burton Mere before coming to West Bexington, where there are toilets and seasonal refreshments.

See Section 71 for details of the alternative Inland Coast Path (South Dorset Ridgeway) between West Bexington and Osmington Mills.

The Coast Path continues along the back of the beach, later passing another car park with toilets and seasonal refreshments and some 200 yards/185m beyond this it turns inland to Abbotsbury. There are alternative routes either going into the village or going south and east of Chapel Hill and missing the village. A permissive path alternative leaves the Coast Path and leads direct to the famous Swannery. Abbotsbury is a beautiful stone-built village with much of historic interest and most facilities.

West Bay - East Cliff

Week 8 - Day 3

OS Maps: Landranger 194; Explorer OL15

	This Walk	Cumulative	This Walk	Cumulative	Grading	Timing
Ascent	955ft	106,662ft	291m	32,511m	Easy. Chesil Beach route strenuous	4 hours official route
Distance	10.9mi	574.9mi	17.5km	925.2km		

For detailed directions see our Abbotsbury to Ferry Bridge Path Description booklet.

This is an untypical Section of the Coast Path. In the west, there is an inland rural high-level field route, giving views over the unusual feature of Chesil Beach and the landlocked Fleet behind. To the east, the path runs along the banks of the Fleet, with pleasant views over this attractive feature, but with views of the sea largely cut off by the shingle bank of Chesil Beach. Although never far from houses or roads, this is often a very quiet Section.

Directions

Buses to and from Abbotsbury and Ferry Bridge link at Weymouth for a potential bus-walk.

It is possible to walk direct from the beach near Abbotsbury to Ferry Bridge at Wyke Regis along the length of Chesil Beach. If this is intended, start at the beach at the inland turn (Day 2) to Abbotsbury, continuing along the beach. However, note that:

Near Abbotsbury

1. It is not possible to get off the beach before Ferry Bridge.
2. It is extremely hard and slow walking.
3. It is necessary to check that firing is not scheduled at the nearby Chickerell Rifle Range; telephone Major Hazard on 01305 783456, ext.8132.
4. The beach is closed to visitors from 1st May to 31st August for the bird nesting season.

Although the Coast Path does not pass through Abbotsbury most walkers will visit the attractive village and its facilities. From the village leave West Street on the path going south adjacent to Chapel Street Stores. Continue on to Nunnery Grove to the signed Coast Path, which now goes inland but is well signed and enjoyable with some excellent views. After Horsepool Farm on the edge of Abbotsbury the path climbs onto the ridge. After about a mile/1.5km turn right off the ridge then left after Hodder's Coppice. Cross a minor road then follow the field headland east then south to the north-east corner of Wyke Wood. The path then heads for the edge of the Fleet - be aware approaching Rodden Hive that the path suddenly goes through a hedge on the left. From here the path follows the edge of the Fleet. At Tidmoor Point follow the red and white posts, unless it is necessary to divert inland because of firing. The diversion is well marked. Approaching Wyke Regis there is a minor deviation behind an MOD Bridging Hard, then the path arrives at the A354 road adjacent to Ferry Bridge, the access for the Isle of Portland, at Wyke Regis, a suburb of Weymouth.

65 · Isle of Portland

Week 8 - Day 4

OS Maps: **Landranger 194; Explorer OL15**

	This Walk	Cumulative	This Walk	Cumulative	Grading	Timing
Ascent	1,112ft	107,774ft	339m	32,850m	Moderate	6 hours
Distance	13.2mi	588.1mi	21.3km	946.5km		

For detailed directions see our Portland Path description booklet.

Portland is different. Different from the rest of Dorset and from the rest of the Coast Path. An almost-island, jutting out into the English Channel, joined to the mainland only by the end of Chesil Beach, it has an isolated air. Formed of limestone, it has been extensively quarried and these workings, some still operational, characterise much of the landscape. Elsewhere, former military buildings and those of Verne Prison and the Young Offenders' Institution are prominent. Portland is not pretty, but it is well worth exploring.

Directions

Bus routes run the length of Portland, making a variety of bus-walks possible. This Section is, in any event, a circular walk in its own right. However, at the time of going to print there were suggestions that the service all the way to the Bill may be discontinued. Check on local bus information.

It is possible to omit this section and continue from Wyke Regis directly into Weymouth. However, Portland is officially part of the National Trail and its interest and sense of being different make it well worth the day's walk.

From Ferry Bridge cross the causeway onto Portland; this is done by simply following the shared footway/cycleway alongside the A354 road or alternatively by crossing the bridge on the A354 to beyond the boatyard and then walking along the raised bed of the old railway on the eastern bank to near the end of the causeway at the roundabout for the access road to Osprey Quay and here returning to the footway/cycleway. At the southern of the two roundabouts at Victoria Square take the main road south and shortly turn right into Pebble Lane then left just before the public toilets. Continue to the Cove House Inn and bear right up onto the promenade. About half way along, at the floodgates, cut back sharp left then right, following Coast Path signs up a steep tarmac path, past the school and up the steep path in the grass incline to the steps to the terraced path that was once the old road. Bear off right onto the signed path running between quarry banks and the cliff face, leading to 3 miles/5km of airy cliff-top walking to Portland Bill. Here, as well as the lighthouse, are refreshments, toilets and buses (but see above).

Continue around the end of the low headland then start northwards, seaward of the wooden chalets, to follow a winding path along the top of low cliffs to join a road above Freshwater Bay after about 1.5 miles/2.5km. Turn right on the road (use the footway on the west side of the road) for 600 yards/550m, past Cheyne Weares car park to a signpost on the right. Follow the zigzag path into the undercliff area and follow the waymarking through disused quarry workings to Church Ope Cove.

Ascend the stepped and signed path up to Rufus Castle. Here the South West Coast Path also becomes the England Coast Path, the first section of which, from here to Lulworth Cove, was formally opened on 30th June 2012. The signposting now usually indicates simply "Coast Path". Some, but not all, of the improvements to the route that the Association sought on Portland can now be walked and the new route is described below. Unfortunately the major alignment around the north-east corner of Portland was not resolved because of legal complications with Portland Ports plc and security issues.

Looking over Isle of Portland Causeway

After Rufus Castle the Coast Path soon joins the track bed of the former Weymouth to Easton railway line. This is then followed northwards for some 1,585 yards/1,450m to a pair of signposts. Here turn left to follow a rocky path that climbs up the cliffs to what appears to be an isolated chimney seen on the skyline above. At the top turn sharp right along the prison road northwards and through a gap in a high wall. On the right is the Old Engine Shed, soon to be converted into a visitor centre. On reaching a narrow road the official route is signed across the road and takes a route across open ground passing disused quarries to reach the perimeter fence of the Verne prison. However, the Association's preferred route here, which is all on public rights of way, can be followed thus:-

At the road turn right and just over the brow of a hill turn left on an access track to compounds. Continue ahead on a grassy path towards a large pinnacle of rock (Nichodemus Knob) after which, at the "rock falls" sign, bear left steeply up onto the higher escarpment, heading for a large communications mast. At the high wire perimeter fence turn left and follow it along then round to the right, to reach the south entrance to Verne Prison. Here rejoin the route of the England Coast Path.

Take a path through a little gap to the left of the entrance, passing beside railings and down steep steps. Bear right along a path that traverses under the grassy banks.

The path drops downhill towards houses to a waymark post. Ignore the left fork and continue on the level on a grass path which then passes through an underpass below a road. Descend steeply down the Castletown Incline (a former quarry tramway), crossing two footpaths and a road. Pass under a footbridge and through another underpass to reach an access road and turn left to a roundabout.

Continue ahead for some 30 yards/27m and then cross to turn right down Liberty Road, signposted to Portland Castle. Go past the castle entrance to the car park and turn right towards the harbour, heading for five black posts. Here join the footway/cycleway to follow the harbour-side to the Sailing Academy, the venue of the sailing events at the 2012 Olympics. Continue on the footway/cycleway to reach the roundabout on the A354 road. From here follow the former railway trackbed to the boatyard before the bridge over the mouth of the Fleet and follow the footway alongside the road to Ferry Bridge.

Week 8 - Day 5

OS Maps: Landranger 194; Explorer OL15

	This Walk	Cumulative	This Walk	Cumulative	Grading	Timing
Ascent	2,385ft	110,159ft	727m	33,577m	Easy to moderate to strenuous	6.25 hours
Distance	14.1mi	602.2mi	22.7km	969.2km		

For detailed directions see our Ferry Bridge to Lulworth Cove Path Description booklet.

This section is part of the first section of the England Coast Path. The signposting generally only refers to "Coast Path".

The western part of this Section is an urban walk along the various lengths of Weymouth's sea front. East of the town is a length of relatively low cliffs but then at White Nothe, two thirds of the way along the section, the coastal geology changes. East of here is a rollercoaster of often sheer white cliffs, the length punctuated by the iconic landmarks of Durdle Door and Lulworth Cove. Both ends of this Section are busy, but in the centre is an often quiet and remote length.

Directions

A regular bus service links Weymouth with Lulworth Cove, also serving Osmington, close to the Coast Path mid-way along this Section, allowing some bus-walk options.

From Ferry Bridge the signed Coast Path follows the footway/cycleway on the old railway trackbed, passing behind the sailing centre. Shortly afterwards bear off right to continue into Old Castle Road. Ignore the footpath sign to the right, a cul-de-sac as the onward cliff path is closed due to a landslip. However, except at high tides the beach can be used to reach a flight of new timber steps that rejoin the former Coast Path beyond the landslip. Instead, continue along the road and 260 yards/240m beyond turn right into Belle Vue Road. Continue for about 600 yards/560m to a crossroads and turn right into Redcliff View. At the end of this road a path leads across a grassed area back to the coast at GR 682 781 (westbound walkers follow the path worn across the grassed area here). Continue on the path to Nothe Fort and bear sharp left then turn down steps on the right to Weymouth harbourside. This is followed to the Town Bridge, which is crossed and the opposite side of the harbour followed back to the Pavilion complex. Bear left to join the Esplanade.

In summer a little ferry may cross the harbour, slightly shortening the route.

Ferry operates (rowing boat) between Easter and June 11:00 to 15:00; during July 09:30 to 17:00; during August 09:30 to 19:00; during September-October 11:00 to 15:00; all weather permitting - telephone 01305 838423.

For ferry details see page 20.

Leave Weymouth along the promenade then, at Overcombe, go up the minor road to Bowleaze Cove. After passing the Spyglass Inn the route now bears right to cross the crest of the grass public open space to reach the Beachside Centre. With the new public access rights now provided the Coast Path follows a signed route through the Beachside Leisure Centre to take a narrow path that squeezes between the

Weymouth - Greenhill Gardens

Riviera Hotel and cliff edge and follows a new signed route to Redcliff Point. A little further on, beyond an education and adventure centre, follow the signed route on a re-established length of the Coast Path. On the downhill approach to Osmington Mills the route avoids another landslip by bearing away from the cliff edge over a stile and down the edge of a field, then crosses two further stiles to meet a narrow road down to the coast.

See Section 71 for details of the alternative Inland Coast Path (South Dorset Ridgeway) between West Bexington and Osmington Mills.

The path goes slightly inland at Ringstead. Beyond the wooden church the route of the Coast Path near Holworth House is now signed to deviate north-east and south although the original route (which is a public right of way) can still be used as a more direct route.

Further on, at the coastguard cottages at White Nothe, take the left fork of the two yellow arrows. The path now traverses some quite severe gradients on its way to Lulworth Cove, passing behind Durdle Door to Hambury Tout. Follow the waymarking here - the route sometimes shown on older maps going south here is not usable. Approaching Lulworth Cove a stone-pitched path leads down through the car park to the Heritage Centre. Turn right here along the cliff past the view into Stair Hole. Pass the Jurassic Coast commemorative stone then turn down towards the Cove in front of the boathouse. Lulworth Cove has toilets and refreshments and most facilities are found here or at West Lulworth a little way inland.

Week 8 - Day 6 (half day)

OS Maps: **Landranger 194 (most); Landranger 195 (eastern end); Explorer OL15**

	This Walk	Cumulative	This Walk	Cumulative	Grading	Timing
Ascent	2,002ft	112,161ft	610m	34,187m	Severe	4 hours
Distance	7.3mi	609.5mi	11.8km	981.0km		

For detailed directions see our Lulworth to Kimmeridge Path Description booklet.

The coast of this Section is of geological interest and importance, largely having been formed by lines of relatively hard limestone having been breached at intervals to form coves and bays as the sea erodes the softer rocks behind. The result is a dramatic coastline of white cliffs and darker coloured coves, some prominent headlands and a succession of extremely steep slopes. Inland, the landscape of the military ranges has been unchanged by farming for some seventy years, though it is perhaps a little too obviously military in a few places.

Directions

Lulworth Cove and Kimmeridge village, about one mile/1.5km inland from Kimmeridge Bay, both have bus links to Wareham, which could provide a bus-walk option.

IMPORTANT: Note that this Section passes through the Lulworth Army Firing Ranges. Before deciding to walk this Section, check that the Ranges are open. PLEASE BE AWARE THE OFFICIAL COAST PATH FOR THIS SECTION MAY BE CLOSED TO WALKERS DURING THE WEEK. However most weekends and during school holidays it is normally open, but please read the section below to check the dates when walkers are allowed access along the official Coast Path.

The Lulworth Range walks, including the Coast Path between Lulworth Cove and Kimmeridge Bay, plus access to Tyneham village, are open to the public every weekend in 2013 WITH THE EXCEPTION OF THE FOLLOWING:-

1. 19th/20th January 2013
2. 9th/10th March 2013
3. 20th/21st April 2013
4. 15th/16th June 2013
5. 28th/29th September 2013
6. 16th/17th November 2013

In addition to the weekends they are OPEN EVERY DAY DURING THE FOLLOWING TIMES IN 2013: ALL DATES ARE INCLUSIVE:-

Christmas/New Year: 22nd December 2012 - 1st January 2013
Easter: 29th March - 7th April 2013
Bank Holiday: 4th - 6th May 2013
Spring: 25th May - 2nd June 2013
Summer: 27th July - 1st September 2013
Christmas/New Year: 21st December 2013 - 5th January 2014.

The exhibitions in Tyneham School and Tyneham Church are open 10.00-16.00. The abandoned village and its historical exhibition are 0.5 mile/800m inland of the Coast Path, and worth the diversion. The gates to the walks are opened as near to 09.00 on the Saturday morning as possible and remain open until 08.00 on the Monday morning when open only at weekends. The gate to Tyneham is locked each night at dusk.

For any further information telephone 01929 404819 or 01929 404712, 0800-1700, Monday to Friday

If the Ranges are closed, it is strongly recommended that schedules are re-arranged so that the Coast Path is walked when open. If, however, this is not possible, two alternative inland diversions are shown below.

Coast Path - Lulworth Cove-Kimmeridge Bay

The Coast Path from Lulworth Cove leaves from behind the cafe. Higher up, a short signed alternative path avoids an eroded area close to the cliff edge. Tide permitting, walking the beach avoids a considerable ascent and descent. At most states of the tide this is possible, going up the path which rises diagonally on the far side of the beach. At the top of the steep ascent off the beach the best route proceeds seawards, the path then turning south-eastwards along the coast to the beginning of the Army Ranges. The route onward is straightforward - just follow the yellow topped posts through the ranges to arrive at Kimmeridge Bay. Here are toilets and seasonal refreshments (or all year refreshments in the village 0.6 mile/1km to the north).

If Ranges Closed - Alternative Option 1 (13.5 miles/22.0km)

This route is safer and quieter but more strenuous than Option 2; it uses mainly Rights of Way plus some permissive paths. Leave the Cove on the road inland, forking right, and take road on the left, by a bus shelter (GR 825 807), and in 100 yards/90m turn right on a footpath that heads north for 0.75 mile/1.2 km. Turn right (east) and after 100 yards/90m turn left (north) to pass Belhuish Coppice and Belhuish Farm, then cross the B3071 road at GR 835 832. At the eastern boundary of Burngate Wood (GR 845 828) use the permissive path (blue) north-east past Park Lodge and go across the road at GR 855 832 onto a bridleway. Continue north-east along the bridleway to GR 865 839, where it veers north and later north-east through Highwood to meet the road at GR872 862. Walk east along the road and then fork right (signposted Stoborough) at GR882 855. Go over the crossroads with the B3070 at GR 886 855 and walk east for a further 1.5 miles/2.5km along Holme Lane to GR 911 854. [(*) Aternative Option 2 below continues from here].

Turn right just before the railway bridge onto Doreys Farm bridleway. After 1.25 miles/2km turn right onto Creech Road. After 1.5 miles/2.5km of this road, walk up a steep gradient to a viewpoint car park. Beyond the car park, at GR 902 815, take the left road that turns back and down over the ridge. (A short cut bridleway at GR 905 817 zigzags down to meet the same road.) As the road levels out, at a left-hand bend at GR 907 812, take the bridleway ahead that leads south through Steeple Leaze Farm. About 200 yards/185m south of the farm, a footpath heads up steeply south to a bridleway on a ridge. Turn left through a gate and look for a narrow path on the right raking steeply downhill and then across three fields towards the coast ahead and Kimmeridge Bay.

If Ranges Closed - Alternative Option 2 (12 miles/19km)

This option is mainly road walking, and care is needed on narrow bends. Leave the Cove to West Lulworth on the B3070, then turn right to East Lulworth and beyond, keeping to the B3070 for some 3 miles/5km to GR 886 855. Here turn right along Holme Lane to GR 911 854. From here, follow the route described from (*) in Option 1 above.

Taxi operators Mike Whittle, Silver Cars, tel. 01929 400409, mobile 07811 328281 Adrian, Valley Taxis, tel. 01929 480507; and K Bay Taxi, tel.01929 480669, mobile 07545 776716, all offer their services in the Lulworth/Kimmeridge area.

Week 8 - Day 6 (half day)

OS Maps: **Landranger 195; Explorer OL15**

	This Walk	Cumulative	This Walk	Cumulative	Grading	Timing
Ascent	1,059ft	113,220ft	323m	34,510m	Severe	3.25 hours
Distance	5.2mi	614.7mi	8.3km	989.3km		

For detailed directions see our Kimmeridge to South Haven Point Path Description booklet.

This is a Section of steeply undulating cliffs, often with quite sheer faces and frequently with rock ledges at the cliff face. Houns-tout Cliff, near the eastern end of the Section, is especially steep. There are some very attractive bays formed by these cliffs, particularly at the eastern end. The tough terrain means that this Section often has a remote character, accentuated by the lack of neighbouring houses and roads.

Directions

Bus-walks are not easily undertaken on this Section. Circular walks using the Coast Path, based on inland villages such as Kimmeridge or Kingston, are possible.

The Coast Path from Kimmeridge Bay eastwards is straightforward, although care may be needed where small lengths have slipped, cracked or may be close to the cliff top. Just beyond Kimmeridge the Clavell Tower has been relocated 27 yards/25m inland and an improved Coast Path installed. There is a very steep climb to Houns-tout and the descent beyond turns inland to avoid dangerous terrain at Chapman's Pool. (For those aiming to end at Worth Matravers, which is about 1.2 miles/2km inland, the Coast Path is left where it crosses the valley at Hill Bottom Cottages. For the village head inland then turn right up a steep track past Renscombe Farm. Worth Matravers has a pub, shop and cafe.)

Clavell Tower

Week 8 - Day 7 (half day)

OS Maps: Landranger 195; Explorer OL15

	This Walk	Cumulative	This Walk	Cumulative	Grading	Timing
Ascent	1,195ft	114,415ft	364m	34,874m	Severe then Moderate	4 hours
Distance	8.1mi	622.8mi	13.1km	1,002.4km		

For detailed directions see our Kimmeridge to South Haven Point Path Description booklet.

The western part of this Section is dominated by St Aldhelm's Head, a flat-topped headland of limestone surmounted by an old chapel. There are extensive views, especially along the coast to the west. East of the headland the cliffs become increasingly disturbed by the remains of small-scale quarrying activity until the Country Park at Durlston Head marks the approach of Swanage.

Directions

Numerous footpaths cross the cliffs to the Coast Path from the outskirts of Swanage and the inland village of Langton Matravers. This allows for bus-walks which combine these link paths with the Coast Path.

(For those starting in Worth Matravers village, walk along the lane westwards past Weston Farm and Renscombe Farm then turn into the valley and on to the Coast Path at Hill Bottom Cottages.)

From the valley at Hill Bottom the Coast Path climbs on a well-signed route steeply up West Hill and on to Emmett's Hill. The path goes out round St Aldhelm's Head, with excellent coastal views west, and on as a fine high level walk to Durlston Head. Signing in Durlston Country Park is limited; keep on the low level path all the way round Durlston Head then, coming up on the north side take the second turning right (the first is a cul-de-sac to a quarry). Durlston Castle has now been converted to a Jurassic Coast Gateway Centre and includes refreshment facilities.

After leaving Durlston Castle follow a broad stony path north through the woods for some 760 yards/700m to a barrier and sign. From here there is a permanent diversion following a cliff fall. Turn left on a good path for some 125 yards/115m to reach Durlston Road at a gate. Turn right and in 185 yards/170m turn right again into Belle Vue Road. Follow the road north-eastwards to the grassed open space leading to Peveril Point. In bad weather or at high tides use the roadway and then down to the footpath at the end of the coastal buildings, otherwise use the foreshore. Continue along Swanage's sea front promenade. Swanage has all facilities.

Week 8 - Day 7 (half day)

OS Maps: **Landranger 195; Explorer OL15**

	This Walk	Cumulative	This Walk	Cumulative	Grading	Timing
Ascent	492ft	114,907ft	150m	35,024m	Moderate	3.5 hours
Distance	7.6mi	630.4mi	12.2km	1,014.6km		

For detailed directions see our Kimmeridge to South Haven Point Path Description booklet.

This is an excellent and scenic Section. The southern, Swanage end comprises increasingly high cliffs, culminating in the length between Ballard Point and Handfast Point, with its offshore stacks. This is an exhilarating length with superb views over Poole Bay to Bournemouth and across the Solent to the matching cliffs of the Needles on the Isle of Wight. The northern end passes along a long sandy beach before arriving at the mouth of Poole Harbour, an enormous enclosed water area and the second largest natural harbour in the world.

Directions

A regular bus service, half hourly in summer and hourly in winter, links Swanage with South Haven Point, making a bus-walk a good option. There are also popular local circuits using the Coast Path in the Swanage-Ballard Down-Studland area.

Swanage has all facilities. The Coast Path passes along the town's sea front, following the main road (Ulwell Road) at the north end by the telephone box where it bears left and on ahead into Redcliff Road at a one-way system. At a shop and post-box turn sharp right into Ballard Way - do not be put off by "Private Estate" signs. Continue forward into the chalet estate and follow signs for the Coast Path, to emerge on a grassed area on the cliff edge. However, from the sea front road, except at very high tides or in severe weather it is possible to keep along the narrow promenade then 200 yards/185m along the beach turn up some rough steps to re-join the official route in a little valley.

The path climbs out to Ballard Down, then the obvious high-level route continues out to Handfast Point and the much-photographed rocks of Old Harry before turning west towards Studland. Studland has toilets and refreshments. For the pub turn up the road from the toilets, otherwise turn right (east) on the outskirts of the village along the signed stony path to South Beach. On reaching the shore, turn left (north) along a terrace in front of beach huts to a seasonal cafe. Continue along the beach for another 90 yards/82m and look for a Purbeck stone waymark between beach huts numbers 59 and 60B, to find a narrow path that ascends steeply up the low cliff. At the top, at another sign, turn right and follow the cliff edge past Fort Henry to join the Middle Beach access road by a barrier. Turn sharp right down to the beach then left by another cafe.

The final 2.6 miles/4.3km are on the sandy beach. Note that further along this beach a length is used by naturists - do not be surprised if nobody else is wearing clothes! There is an alternative, the Heather Walk, through the dunes, marked by yellow-topped posts, but the soft sand is tiring walking and part of the naturist area is still visible. The beach route curves round to the point at the mouth of Poole

South West Coast Path end marker

Harbour. This is South Haven Point, the end (or beginning) of the Coast Path, with an impressive commemorative marker. A ferry links the Point with Sandbanks on the opposite shore, which is linked to Poole and Bournemouth.

The ferry operates all year daily every 20 minutes, from Shell Bay (South Haven Point) 07:10 to 23:10; from Sandbanks 07:00 to 23:00; Christmas Day every half hour - telephone 01929 450203.; website www.sandbanksferry.co.uk.

Note that the ferry is usually scheduled to undergo maintenance during late October or November and may be closed for approximately four weeks. If you intend to use the ferry at this time check the Association's website under Path News or the ferry company's website above.

For ferry details see page 21.

Postscript

For those who have been with us all the way from Minehead, be it in one go or in bits and pieces over a period, a final few words seem appropriate. Alfred Wainwright, at the end of his work on the Pennine Way, said; "You have completed a mission and satisfied an ambition. You have walked the Pennine Way, as you have dreamed of doing. This will be a very satisfying moment in your life. You will be tired and hungry and travel stained. But you will feel great, just great." Just substitute the South West Coast Path for the Pennine Way and Wainwright's words will doubtless ring true. You will be glad and proud that you have walked and finished Britain's longest and finest footpath. As Wainwright said of the Pennine Way, it's a longer step than most take in their lifetime!

Alternative Inland Coast Path

OS Maps: Landranger 194; Explorer OL15

	This Walk	This Walk	Grading	Timing
Ascent	2,290ft	698m	Moderate	8 hours
Distance	16.8mi	27.0km		

For detailed directions see our West Bexington to Osmington Mills Path Description booklet.

This is a very scenic walk, parallel to the coast and a varying distance inland. For most of its length quite extensive coastal views are obtained beyond a green and rural foreground. Substantial lengths follow chalk ridges and these give impressive views north as well. Coastal features such as Portland and Chesil Beach are clearly seen, as are the flanks of the enormous Iron Age Maiden Castle inland. This is a quiet route, often feeling quite remote, and with usually no refreshments on its length it requires preparation. It is, nevertheless, a superb experience.

Directions

A regular bus service links Swyre (for West Bexington) and Osmington Mills, making this a perfect opportunity for a bus-walk.

The Dorset element of the Coast Path is unique in having an official alternative route for part of its length. This was often referred to by the apparently contradictory name of the "Inland Coast Path". It is, however, now known as the South Dorset Ridgeway (SDR) and the signposting now uses that name almost throughout. The waymarking has also been replaced and incorporates the name of the South Dorset Ridgeway. The length of the Section, and the fact that the two ends are linked by a regular bus service, make it an ideal long day's walk. However, be aware that other than one seasonal mobile refreshment van if the timing is right, no facilities are found anywhere along the route other than at the two ends, so it is necessary to be well prepared. A detailed route description is given below.

At West Bexington car park turn inland up the road and where the road turns left continue forward up the stony track, signposted "SDR. For Hardy Monument 6 Osmington Mills 16".

Near the top of the hill take the right-hand fork to reach a lay-by on the B3157 road. Take the gate or stile to the right and follow a faint path that follows the edge of the escarpment of the hill passing three waymark posts. After passing through a wall start to bear upwards to the left towards a signpost near the road. Continue eastwards through the field to reach a gate by the corner of a wall. Continue through the gate and almost immediately emerge on the B3157 road at a signpost. Cross and leave through a gate, again signposted "Hardy Monument".

Approaching Abbotsbury Castle prehistoric hill fort, where the grass path divides, take the upper, slightly right-hand fork along the top of the southern earthwork of the fort, past the trig point, from where there are superb views in all directions. It should be possible to see the Hardy Monument clearly in the distance.

Continue eastwards along the top of the earthwork and cross a minor road, signposted "SDR Hardy Monument". Proceed in an approximately easterly direction along the ridge of Wears Hill and the crest of White Hill for about 2 miles/3.2km, following the signing. Be careful not to follow any signs indicating routes down to the village of Abbotsbury in the valley below and its adjacent hilltop chapel. At the east end of White Hill bear north-east as signed and leave the field in the north-east corner through a gate on to a minor road. Continue north-east along this road for some 50 yards/46m and then turn right as signposted.

Follow the narrow and rough bridleway along the wire fence above the scrub to a path junction; where the bridleway bears right take the yellow waymarked footpath to the left and cross a stile. At the end of this short section take a headland path north-east. At the far side of the field the track then leads approximately 50 yards/46m to a further gate with a stile and waymark. Immediately adjacent to this gate is a prehistoric stone circle, a scheduled ancient monument. Continue forward on the track, leaving a small wood to the left, to reach the road between Portesham and Winterbourne Steepleton. Turn left along the road for about 60 yards/55m and then turn right over a stile into a field, signed "Hardy Monument". Continue eastwards through four fields. At a small wooded area before Black Down Barn (ruin) turn north at a signpost to Hardy Monument. Climb through the woods to the recently renovated monument. In season it may be possible to find a mobile refreshment van here.

To continue find a roadside signpost 30yards/32m east of the car park entrance. Cross the road and descend eastward on a narrow path through the bracken. Reaching the same road again, ignore the signpost "Bridleway to Coast Path" and the track opposite and turn left along the road then in another 30 yards/32m turn right, signposted "Inland Route or SDR to Bincombe" .

Now there is a good ridgeway path for some 3 miles/4.8km, with excellent views to seaward. At a point some 550 yards/500m after passing under the second set of HV power lines take the gate north of a large tumulus to stay on the north side of the fence running along the ridge. On reaching the B3159 road, marked by the Borough of Weymouth boundary stone, continue across as signposted and towards the A354 road.

Major road construction has now been completed and a new section of the busy A354 road opened over Ridgeway Hill. The former very difficult crossing of the old road has been replaced with a fine new bridleway bridge (locally known as Green Bridge). Cross the new bridge and take a new bridleway south, that at first rises and then falls, down the perimeter fence on the east side of the new road. About halfway down the hill look out for and take the old bridleway on the left.

Continue eastwards, then before the farm, with its adjacent radio mast, take care to go through the gate on the right, marked with a blue arrow. After crossing the field, leaving two tumuli on the left, reach a metalled road and turn right. At the junction at the corner of Came Wood turn right at the signpost "Bridleway to Bincombe". At the end of the path join a metalled lane and at the road junction turn left, signposted "South Dorset Ridgeway".

Alternative Inland Coast Path (continued)

Drop down the road into the village of Bincombe and where the road turns right take the track forward leaving the small church on the right. Where the path splits take the left-hand fork, marked with a blue arrow and acorn. After the overhead HV power lines, pass through a small signposted wooden gate and then proceed forward through one field, into the next to a footpath sign. Here turn left and there is a choice of routes for the next couple of hundred yards/m.

For the best option, at a waymark post turn sharp right down a steep grassy slope to a stile at a road ahead. Cross the road to go over another stile to follow a grassy path that contours around the south and east sides of Green Hill. On reaching a road at a gate and stile turn left and in 50 yards/46m turn right through a gate signposted "White Horse Hill - Osmington Mills". The path is now easy to follow with extensive views to seaward over Weymouth and Portland. On passing a ruined building on the left the route reaches a broad track; here turn right, signposted "Osmington" and after about 200 yards/185m go through a gate as signposted. Shortly afterwards pass a trig point on the right and at the next field gate bear left and follow the field boundary along White Horse Hill. Just beyond the next gate fork right, signposted "For Osmington".

Descend to Osmington and follow the signs through the village. On reaching the main Weymouth road near the Sun Ray Inn turn left and in about 250 yards/230m turn right at a signpost, over a stile and footbridge. Follow the field boundary on the left through two fields - at the top look back to see the Hardy Monument in the distance and the white horse on the hillside. Go over the stile to the footpath sign, then turn half right to cross the field at an angle to a further stile. Cross it and turn left along the hedge side to the bottom. At the end of the field there is a very short length of enclosed footpath to the road; turn right along it, descending to Osmington Mills.

Hardy Monument

Old Harry Rocks

Accommodation

This list of accommodation has been prepared in path order.

The majority of our B&B addresses have been recommended by Coast Path walkers. The fact that they are included in this book does not indicate a recommendation by The South West Coast Path Association and their inclusion is merely for information purposes. We cannot, for financial and practical reasons, introduce vetting, inspection or any form of `Star' rating. We do have a system whereby addresses can be removed from the list. All the contact information in the following pages has been supplied by the accommodation providers themselves.

RED DISC

Many of the accommodation addresses are highlighted with a red disc. This indicates that they have joined the Association as Business Members, with a large proportion of their membership fee going towards improvements on the Coast Path.

In return for their support for the Path, we urge you to support them and use their accommodation and facilities on your walk wherever possible. Your support for them will in turn encourage them to stay with us as Business Members, with all that means for our Path Improvement Funds.

B&B Key

Facilities:

O	Open All Year
EM	Evening Meal
CP	Car Parking
DW	Dogs Welcome
PD	Pick Up/Drop Service
D	Drying Facilities for wet clothes
PL	Packed Lunches
LSP	Long Stay Parking
KT	Kit Transfer
LT	Luxury Tent
SO	Single Occupancy
PR	Per Room

Room Type:

D	Double
S	Single (SS Single Supplement)
ES	Ensuite
T	Twin
F	Family
SC	Self Catering

Campsite Key

Facilities:

T	Toilets
G	Grocery Shop
LSP	Long Stay Parking
O	Open All Year
KT	Kit Transfer
S	Showers
CP	Car Parking
LY	Laundry
DW	Dogs Welcome
PD	Pick Up/Drop Service

Colour coding by walk regions

- Exmoor
- North Devon
- North Cornwall
- West Cornwall
- South Cornwall
- South Devon
- Dorset

Kit Transfer (KT)

A service being offered by some of our accommodation providers is to transfer your kit to your next accommodation. This could prove useful to you. A fee may be levied for this service. Please request this service at the time of booking and ensure that the accommodation to which your kit is to be sent is aware of the arrangements you have made. See also the information on page 24 about kit transfer.

Pick Up/Drop (PD)

This code appears following the distance from the path and denotes a facility whereby your host is prepared to collect and return you to the Coast Path within reasonable distance. No fee should be charged for this service. Where this facility is offered, you may consider booking for two or three nights and asking them to collect you from your finishing point and return you there for your start the next day. This way the B&B gets you for more than one night and you can get to walk for a day or more with a lighter day sack. Again no fee should be charged for this service.

Distance from Path - please remember these are only approximate and may not be accurate.

Luxury Tent (LT)

Due to the Eden Project there may be accommodation problems in the St Austell Bay area, and some providers have installed superb tents in their gardens/paddocks. You will not need sleeping bags or any camping out gear.

Listed Information

The part of the address in CAPITALS is an aid to location; it does not signify the postal town. The extreme left-hand column refers to the appropriate section in the 'Coast Path Walks'; we feel it may help you to find addresses quickly. The amount quoted gives an indication of the starting rate for bed and breakfast, and may well rise. **If working on a tight budget, it is best to ask first.**

Tourist Information Centres can be an additional source of accommodation addresses. We have provided a list of TICs along the Coast Path for your use on page 181.

Most of the B&B providers operate from their own private homes so do not expect plenty of staff as there are in hotels and large guesthouses. They work hard to make you comfortable, welcome, dry you out and make you feel like one of the family.

If your chosen address does not supply evening meals you should ask, when booking, how far it is to your evening meal - you can then decide if you want to stay there.

We wish to develop this list and suggestions for inclusion in our next guide will be welcome. Details of any new accommodation should be addressed to the Administrator. Our list is not comprehensive and walkers will find many B&Bs in towns and villages along the Coast Path that are not recorded in this book.

Although there are a lot of addresses that state they are 'open all the year', some of these close for the Christmas period. Walkers should remember that during the holiday season many of our accommodation addresses could be fully booked up in advance by holidaymakers staying for a week or two. Conversely a walker could book for one night only in good time, thus preventing a guest house proprietor from taking a week or more booking later on. Accommodation problems can be frustrating to all parties concerned so bear these facts in mind when hunting for one night only.

Campsites

Individuals - but we stress not parties - usually find no problem in obtaining leave to camp away from official camp sites if they request permission to do so. In fact, our correspondence has many examples of extra kindnesses extended by farmers and others to campers. We would, however, very much emphasise the requesting of permission first. If would be so easy for the thoughtlessness of a few to undo the good relationships of many others built up over some years.

The list of campsites is thin in many areas. Suggestions for inclusions in future lists will always be welcome. Information should be addressed to the Administrator.

Important

If having booked ahead, and for any reason you are unable to get to your accommodation address, please telephone and explain your absence to your intended host. We have known instances where the host has become so worried about the non-appearance of walkers that they have informed the emergency services. The last thing we want is the emergency services out on a wild goose chase.

Walk No.	Contact name Establishment name Address Region/Postcode	Telephone no. Mobile no. Email Website	OS Map Ref. Dist. from path	Starting price Facilities Room types No. of en-suite rooms
1 BUSINESS MEMBER	Mr A Brunt The Yarn Market Hotel High Street **DUNSTER** TA24 6SF	01643 821425 hotel@yarnmarkethotel.co.uk www.yarnmarkethotel.co.uk	993 438 4km PD	£45.00 O D EM PL CP DW KT PD 16D 6T 3S 2F ALL ES
1	Mr E Moulder Montrose Guest House 14 Tregonwell Road **MINEHEAD** TA24 5DU	01643 706473 montroseminehead@btinternet.com www.montroseminehead.co.uk	972 460 900m	£40.00 based on 2 sharing, SS D CP KT O D(4)(4ES) T(1)(1ES) ALL ES
1	Mrs J Bakker Beverleigh Beacon Road **MINEHEAD** TA24 5SE	01643 708450 beverleighminehead@gmail.com www.beverleigh.co.uk	968 469 200m	£32.50 single occupancy £40.00 PL D LSP CP KT PD O D(2)(2ES) T(1)(1ES) ALL ES
1	Mr & Mrs S Poingdestre Kenella House 7 Tregonwell Road **MINEHEAD** TA24 5DT	01643 703128 kenellahouse@fsmail.net www.kenellahouse.co.uk	972 462 500m	£32.50 SS PL EM CP KT O D(4)(4ES) T(2)(2ES) ALL ES
1	Mr & Mrs P Thompson Glendower House 30-32 Tregonwell Road **MINEHEAD** TA24 5DU	01643 707144 info@glendower-house.co.uk www.glendower-house.co.uk	973 460 1km	 D LSP CP KT S(3)(3ES) D(5)(5ES) T(3)(3ES) ALL ES
1	Mr & Mrs G Hayes Tigoni The Ball **MINEHEAD** TA24 5JJ	01643 708852 g_w_hayes@yahoo.co.uk	967 466 400m	£27.00 D LSP CP KT O S(1)(0ES) T(1)(0ES)
1 BUSINESS MEMBER	Mr & Mrs R Webber Hindon Organic Farm Near Selworthy **MINEHEAD TA24 8SH**	01643 705244 info@hindonfarm.co.uk www.hindonfarm.co.uk	933 467 800m	£45.00 PL DW D LSP CP O D(2)(2ES) T(1)(0ES)
1	Mr & Mrs A Shaw Tudor Cottage **BOSSINGTON** TA24 8HQ	01643 862255 07855 531593 bookings@tudorcottage.net www.tudorcottage.net	898 479 100m	£35.00 single occupancy £50.00 PL EM D LSP CP KT O S(1)(0ES) D(2)(1ES) T(1)(0ES)
1	Mr M Lawrence Cross Lane House **ALLERFORD** Minehead TA24 8HW	01643 863276 info@crosslanehouse.com www.crosslanehouse.com	905 469 1km PD	£95.00 PL EM DW D LSP CP KT PD O D(3)(3ES) ALL ES
1 BUSINESS MEMBER	Mr & Mrs N Southwood Myrtle Cottage High Street **PORLOCK** TA24 8PU	01643 862978 07884 233422 enquiries@myrtleporlock.co.uk www.myrtleporlock.co.uk	885 467 1km	£30.00 SS £5.00 O DW CP 4D/T/S/F[4]
1	Mrs C Gladstone The Cottage High Street **PORLOCK** TA24 8PU	01643 862996 cottageporlock@aol.com www.cottageporlock.co.uk	885 467 400m	£27.50 SS D LSP CP KT O PL to be pre-booked S(1)(0ES) T(2)(0ES) F(1)(0ES)
1	Mrs Jane Richards Silcombe Farm **PORLOCK WEIR** TA24 8JN	01643 862248	833 482 750m PD above Culbone Woods on old route of Coast Path	£27.00 £30 single PL EM DW LSP CP KT PD O S(1)(0ES) D(1)(1ES) T(1)(1ES)

Walk No.	Contact name Establishment name Address Region/Postcode	Telephone no. Mobile no. Email Website	OS Map Ref. Dist. from path	Starting price Facilities Room types No. of en-suite rooms
1	Mrs J E Richards Ash Farm **PORLOCK WEIR** TA24 8JN	01643 862414	842 478 750m PD	£25.00 PL D LSP CP S(1)(0ES) T(1)(0ES) F(1)(0ES)
2 BUSINESS MEMBER	Mr A Allen & Rachel Williams The Bath Hotel **LYNMOUTH** EX35 6EL	01598 752238 info@bathhotellynmouth.co.uk www.bathhotellynmouth.co.uk	727 495 100m	£37.50 SS £7.50 PL EM DW D CP KT O S(1)(1ES) D(10)(10ES) T(7)(7ES) F(4)(4ES) ALL ES
2 BUSINESS MEMBER	Mr & Mrs C Parker The Old Sea Captain's House, 1 Tors Road **LYNMOUTH** EX35 6ET	01598 753369 thecaptainshouse@btinternet.com www.thecaptainshouseinlynmouth.co.uk	727 494 50m	£28.00 D LSP CP KT O PL DW by prior arrgt S(1)(1ES) D(6)(6ES) T(1)(1ES) F(1)(1ES) ALL ES
2	Mr & Mrs A Francis Glenville House 2 Tors Road **LYNMOUTH** EX35 6ET	01598 752202 tricia@glenvillelynmouth.co.uk www.glenvillelynmouth.co.uk	727 494 200m	£30.00 SS D D(3)(3ES) T(1)(0ES)
2	Dr J Batch Bonnicott House 10 Watersmeet Road **LYNMOUTH** EX35 6EP	01598 753346 stay@bonnicott.com www.bonnicott.com	725 493 180m	£30.00 £33.00 Apr-Sept PL EM DW D LSP CP KT O D(7)(6ES) T(1)(1ES)
2	Miss D Smith Hillside House 22 Watersmeet Road **LYNMOUTH** EX35 6EP	01598 753836 gjbanfield@aol.com www.hillside-lynmouth.co.uk	725 493 200m	£28.00 SS PL DW D KT O S(1)(1ES) D(3)(3ES) T(1)(1ES) ALL ES
2 BUSINESS MEMBER	Mrs C Sheppard River Lyn View 26 Watersmeet Road **LYNMOUTH** EX35 6EP	01598 753501 riverlynview@aol.com www.riverlynview.com	725 493 150m	£28.00 seasonal supplement PL D CP KT O D(3)(0ES)
2	Mr & Mrs J McGowan The Denes Longmead **LYNTON** EX35 6DQ	01598 753573 j.e.mcgowan@btinternet.com www.thedenes.com	715 494 400m PD	£32.00 SS PL D LSP by prior arrgt CP KT O D(5)(4ES) T(2)(2ES)
2	Mr & Mrs N Firman Sinai House Lynway **LYNTON** EX35 6AY	01598 753227 enquires@sinaihouse.co.uk www.sinaihouse.co.uk	721 492 400m	£36.00 SO £45.00 PL EM D CP KT O S(2)(0ES) D(5)(5ES) T(1)(1ES)
2	Mr & Mrs A Mundell Castle Hill Guest House Castle Hill **LYNTON** EX35 6JA	01598 752291 castlehillbiz@gmail.com www.castlehill.biz	720 493 50m	£32.50 PL D KT O D(5)(5ES) T(2)(2ES) F(1)(1ES) ALL ES
2 BUSINESS MEMBER	Mrs A Wilford Gable Lodge 35 Lee Road **LYNTON** EX35 6BS	01598 752367 gablelodge@btconnect.com www.gablelodgelynton.co.uk	717 495 400 mts PD	£33.00 SS £10 PL EM D CP KT PD O D(4)(4ES) T(1)(1ES) F(1)(1ES) ALL ES
2 BUSINESS MEMBER	Mr & Mrs J Hodges Chough's Nest Hotel North Walk **LYNTON** EX35 6HJ	01598 753315 relax@choughsnesthotel.co.uk www.choughsnesthotel.co.uk	718 497 on path	£48.00 PL EM D LSP CP PD O D(5)(5ES) T(3)(3ES) ALL ES

Walk No.	Contact name Establishment name Address Region/Postcode	Telephone no. Mobile no. Email Website	OS Map Ref. Dist. from path	Starting price Facilities Room types No. of en-suite rooms
3	Mrs Dallyn Mannacott Farm Nr Hunters Inn **MARTINHOE** EX31 4QS	01598 763227	662 481 800m	£26.00 SO £28.00 D CP KT O 1D 1T ALL ES
3 (BUSINESS MEMBER)	Mrs R Brown Blair Lodge Moory Meadow **COMBE MARTIN** EX34 0DG	01271 882294 info@blairlodge.co.uk www.blairlodge.co.uk	579 473 on path	£30.00 PL EM D LSP CP KT O S(1)(0ES) D(5)(5ES) T(3)(3ES) F(1)(1ES)
3	Mr J James & Ms P Palmer Mellstock House Woodlands **COMBE MARTIN** EX34 0AR	01271 882592 enquiries@mellstockhouse.co.uk www.mellstockhouse.co.uk	573 472 on path	£27.00 SS £5.00 PL EM D LSP CP KT O D(3)(3ES) T(2)(2ES) F(1)(1ES) ALL ES
3	Mrs L Leyland Channel Vista Woodlands **COMBE MARTIN** EX34 0AT	01271 883514 channelvista@btconnect.com www.channelvista.co.uk	574 470 100m	£31.00 PL EM DW D CP KT O LSP by prior arrgt S(2)(2ES) D(4)(4ES) T(2)(2ES) F(1) (1ES) ALL ES
3 (BUSINESS MEMBER)	Mr & Mrs M J Lethaby The Royal Marine Public House, Seaside **COMBE MARTIN** EX34 0AW	01271 882470 theroyal.marine@btconnect.com www.theroyalmarinehotel.co.uk	576 472 200m	£35.00 SC apartments available PL EM D LSP CP PD O Free KT D(3)(3ES) T(2)(2ES) F(1)(1ES) ALL ES
3	Mrs R Irwin Trenode House High Street **COMBE MARTIN** EX34 0EQ	01271 883681 07967 998191 rmirwin@btinternet.co.uk	583 467 350m	£20.00 SS PL EM D LSP KT PD O D(1)(1ES) F(2)(0ES)
3	Mrs L Miller Brooklands Buzzacott Lane **COMBE MARTIN** EX34 0NL	01271 883578 lindam1@operamail.com www.visitcombemartin.co.uk	597 459 1500m PD	£30.00 SS £5.00 PL D LSP CP KT O S(1)(1ES) D(1)(1ES) T(1)(1ES) ALL ES
3	Mrs S Davey Fontenay Woodlands **COMBE MARTIN** EX34 0AT	01271 889368 07814 769845 sarah@visitfontenay.co.uk www.visitfontenay.co.uk	575 470 200m	£24.00 DW CP O PL by arrgt S(1)(0ES) D(1)(0ES) T(1)(0ES)
3	Mrs L Heard Park View, Sunnyside **COMBE MARTIN** EX34 0JH	01271 883006 luzia.heard@yahoo.co.uk www.parkview-bandb.com	587 464 800m PD	 PL D CP KT PD O D(1)(1ES) F(1)(1ES) ALL ES

Heddon's Mouth

For Combe Martin addresses see Exmoor B&Bs.

Walk No.	Contact name Establishment name Address Region/Postcode	Telephone no. Mobile no. Email Website	OS Map Ref. Dist. from path	Starting price Facilities Room types No. of en-suite rooms
4 BUSINESS MEMBER	Mr & Mrs D Jenkins Avalon 6 Capstone Crescent **ILFRACOMBE** EX34 9BT	01271 863325 avalon_ilfracombe@yahoo.co.uk www.avalon-hotel.co.uk	522 478 200m	£28.00, Single £33.00 O no LSP Jul & Aug
4	Mr & Mrs G W Pannell Sherborne Lodge Torrs Park **ILFRACOMBE** EX34 8AY	01271 862297 07779 324329 visit@sherborne-lodge.co.uk www.sherborne-lodge.co.uk	514 475 200m	£32.50 SS DW D LSP CP KT O S(1)(1ES) D(3)(3ES) T(1)(1ES) F(4) (4ES) ALL ES
4	Mr & Mrs J Brown Avoncourt Hotel Torrs Walk Avenue **ILFRACOMBE** EX34 8AU	01271 862543 johnbrown735@btinternet.com www.avoncourtilfracombe.co.uk	513 476 on path	£32.00 PL EM DW D LSP KT O S(2)(2ES) D(6)(6ES) T(1)(1ES) F(1) (1ES) ALL ES
4	Mr & Mrs C Burley Rosedale Bed & Breakfast 33 St Brannocks Road **ILFRACOMBE** EX34 8EQ	01271 855550 jillybee@hotmail.com www.rosedalebandb.co.uk	515 468 800m	£30.00 SS D LSP CP O Some PD S(1)(0ES) D(2)(1ES) T(1)(1ES)
4	Mrs C Pearson Lyncott House 56 St Brannocks Road **ILFRACOMBE** EX34 8EQ	01271 862425 www.lyncotthouse.co.uk	515 468 1km	£35.00 SS £10.00 PL D CP O D(4)(4ES) T(1)(1ES) F(1)(1ES) ALL ES
4	Mr & Mrs D Furmston The Collingdale 13 Larkstone Terrace **ILFRACOMBE** EX34 9NU	01271 863770 stay@thecollingdale.co.uk www.thecollingdale.co.uk	526 475 30m	£35.00 SS PL D KT O D(3)(0ES) T(3)(0ES) F(3)(0ES)
4	Ms A Tappenden Ocean Backpackers Hostel 29 St James Place **ILFRACOMBE** EX34 9BJ	01271 867835 info@oceanbackpackers.co.uk www.oceanbackpackers.co.uk	522 478 25m	£13.50 w/e £15.00 D CP O DW D(1)(1ES) F(1)(1ES) SC(6)(5ES) kitchen for self catering
5	Mrs J Jackson Pensport Rock Lincombe Lee **LEE BAY** Ilfracombe EX34 8LL	01271 863419 07977 243026 pensport_rock@talktalk.net www.pensportrock.com	498 459 1km	£33.00 D CP KT PD O D(2)(2ES) ALL ES
5	Mrs J Penman Bellacombe Western Rise **WOOLACOMBE** EX34 7AG	01271 870324 07967 049829 bellacombe@gmail.com www.bellacombe.co.uk	465 438 750m PD	£37.50 SS £12.50 PL D LSP CP KT PD O D(2)(2ES) T(1)(1ES) F(1)(1ES) ALL ES
5 BUSINESS MEMBER	Mr P Milton, Trimstone Manor Country House Hotel, **TRIMSTONE** Nr Woolacombe EX34 8NR	01271 862841 info@trimstone.co.uk www.trimstone.co.uk	499 434	£54.00 SC & PD from C Martin to Bnstple EM DW LSP CP PD O S(1)(1ES) D(10)(10ES) T(2)(2ES) F(1)(1ES) ALL ES
6 BUSINESS MEMBER	Mrs G Adams Combas Farm **PUTSBOROUGH** Croyde EX33 1PH	01271 890398 combasfarm@hotmail.co.uk www.combasfarm.co.uk	449 396 900m	£33.00 SS high season PL D LSP CP KT O D(2)(2ES) T(1)(1ES) F(1)(1ES)
6	Mrs V Learmonth Chapel Farm Guest House Hobbs Hill **CROYDE** EX33 1NE	01271 890429 vall52@yahoo.co.uk www.chapelfarmcroyde.co.uk	444 390 1km	£35.00 also self catering O D(4)(3ES) T(2)(1ES) F(1)(1ES)

Walk No.	Contact name Establishment name Address Region/Postcode	Telephone no. Mobile no. Email Website	OS Map Ref. Dist. from path	Starting price Facilities Room types No. of en-suite rooms
6	Mr & Mrs F Cannock Sandbourne Down End **CROYDE** EX33 1QE	01271 890536 fredcannock@tiscali.co.uk	436 386 300m	£35.00 PL D CP KT O D(2)(1ES) T(1)(1ES)
7 BUSINESS MEMBER	Mrs J Watkins North Cottage 14 North Street **BRAUNTON** EX33 1AJ	01271 812703 07779 842367 north_cottage@hotmail.com	485 367 750m	£28.50 PL DW D CP KT O S(2)(0ES) D(2)(2ES) T(1)(1ES)
7	Mrs K Mitchell Folly Farm Cottage 48 Saunton Road **BRAUNTON** EX33 1HD	01271 812148 07737 420311 follyfarm48@gmail.com www.follyfarmcottage.com	481 366	£34.00 Single £48.00 PL D CP O D(2)(2ES) T(1)(1ES) ALL ES
7 BUSINESS MEMBER	Mr & Mrs J Benning The Firs Higher Park Road **BRAUNTON** EX33 2LG	01271 814358 alisonbenning@btinternet.com www.bennings.co.uk	498 364 2km PD	£32.50 SS PL DW D LSP CP KT PD O D(1)(1ES) T(1)(1ES) ALL ES
7 BUSINESS MEMBER	Mr & Mrs C Brookes The Brookfield South Street **BRAUNTON** EX33 2AN	01271 812382 info@thebrookfield.co.uk www.thebrookfield.co.uk	487 362 400m	£31.50 SS PL D CP KT O S(4)(4ES) D(5)(5ES) T(5)(5ES) F(1) (1ES) ALL ES
7	Mr J Moran The George Hotel Exeter Road **BRAUNTON** EX33 2JJ	01271 812029 georgehoteldevon@btconnect.com www.thegeorgehotel-braunton.co.uk	488 365 1km	£38.00 SS EM DW LSP CP O PL by arrgt D(2)(2ES) T(4)(2ES) ALL ES
8	Mrs J Manning Herton Guesthouse Lake Hill **BARNSTAPLE** EX31 3HS	01271 323302 janice@janicemanning93.wanadoo.co.uk www.herton-guesthouse.co.uk	554 322 500m	£29.00 SS PL D LSP CP KT O D(3)(2ES) T(1)(1ES) F(1)(1ES)
8	Mr P Chappell Yeo Dale Hotel Pilton Bridge **BARNSTAPLE** EX31 1PG	01271 342954 stay@yeodalehotel.co.uk www.yeodalehotel.co.uk	557 338 600m	£42.50 PL D CP KT O EM & LSP by arrgt S(3)(3ES) D(7)(7ES) T(2)(2ES) F(2) (2ES) ALL ES
8 BUSINESS MEMBER	Mr B Abell The Old Vicarage B&B Barbican Terrace **BARNSTAPLE** EX32 9HQ	01271 328504 theoldvicaragebarnstaple@gmail.com www.oldvicaragebarnstaple.co.uk	561 328 200m	£35.00 SS £10.00 D LSP CP S(1)(1ES) D(1)(1ES) T()(1ES) F(2) (2ES)
9 BUSINESS MEMBER	Mr P Day Lower Yelland Farm **FREMINGTON** Barnstaple EX31 3EN	01271 860101 peterday@loweryellandfarm.co.uk www.loweryellandfarm.co.uk	492 322 200m	£35.00 DW D LSP CP O S(2)(2ES) D(3)(3ES) T(2)(2ES)
9	Mrs A Grigg Lovistone Cottage 3 Lyndale Terrace **INSTOW** EX39 4HS	01271 860676 martinandangela@lovistone.co.uk www.lovistone.co.uk	475 305 80m	£35.00 SS £45.00 CP KT O D(3)(0ES)
9	Ms V Ashford 54 Grove Cottages West Yelland **INSTOW** EX31 3HF	01271 861598 07879 884027 val@oaktreecottage.eclipse.co.uk www.instow.net/thesquirrels	484 316 300m	£45.00 SS £35.00 DW LSP CP KT PD O T(2)(2ES) ALL ES

Walk No.	Contact name Establishment name Address Region/Postcode	Telephone no. Mobile no. Email Website	OS Map Ref. Dist. from path	Starting price Facilities Room types No. of en-suite rooms
10	Mrs S Chapman Orchard Cottage Old Barnstaple Road **BIDEFORD** EX39 4ND	01237 422427 sylvia@orchardstudiobideford.co.uk www.orchardstudiobideford.co.uk	463 267 200m	£33.00 CP O also SC T(1)(1ES) SC
10	Mrs S Wright Old Barn Heywood Road **BIDEFORD** EX39 3QB	01237 478704 sue@oldbarnbideford.co.uk www.oldbarnbideford.co.uk	449 282 800m	£60.00 SS PL D LSP CP KT O D(1)(0ES) F(1)(0ES)
10	Ms P Lucraft 19 Bude Street **APPLEDORE** EX39 1PS	01237 477127 peejay87@hotmail.com www.torridgehouseappledore.com	464 304 75m	£35.00 SS PL EM DW D PD O D(2)(2ES) T(1)(1ES) ALL ES
10 BUSINESS MEMBER	Mr & Mrs M Thomson Culloden House Fosketh Hill **WESTWARD HO!** EX39 1UL	01237 479421 cullodenhouse@gmail.com www.culloden-house.co.uk	432 289 100m	£70.00 PR Single £56.00 KT O DW by arrgt D(4)(4ES) T(2)(2ES) F(2)(2ES) ALL ES
10 BUSINESS MEMBER	Mrs L Batten Penkenna House 11 Nelson Road **WESTWARD HO!** EX39 1LF	01237 470990 penkenna@hotmail.co.uk www.penkennahouse.com	431 291 180m	£30.00 SS CP KT O D(1)(1ES) T(1)(1ES) F(1)(1ES) ALL ES
10	Mr & Mrs P Snowball Brockenhurst 11 Atlantic Way **WESTWARD HO!** EX39 1HX	01237 423346 info@brockenhurstindevon.co.uk www.brockenhurstindevon.co.uk	432 291 200m	£35.00 SS £10.00 PL D CP KT O D(2)(2ES) T(1)(1ES) ALL ES
11	Mrs S Park Lower Worthygate Horns Cross **BIDEFORD** EX39 5EA	01237 451246 lowerworthygate@tiscali.co.uk www.lowerworthygatefarm.co.uk	367 232 500m	£28.00 PL EM DW D CP KT O D(1)(0ES) T(1)(0ES)
11 BUSINESS MEMBER	Mr & Mrs C West Pillowery Park Burscott, **HIGHER CLOVELLY** EX39 5RR	01237 431668 info@clovellyaccommodation.com www.clovellyaccommodation.com	312 241 1.5km	£26.00 SS £10.00 PL D LSP CP KT O D(1)(1ES) T(2)(0ES)
11	Mr & Mrs T D Curtis Fuchsia Cottage Burscott Lane, **HIGHER CLOVELLY** EX39 5RR	01237 431398 tom@clovelly-holidays.co.uk www.clovelly-holidays.co.uk	313 242 1km PD	£30.00 £35.00 single PL D LSP CP KT O S(1)(0ES) D(1)(1ES) T(1)(1ES)
11	Mr & Mrs N Sanders The Old Police House Burscott Road, **HIGHER CLOVELLY** EX39 5RR	01237 431256 norman.sanders@btinternet.com www.clovellybandb.co.uk	313 241 500m	£30.00 SS £5.00 PL EM DW D LSP CP KT O D(1)(0ES) T(1)(1ES)
11 BUSINESS MEMBER	Mrs M McColl 1 Southdown Cottage **HIGHER CLOVELLY** EX39 5SA	01237 431504 maryfmcoll@hotmail.com	297 236 4km PD	£31.00 SS £14.00 PL EM DW D LSP CP KT PD O D(1)(1ES) T(1)(1ES) ALL ES
12 BUSINESS MEMBER	Mr & Mrs J W George Gawlish Farm Gawlish **HARTLAND** EX39 6AT	01237 441320	256 263 300m PD	£30.00 SS £5.00 PL EM D LSP CP KT O D(2)(2ES) T(2)(2ES) ALL ES

Walk No.	Contact name Establishment name Address Region/Postcode	Telephone no. Mobile no. Email Website	OS Map Ref. Dist. from path	Starting price Facilities Room types No. of en-suite rooms
12 BUSINESS MEMBER	Mrs Y Heard West Titchberry Farm **WEST TITCHBERRY** Hartland Point EX39 6AU	01237 441287	242 272 250m PD	£27.50 SS £5.00 Closed Christmas PL EM D LSP CP PD O D(1)(0ES) T(1)(0ES) F(1)(1ES)
12 BUSINESS MEMBER	Ms M Chesterman 2 Harton Manor The Square **HARTLAND** EX39 6BL	01237 441670 07771 610982 merlyn@twohartonmanor.co.uk www.twohartonmanor.co.uk	258 245 3 km PD	£30.00 PL DW D LSP CP KT PD O PD Hartland Quay S(1)(0ES) D(1)(1ES) T(1)(1ES)
12	Mrs T Goaman Elmscott Farm **HARTLAND** EX39 6ES	01237 441276 john.goa@virgin.net www.elmscott.org.uk	231 215 400m PD	£30.00 PL EM D LSP CP KT PD O YHA Elmscott & Winter Bookings available D(2)(2ES) T(1)(1ES)
12	Mrs J Yeates 7 Goaman Park **HARTLAND** EX39 6DF	01237 440005 richard.yeates@tiscali.co.uk	267 241 3.5km	£25.00 SS £5.00 PL D CP KT PD O D(1)(1ES) ALL ES
13	Mrs A Dart 1 Coastguard Cottages **STOKE**, Hartland EX39 6DU	01237 441011 annajon@btinternet.com www.coastguardcottagestoke.com	235 246 500m	£30.00 SS £5.00 PL EM DW D LSP CP KT O D(2)(2ES) ALL ES
13	Mr & Mrs A Jones Cranham House **WELCOMBE** Hartland EX39 6ET	01288 331351 info@cranhamhouse.co.uk www.cranhamhouse.co.uk	224 192 800m	£37.50 SS SC barn available PL EM D LSP CP KT O D(2)(2ES) SC(2)(2ES) ALL ES

For addresses between Welcombe and Bude see North Cornwall B&Bs.

Hartland Lighthouse

Walk No.	Contact name Establishment name Address Region/Postcode	Telephone no. Mobile no. Email Website	OS Map Ref. Dist. from path	Starting price Facilities Room types No. of en-suite rooms
13 BUSINESS MEMBER	Mrs Heywood Cornakey Farm **CORNAKEY** Morwenstow EX23 9SS	01288 331260 cornakeyfarm@hotmail.co.uk	208 160 500m	£32.00 SS PL D LSP CP KT O D(1)(1ES) F(1)(1ES) ALL ES
13	Mrs E Cole Jays **WOOLLEY** Morwenstow Bude EX23 9PP	01288 331540 cole.jays@talk21.com www.martincoleguitars.co.uk/jaysbarn.html	254 168 4km PD	£31.00 WiFi AVAILABLE PL EM DW D LSP CP KT O S(2)(2ES) D(1)(1ES) ALL ES
13 BUSINESS MEMBER	Mr Rob Tape The Bush Inn, Crosstown **MORWENSTOW** Bude EX23 9SR	01288 331242 www.bushinn-morwenstow.co.uk	208 150 600m	£44.00 £50.00 single charge PL EM DW D LSP CP PD O KT by arrgt S(4)(4ES) D(4)(4ES) T(2)(2ES) F(2) (2ES) SC()(ES) Also Self Catering
13	Mrs C White Trelawney, Crosstown **MORWENSTOW** Bude EX23 9SR	01288 331453	208 150 800m	£30.00 SS £5.00 O D PL CP KT 1D 1T
13	Mr & Mrs Bramhill West Point, **CRIMP** Morwenstow EX23 9PB	01288 331594 bramhill@supanet.com www.budebedandbreakfast.co.uk	255 155 5.5km PD	£30.00 PL LSP CP KT PD O D(1)(1ES) T(1)(1ES) F(1)(1ES) ALL ES
13	Mrs B Dunstan Strands **STIBB** Bude EX23 9HW	01288 353514 07896 483078 brendadunstanbude@yahoo.co.uk www.strandatstibb.co.uk	217 107 2.5km PD	£26.00 also SC PL D CP KT O D(1)(1ES) F(1)(1ES) ALL ES
13	Mr M E Payne Pencarrol Guest House 21 Downs View **BUDE** EX23 8RF	01288 352478 pencarrolbude@aol.com	209 070 300m	£33.00 SS in D PL D KT O S(1)(0ES) D(2)(2ES) T(2)(2ES) F(1) (1ES)
13	Mr & Mrs M Fly Fairway Guest House 8 Downs View **BUDE** EX23 8RF	01288 355059 enquiries@fairwayguesthouse.co.uk www.fairwayguesthouse.co.uk	209 070 300m	 PL D KT O(Feb-Nov) PL by arrgt S(3)(1ES) D(5)(5ES) T(2)(2ES) F(1)(1ES)
13 BUSINESS MEMBER	Mr & Mrs D Steadman Tee-side Guest House 2 Burn View **BUDE** EX23 8BY	01288 352351 teeside.bude@gmail.com www.tee-side.co.uk	208 066 400m	£30.00 PL D KT O D(2)(2ES) T(2)(2ES) ALL ES
13 BUSINESS MEMBER	Mr M Safdar-Wallace Sea Jade 15 Burn View **BUDE** EX23 8BZ	01288 353404 seajadeguesthouse@yahoo.co.uk www.seajadeguesthouse.co.uk	209 065 450m	£30.00 SS £3.00 Rooms are D/T/F PL EM D KT PD O D(7)(4ES)
13	Mrs L Kelly Links Side 7 Burn View **BUDE** EX23 8BY	01288 352410 linksidebude@hotmail.com www.linkssidebude.co.uk	208 067 400m	£25.00 PL D CP KT O S(1)(1ES) D(4)(3ES) T(1)(1ES) F(1) (1ES) ALL ES
14 BUSINESS MEMBER	Mr & Mrs R Holmes Bears & Boxes Penrose, **DIZZARD** St Gennys EX23 0NX	01840 230318 rwfrh@btinternet.com www.bearsandboxes.com	168 990 500 mts PD	£37.00 PL EM DW D LSP CP O S(2)(2ES) D(2)(2ES) ALL ES

Walk No.	Contact name Establishment name Address Region/Postcode	Telephone no. Mobile no. Email Website	OS Map Ref. Dist. from path	Starting price Facilities Room types No. of en-suite rooms
14 BUSINESS MEMBER	Mr R Tape The Old Wainhouse Inn Wainhouse Corner **ST GENNYS** Bude EX23 0EA	01840 230711 wainhouse10@yahoo.co.uk www.oldwainhouseinn.co.uk	220 006 2.5km	£40.00 SS £10.00 PL EM DW D LSP CP KT PD O S(1)(1ES) D(1)(1ES) T(2)(2ES) ALL ES
14	Mr & Mrs F Mussell Trewartha by Chy St Gennys **CRACKINGTON HAVEN** EX23 0NN	01840 230420 francismussell@btinternet.com	150 967 750m	£30.00 some chalet accommodation PL EM DW D LSP CP KT PD O S(2)(1ES) D(2)(1ES) T(1)(1ES)
14	Mr & Mrs J May Ludon Hill **CRACKINGTON HAVEN** EX23 0JZ	01840 230584 johnanniemay@btinternet.com	144 966 300m	£30.00 D KT O D(1)(0ES) T(1)(0ES)
14	Mrs S Bennett The Lodge **CRACKINGTON HAVEN** EX23 0JW	01840 230347 c.haven@tiscali.co.uk www.thelodgecrackingtonhaven.co.uk	158 958 2 km PD	£30.00 SS £5.00 PL CP KT PD O D(1)(1ES)
14	Mr & Mrs G Morris 14 Lundy Drive **CRACKINGTON HAVEN** EX23 0PA	01840 230106 geoff@crackingtonhavenbandb.co.uk www.crackingtonhavenbandb.co.uk	154 959 1.5km	£27.50 PL D LSP CP PD O D(1)(1ES) T(1)(0ES)
15 BUSINESS MEMBER	Mr J Scott The Wellington Hotel The Harbour **BOSCASTLE** PL35 0AQ	01840 250202 info@wellingtonhotelboscastle.com www.wellingtonhotelboscastle.com	098 913 200m	 PL EM DW D CP KT O S(3)(3ES) D(9)(9ES) T(3)(3ES) F(1) (1ES) ALL ES
15	Mr & Mrs G Barratt Orchard Lodge Gunpool Lane **BOSCASTLE** PL35 0AT	01840 250418 orchardlodgeboscastle@gmail.com www.orchardlodgeboscastle.co.uk	906 099 500m	£37.50 PL D CP KT O D(3)(3ES) T(2)(2ES) ALL ES
15	Mrs J Horwell The Old Coach House Tintagel Road **BOSCASTLE** PL35 0AS	01840 250398 stay@old-coach.co.uk www.old-coach.co.uk	098 906 400m	£36.00 Price based on 2 sharing PL D KT O D(3)(3ES) T(3)(3ES) F(2)(2ES) ALL ES
16	Mrs A Jones Grange Cottage **BOSSINEY** Tintagel PL34 0AX	01840 770487	066 888 200m	£34.00 PL CP O S(1)(0ES) D(1)(1ES)
16	Mrs P Tinney Bossiney Cottage **BOSSINEY** Tintagel PL34 0AY	01840 770327 bossinney@tinney.org	066 888 200m	£30.00 PL EM D CP KT O S(1)(0ES) D(1)(0ES) F(1)(0ES)
16	Mr & Mrs N Chamberlain Westcote House **BOSSINEY** Tintagel PL34 0AX	01840 779194 nevchamberlain@btinternet.com www.westcotehouse.co.uk	064 888 450m	 D LSP CP KT O D(1)(1ES) T(1)(1ES) ALL ES
16 BUSINESS MEMBER	Mr & Mrs K Walker Bosayne Guest House Atlantic Road **TINTAGEL** PL34 0DE	01840 770514 enquiries@bosayne.co.uk www.bosayne.co.uk	056 888 300m	£26.00 PL D CP KT O S(3)(0ES) D(3)(3ES) T(1)(1ES) F(1) (0ES)

Walk No.	Contact name Establishment name Address Region/Postcode	Telephone no. Mobile no. Email Website	OS Map Ref. Dist. from path	Starting price Facilities Room types No. of en-suite rooms
17	Mr & Mrs B Nutt Hillscroft, **TREKNOW** Tintagel, Near Trebarwith Strand PL34 0EN	01840 770551 brian.nutt@btinternet.com	056 866 800m PD	£30.00 SS £10.00 PL LSP CP KT PD O D(1)(1ES)
17	Mrs M Andrews Hathaway B&B Roscarrock Hill **PORT ISAAC** PL29 3RG	01208 880416 marion.andrews1@btopenworld.com www.cornwall-online.co.uk/hathaway	995 807 50m	£38.00 single occupancy £66.00 CP O D(1)(0ES) T(3)(3ES)
17	Mrs N March Penderris House B&B 7 Tintagel Terrace **PORT ISAAC** PL29 3SE	01208 880419 07816 918041 nancymarch@live.com	999 808	£30.00 SS £10.00 PL DW LSP CP KT O D(1)(1ES) T(2)(0ES)
17 BUSINESS MEMBER	Mr & Mrs N Monk Lane End Farm Pendoggett **PORT ISAAC** PL30 3HH	01208 880013 07724 133820 nabmonk@tiscali.co.uk www.laneendcornwall.co.uk	026 793 2.5km PD	£35.00 Also SC PL D LSP CP KT PD O S(1)(1ES) T(1)(1ES) ALL ES
18	Mrs P White Seaways **POLZEATH** PL27 6SU	01208 862382 pauline@seaways99.freeserve.co.uk www.seawaysguesthouse.co.uk	939 788 350m	£40.00 SS in D room D LSP CP KT O S(1)(0ES) D(1)(1ES) T(2)(1ES)
18	Mr & Mrs P Cullinan 4 Riverside PADSTOW PL28 8BY	01841 532383 cullinan@madasafish.com www.southquaybedandbreakfastpadstow.co.uk	920 754 190m	£35.00 SS O DW in one room only D(2)(1ES)
18	Mrs A Crowley Trealaw Guest House & Tea Room, 22 Duke St **PADSTOW** PL28 8AB	01841 533161 www.trealaw.com	918 754 300m	£80.00 price per room, single £50 PL EM O D(1)(1ES) ALL ES
18	Mrs E Cortis 'Ere Tis 3 Egerton Road **PADSTOW** PL28 8DJ	01841 532320	920 748 200m	 D LSP CP S(1)(0ES) D(1)(1ES) T(1)(0ES)
20	Mrs E Kennerley Penhalonga **CONSTANTINE BAY** PL28 8JG	01841 521122 07815 833158 lizkennerley@btinternet.com	869 743	£70.00 Price for 2 sharing SS £40.00 PL LSP CP O S(1)(1ES) D(1)(1ES) T(1)(1ES) ALL ES
20	Mrs M Neale Penlan **PORTHCOTHAN BAY** PL28 8LP	01841 520440 07525 940404 mary@idenna.com www.porthcothanbay.co.uk	859 719 150m	£35.00 PL EM DW D LSP CP KT O D(2)(2ES) T(1)(0ES)
20	Mrs P Mcowen Greylands, Treburrick St Eval **PORTHCOTHAN** PL27 7UR	01841 540451 pam.mcowen@btopenworld.com	862 707 500m PD	£65.00 per room £45 sing occup PL EM DW D LSP CP KT PD O D(2)(1ES)
21	Mrs K L Page Seavista **MAWGAN PORTH** TR8 4AL	01637 860276 enquiries@seavista.co.uk www.seavista.co.uk	849 668 200m	£55.00 per room discount sing occup PL D CP PD O S(1)(1ES) D(5)(5ES) T(1)(1ES) ALL ES

Walk No.	Contact name Establishment name Address Region/Postcode	Telephone no. Mobile no. Email Website	OS Map Ref. Dist. from path	Starting price Facilities Room types No. of en-suite rooms
21 BUSINESS MEMBER	Mr & Mrs C Vickers Trevarrian Lodge Trevarrian **MAWGAN PORTH** TR8 4AW	01637 860156 trevarrianlodge@gmail.com www.trevarrianlodge.com	850 661 400m	£30.00 PL D LSP CP KT O DW by arrgt S(1)(1ES) D(1)(1ES) T(2)(2ES) F(2) (2ES)
21	Mrs B Bradley Dimora Gwel-an-Mor **MAWGAN PORTH** TR8 4DW	01637 860511 info@dimora-bed-breakfast.co.uk www.dimora-bed-breakfast.co.uk	853 674 500m	PL DW D LSP CP O S(1)(0ES) D(1)(1ES) F(1)(0ES)
21	Mrs Y Moore Porth Cove Watergate Road **PORTH** TR7 3LX	01637 859314 porthcove@talktalk.net www.porthcove.co.uk	832 632 30m	£35.00 LSP CP KT S(3)(3ES) D(8)(8ES) T(2)(2ES) F(1) (1ES) ALL ES
21	Miss L Balls Kenton Hotel Watergate Road **PORTH** TR7 3LX	01637 872736 info@hotelsinnewquay.co.uk www.hotelsinnewquay.co.uk	532 632 100m	£37.00 SS in August EM DW CP KT O S(2)(2ES) D(5)(5ES) T(5)(5ES) F(4) (4ES) ALL ES
21 BUSINESS MEMBER	Mr G Dolan The Three Tees Hotel 21 Carminow Way NEWQUAY TR7 3AY	01637 872055 greg@3tees.co.uk www.3tees.co.uk	824 621 250m	£34.00 PL DW LSP CP KT O D D(4)(4ES) T(2)(2ES) F(3)(3ES)
21	Mrs M Dewolfreys Dewolf Guesthouse 100 Henver Road **NEWQUAY** TR7 3BL	01637 874746 holidays@dewolfguesthouse.com www.dewolfguesthouse.com	828 620 500m	£30.00 £35 single also SC LSP CP KT O PL & DW by arrgt S(3)(3ES) D(2)(2ES) T(2)(2ES) F(1) (1ES) ALL ES
21	Mr & Mrs G Brown Trevellis Guest House 21 Trebarwith Crescent **NEWQUAY** TR7 1DX	01637 874338 seasurfer@talktalk.net www.trevellisbedandbreakfast.com	812 617 50m	£30.00 O S(3)(0ES) D(2)(2ES) T(1)(1ES) F(1) (1ES)
22	Mr & Mrs B Clark Carden Cottage Halwyn Hill **CRANTOCK** TR8 5RR	01637 830806 cardencottage@btinternet.com www.cardencottagecrantock.com	791 603 500m	£40.00 £4 supplement for D ES PL D LSP CP KT PD O D(2)(2ES) T(1)(1ES) ALL ES
23	Mrs M Burch Cliffside Hotel Cliff Road **PERRANPORTH** TR6 0DR	01872 573297 www.cliffsideperranporth.co.uk	754 544 on path	£30.00 DW D O S(2)(1ES) D(4)(4ES) T(2)(2ES) F(2)(2ES) ALL ES
23	Mrs Stirling & Mrs Lawrie St George's Country Hotel St George's Hill **PERRANPORTH** TR6 0ED	01872 572184 info@stgeorgescountryhouse.co.uk www.stgeorgescountryhouse.co.uk	746 533 400 mts PD	£40.00 PL EM D LSP CP KT PD O DW by arrgt D(5)(5ES) F(2)(2ES)
24	Mr & Mrs N York Kimberley West Polberro **ST AGNES** TR5 0SS	01872 552044 07790 048616 kimberley_sta@hotmail.com www.kimberleybedandbreakfast.co.uk	716 515 500m	£65.00 £45 SO, 4 night discount D LSP CP KT O D(2)(1ES) T(1)(1ES) ALL ES
24	Mrs M Urban Moor House Bridge Moor **PORTREATH** TR16 4QA	01209 843120 maria.urban@earthlink.net www.moor-house-uk.com	664 452 800m	£40.00 SS PL LSP CP KT O S(1)(1ES) D(2)(2ES) ALL ES

Walk No.	Contact name Establishment name Address Region/Postcode	Telephone no. Mobile no. Email Website	OS Map Ref. Dist. from path	Starting price Facilities Room types No. of en-suite rooms
25 BUSINESS MEMBER	Mr & Mrs S Haywood Cliff House Cliff Terrace **PORTREATH** TR16 4LE	01209 842008 simon.viv.haywood@gmail.com www.cliffhouseportreath.co.uk	656 455 on path	£35.00 SS PL DW CP KT O S(2)(0ES) D(2)(2ES) T(2)(2ES) F(1)(1ES)
25	Mr & Mrs E Berriman Dolphin House Cliff Terrace **PORTREATH** TR16 4LE	01209 842936 dolphinhouse@me.com www.dolphinhouse.me	656 453 on path	£69.00 price per D room single £39 PL D LSP CP PD O DW by prior arrgt D(2)(0ES) F(1)(0ES)

Sunset at Porteath

West Cornwall B&Bs

For Portreath addresses see North Cornwall B&Bs.

Walk No.	Contact name Establishment name Address Region/Postcode	Telephone no. Mobile no. Email Website	OS Map Ref. Dist. from path	Starting price Facilities Room types No. of en-suite rooms
25	Mr T Greenaway Godrevy House Prosper Hill **GWITHIAN** TR27 5BW	01736 755493 enquiries@gwithianholidays.com www.gwithianholidays.com	588 409 1km	£30.00 DW CP KT PD O D(2)(2ES) F(2)(2ES) ALL ES
25 (BUSINESS MEMBER)	Mrs L Davies Nanterrow Farm **GWITHIAN** TR27 5BP	01209 712282 nanterrow@hotmail.com www.nanterrowfarm.co.uk	599 412 1.5km PD	£35.00 SS D LSP CP PD O S(1)(0ES) D(1)(0ES) F(1)(0ES)
25	Mrs P Ellis The Mad Hatter 73 Fore Street **HAYLE** TR27 4DX	01736 754241 07871 165381 paulineellis-madhatter.org@tesco.net www.cornwall-online.co.uk/madhatter	566 378 1km	£30.00 PL EM DW D LSP CP PD O S(2)(1ES) D(2)(1ES) T(2)(1ES) F(1)(0ES)
25	Mrs A Cooper 54 Penpol Terrace **HAYLE** TR27 4BQ	01736 752855 jacoop@talktalk.net	558 374 on path	£35.00 PL D LSP CP O T(1)(0ES)
26	Mr & Mrs M Laywood Halwell Fore Street **LELANT** TR26 3EL	01736 752003 jmlaywood@aol.com www.halwelllodge.com	544 370 on path	£75.90 price per room SS PL EM D CP KT O D(4)(4ES) T(1)(1ES) F(1)(1ES) ALL ES
26	Mr C England The Anchorage 5 Bunkers Hill **ST IVES** TR26 1LJ	01736 797135 info@anchoragestives.co.uk www.anchoragestives.co.uk	518 407 on path	£45.00 PL D LSP KT O S(1)(0ES) D(3)(3ES) T(1)(1ES)
28	Mrs L Bowden 5b Carlill 9 Porthminster Terrace **ST IVES** TR26 2DQ	01736 796738 07818 661837 carlillguesthouse@hotmail.co.uk www.carlillguesthouse.co.uk	517 402 250m	£40.00 seasonal SS PL LSP CP KT O S(1)(1ES) D(2)(2ES) T(2)(2ES) F(1)(1ES)
26	Mrs S Martin 8 Ayr Lane **ST IVES** TR26 1JL	01736 793172	517 405 100m	£30.00 D PL O S(1)(1ES) T(1)(1ES) ALL ES
26	Mr A Biss & Ms A Pascoe Primrose Valley Hotel Porthminster Beach **ST IVES** TR26 2ED	01736 794939 info@primroseonline.co.uk www.primroseonline.co.uk	519 399 50m	£42.50 PL D LSP CP KT O S(2)(2ES) D(5)(5ES) T(2)(2ES) ALL ES
27	Mrs N Mann Trewey Farm **TREWEY** Zennor TR26 3DA	01736 796936	456 381 700m	£38.00 Single £40.00 PL D CP S(1)(1ES) D(2)(2ES) T(1)(1ES) F(2)(2ES)
27	Dr Thompson Boswednack Manor **BOSWEDNACK** Zennor TR26 3DD	01736 794183 boswednack@ravenfield.co.uk www.boswednackmanor.co.uk	442 378 1.5km	£27.00 also SC PL CP KT O S(1)(0ES) D(2)(2ES) T(1)(0ES) F(1)(0ES) SC()(ES)
28 (BUSINESS MEMBER)	Ms H Hurkett, Gypsy Caravan B&B, Primrose Cot. Levant Rd, **TREWELLARD** Pendeen TR19 7SU	01736 787585 07900 631268 holiday@gypsycaravanbandb.co.uk www.gypsycaravanbandb.co.uk	373 339 300m	£28.00 £5 charge for dog D LSP CP KT O S(1)(0ES) D(1)(0ES) cold supper provided on request

Walk No.	Contact name Establishment name Address Region/Postcode	Telephone no. Mobile no. Email Website	OS Map Ref. Dist. from path	Starting price Facilities Room types No. of en-suite rooms
28 BUSINESS MEMBER	Mrs J Hoather The Old Chapel **BOSCASWELL DOWNS** Pendeen TR19 7DR	01736 786006 07789 547806 geoffgoatherd@aol.com www.cornwallfarwest.co.uk	385 344 1km	£30.00 also self catering DW D LSP CP O D(2)(2ES) T(2)(2ES) ALL ES
28	Mr E J Coak The North Inn **PENDEEN** TR19 7DN	01736 788417 ernestjohncoak@aol.com www.thenorthinnpendeen.co.uk	383 344 1km	 PL EM DW LSP CP O D(1)(1ES) T(3)(3ES) Also camping
28	Mr & Mrs T Dymond The Old Count House **BOSCASWELL DOWNS** Pendeen TR19 7EE	01736 788058 dymondep@aol.com www.cornwallonline.co.uk	383 344 1km	£30.00 PL D LSP CP KT O D(2)(0ES)
28 BUSINESS MEMBER	Mr & Mrs P Michelmore St Just B&B 2 Fore Street **ST JUST** TR19 7LL	01736 787784 wendy.michelmore@tesco.net www.stjustbandb.com	372 314 1.75km	£32.50 Single £45 PL KT O D(1)(0ES) T(1)(0ES) F(1)(0ES)
28	Mrs H Davies 34 Queen Street **ST JUST** TR19 7JW	01736 788088 07927 917849	367 313 1km	£25.00 EM O T(1)(0ES) F(1)(0ES)
28	Mrs J Eccleston Nanquidno Farm **ST JUST** Penzance TR19 7NU	01736 788463 joeeccleston3@hotmail.co.uk www.nanquidnofarm.co.uk	363 292 695m	£25.00 EM DW D CP KT O D(1)(0ES) T(1)(0ES)
28	Mr & Mrs A Collinson Bosavern House **BOSAVERN** St Just TR19 7RD	01736 788301 info@bosavern.com www.bosavern.com	370 305 1km	£38.00 SS PL D CP KT O PL by arrgt S(1)(1ES) D(3)(3ES) T(2)(1ES) F(2)(2ES) ALL ES
28	Mr & Mrs B Harrison Weavers **SENNEN** Penzance TR19 7AQ	01736 871565 weaversbb@btinternet.com www.cornwallfarwest/weavers	355 248 750m	£38.00 SS D LSP CP KT O D(1)(1ES)
28	Mrs J Pengelly Pengelly House **SENNEN COVE** TR19 7DF	01736 871866 07810 361739 stay@pengellyhouse.com www.pengellyhouse.com	352 265 40m	£30.00 Continental breakfast in room PL D LSP CP KT PD O S(1)(1ES) D(1)(1ES) T(1)(1ES) ALL ES
28 BUSINESS MEMBER	Mrs J Mitchell Mayon Farmhouse **SENNEN** TR19 7AD	01736 871757 mayonfarmhouse@hotmail.co.uk www.mayonfarmhouse.co.uk	356 257 400m	£42.50 SS PL D LSP CP KT O D(3)(3ES) T(1)(0ES) F(1)(1ES)
29 BUSINESS MEMBER	Mr & Mrs D Hicks Land's End Hostel Accom Mill Barn, Trevescan **NR LAND'S END** TR19 7AQ	07519 309 908 susie@landsendhostelaccommodation.co.uk www.landsendhostelaccommodation.co.uk	355 248 500m	£25.00 Hostel Accommodation DW CP KT O S(1)(0ES) D(1)(1ES) T(1)(1ES) F(2)(1ES)
29 BUSINESS MEMBER	Mr & Mrs C Bishop Sea View House The Valley **PORTHCURNO** TR19 6JX	01736 810638 svhouse@btinternet.com www.seaviewhouseporthcurno.com	383 227 400m PD	£38.00 SS PL D LSP CP KT PD 2D(2) 2T(1) 1S

For Portreath addresses see North Cornwall B&Bs.

Walk No.	Contact name Establishment name Address Region/Postcode	Telephone no. Mobile no. Email Website	OS Map Ref. Dist. from path	Starting price Facilities Room types No. of en-suite rooms
29	Mr & Mrs F M Byott Treville, The Valley **PORTHCURNO** TR19 6JY	01736 810167 jbyott@live.co.uk	382 229 500m	£35.00 SS £10.00 PL D O D(1)(0ES)
29	Mrs S Wear The Wearhouse The Valley **PORTHCURNO** TR19 6JX	01736 810129 susan.wear@me.com	383 226 200m	£35.00 D LSP CP KT O D(2)(2ES)
29	Mr & Mrs C Hatton Rose Cottage **PORTHCURNO** TR19 6JY	01736 810082 07926 084610 chris@chrisswcpa.co.uk www.porthcurno.org.uk	382 229 500m	£28.00 PL D CP KT PD O S(1)(0ES) D(1)(0ES) guided walks offered Land's End & Lizard
30	Mrs R Hood Castallack Farm **LAMORNA** Penzance TR19 6NL	01736 731969 info@castallackfarm.co.uk www.castallackfarm.co.uk	452 254 1.75km	£35.00 SS PL EM DW D LSP CP KT O D(2)(2ES) T(1)(1ES) ALL ES
31	Mrs E Reynolds Renovelle 6 The Parade **MOUSEHOLE** TR19 6PN	01736 731258	469 264 on path	£28.00 Easter-Oct PL D CP KT O S(1)(0ES) D(2)(1ES)
31	Mrs D Waters White Gates Cliff Lane **MOUSEHOLE** TR19 6PU	01736 731691	471 267 on path	£35.00 SS PL DW D CP O D(2)(1ES) T(1)(0ES) F(1)(1ES)
31 BUSINESS MEMBER	Ms L Brown Panorama Guest House Chywoone Hill, **NEWLYN** Penzance TR18 5AR	01736 360798 lyndabrown1806@btinternet.com www.panorama-guesthouse.co.uk	461 283 400m	£42.50 SS DW £5 PL EM DW D LSP CP KT O S(2)(2ES) D(2)(2ES) T(1)(1ES) F(1)(1ES) ALL ES
31	Mr M Martens Cornerways 5 Leskinnick Street **PENZANCE** TR18 2HA	01736 364645 mobile 07582 722510 enquiries@cornerways-penzance.co.uk www.cornerways-penzance.co.uk	475 308 800m	£35.00 SS PL D O S(2)(2ES) D(1)(1ES) T(1)(1ES) ALL ES
31	Mr & Mrs H Robinson Honeydew Guest House 3 Leskinnick Street **PENZANCE** TR18 2HA	01736 364206 07856 685053 info@honeydewguesthouse.co.uk www.honeydewguesthouse.co.uk	475 306 200m	£70.00 SS Single £40 PL DW KT PD O S(1)(0ES) D(1)(1ES) T(1)(1ES) F(1)(1ES)
31	Mr & Mrs Cavanagh-Wilson Warwick House 17 Regent Terrace **PENZANCE** TR18 4DW	01736 363881 enquiry@warwickhousepenzance.co.uk www.warwickhousepenzance.co.uk	475 298 50m	£44.00 SS PL LSP CP O WiFi DVD library S(2)(2ES) D(3)(3ES) T(2)(2ES) SC(2)(2ES) ALL ES
31 BUSINESS MEMBER	Mr & Mrs A Stott Glencree House 2 Mennaye Road **PENZANCE** TR18 4NG	01736 362026 stay@glencreehouse.co.uk www.glencreehouse.co.uk	469 297 50m	 PL D KT O S(2)(1ES) D(3)(3ES) T(1)(1ES) F(1)1ES)
31 BUSINESS MEMBER	Mrs C Edwards Tremont Guest Accom Alexandra Road **PENZANCE** TR18 4LZ	01736 362614 info@tremonthotel.co.uk www.tremonthotel.co.uk	465 300 500m	£34.00 SS PL D KT O S(2)(2ES) D(3)(3ES) T(3)(3ES) ALL ES

Walk No.	Contact name Establishment name Address Region/Postcode	Telephone no. Mobile no. Email Website	OS Map Ref. Dist. from path	Starting price Facilities Room types No. of en-suite rooms
31 BUSINESS MEMBER	Mrs A Channing-Williams Netherleigh Fore Street **MARAZION** TR17 0AL	01736 711880 07845 739109 anniecw@btinternet.com	520 307 on path	£30.00 SS EM D CP KT O D(2)(1ES) ALL ES
31	Mr & Mrs P Vincent Blue Horizon Fore Street **MARAZION** TR17 0AW	01736 711199 bluehorizon1@btinternet.com www.holidaybreaksmarazion.co.uk	521 306 on path	PL D CP PD O PD & LSP low season S(1)(0ES) D(3)(3ES) T(2)(2ES)
32 BUSINESS MEMBER	Mrs M Foy Mzima Penlee Close **PRAA SANDS** TR20 9SR	01736 763856 marianfoy@prussia-cove-holiday.com	581 287 800m PD	£27.00 PL D CP KT PD O T(1)(0ES) F(1)(0ES)
32	Mrs V Hocking Dingley Dell, Pengersick Lane, **PRAA SANDS** Nr Penzance TR20 9SL	01736 763527 valhocking@uwclub.net www.dingleydell.eu	582 284 650m	£30.00 based on 2 sharing PL D CP PD O D(1)(1ES) T(1)(1ES) SC(1)(1ES) ALL ES
32 BUSINESS MEMBER	Miss Kelynack & Mr Perkins An Mordros Hotel Peverell Terrace **PORTHLEVEN** TR13 9DZ	01326 562236 info@anmordroshotel.com www.anmordroshotel.com	630 255 100m	£34.50 SS PL D O D(5)(5ES) T(1)(1ES) ALL ES
33	Mr & Mrs I Paterson Tregathenan House B&B The Old Farmhouse Tregathenan **HELSTON** TR13 0RZ	01326 569840 tregathenan@hotmail.com www.tregathenan.co.uk	654 306 3km PD to Falmouth	£28.50 PL D LSP CP PD O D(2)(1ES) T(1)(1ES) ALL ES
33	Mr & Mrs T Payne Lyndale Cottage Guest Hse 4 Greenbank, Meneage Rd **HELSTON** TR13 8JA	01326 561082 enquiries@lyndalecottage.co.uk www.lyndalecottage.co.uk	662 269 3.5km	£35.00 SS CP O S(1)(1ES) D(3)(3ES) T(2)(2ES) ALL ES
33 BUSINESS MEMBER	Ms S Allen Mullion Cove Hotel **MULLION COVE** Nr Helston TR12 7EP	01326 240328 enquiries@mullion-cove.co.uk www.mullion-cove.co.uk	668 181 on path	£65.00 SS PL EM DW LSP CP KT O D(17)(17ES) T(10)(10ES) F(3)(3ES) ALL ES
33	Mr & Mrs P W Savage The Mounts Bay Guest House & Inn, Churchtown **MULLION** TR12 7HN	01326 241761 mountsbaybandb@btinternet.com www.mountsbayguesthouse.co.uk	678 192 1km	£35.00 EM D KT O S(1)(1ES) D(4)(4ES) T(2)(2ES) F(1)(1ES) ALL ES
34	Mrs A Bennett Stormfield **THE LIZARD** TR12 7NZ	01326 290806 alison.b60@btinternet.com www.cornwall-online.co.uk	703 126 400m	£35.00 SS PL DW D LSP CP KT PD O T(1)(0ES) F(1)(0ES)
34	Mr & Mrs A H Pratt The Caerthillian **THE LIZARD** TR12 7NQ	01326 290019 caerthillian@hotmail.com www.thecaerthillian.co.uk	703 125 500m	£32.50 SS £12.50 PL DW D CP KT O S(1)(0ES) D(2)(2ES) T(1)(1ES) F(1)(1ES)
35	Mrs A Rogers Fernleigh Chymbloth Way **COVERACK** TR12 6TB	01326 280626 sudan-ann03@hotmail.co.uk www.fernleighcoverack.co.uk	781 183 50m	£35.00 PL EM DW D LSP CP KT O D(2)(1ES) T(1)(1ES) F(1)(1ES) ALL ES

For Portreath addresses see North Cornwall B&Bs.

Walk No.	Contact name Establishment name Address Region/Postcode	Telephone no. Mobile no. Email Website	OS Map Ref. Dist. from path	Starting price Facilities Room types No. of en-suite rooms
35	Mrs G Wood Arlyn Wartha **COVERACK** TR12 6TB	01326 280926 woodpgs@tesco.net www.coverack.org.uk/pages/Arlyn.html	781 183	£30.00 D LSP CP O D(2)(1ES) F(1)(0ES)
35	Mr & Mrs D Powell Penmarth House **COVERACK**, The Lizard Peninsula TR12 6TQ	01326 280240 francine@coverack-bandb.co.uk www.coverack-bandb.co.uk	781 185 150m	£25.00 SS PL EM D LSP CP KT O D(2)(2ES) T(2)(2ES) F(1)(1ES) ALL ES
35	Mr & Mrs A Marsland Herons Pool Trevothen **COVERACK** TR12 6SD	01326 280924 tony.marsland@btinternet.com www.heronspool.co.uk	771 179 1.3km	£34.50 SS CP KT O D(1)(1ES)
36	Mr & Mrs W Sanger Tregoning Lea **LADDENVEAN** St Keverne Helston TR12 6QE	01326 280947 waltersanger@aol.com	788 214 1.5km PD	£30.00 Supplement for D or T PL DW D LSP CP KT PD O S(1)(0ES) D(1)(0ES) T(1)(0ES)
36	Ms A Strickland Gallen-Treath Guest House **PORTHALLOW** St Keverne Near Helston TR12 6PL	01326 280400 gallentreath@btclick.com www.gallen-treath.com	797 232 450m PD	£36.00 single & DW supplement PL EM DW CP KT O S(1)(0ES) D(2)(2ES) T(2)(2ES) F(1)(1ES)
36 BUSINESS MEMBER	Mr & Mrs D Lambrick The Five Pilchards Inn **PORTHALLOW** TR12 6PP	01326 280256 fivepilchards@btinternet.com www.fivepilchards.co.uk	796 232 5m	PL EM D LSP CP KT O T(4)(4ES) ALL ES
36	Mrs E Whale Porthvean **GILLAN** TR12 6HL	01326 231204 ewhale@hotmail.co.uk	782 252 on path	£25.00 PL DW D LSP CP KT O T(1)(1ES) facilities to prepare own EM
36	Mrs J Phelps Karenza Tregildry Lane **GILLAN** TR12 6HG	01326 231712 phelps950@btinternet.com www.cornwall-online.com	783 249 400m	£40.00 PL EM CP KT O S(1)(1ES) D(1)(1ES) ALL ES
36	Mrs P Royall **POINT** Helford TR12 6JY	01326 231083 pamroyall@btinternet.com	768 263 on path	£37.00 SS D CP O T(1)(1ES) ALL ES
37	Mrs C Spike Carwinion Vean Grove Hill **MAWNAN SMITH** TR11 5ER	01326 250513 christinespike@fsmail.net www.carwinionvean.co.uk	777 283 1.6km	£35.00 PL D LSP CP O DW by prior arrgt D(3)(1ES) T(3)(1ES) ALL ES
37	Mrs S P Annan Chynoweth Carwinion Lane **MAWNAN SMITH** TR11 5JB	01326 250534 07900 274230 sallyannan2@gmail.com www.chynoweth.helfordriver.net	781 283 800m PD	£35.00 Single £50.00 D CP KT O D(1)(1ES) T(1)(1ES) ALL ES
37	Mrs C Lake Gold Martin Carlidnack Road **MAWNAN SMITH** TR11 5HA	01326 250666 gold_martin@hotmail.com www.goldmartin.co.uk	779 291 1.6km PD	£34.00 Single only let with dble rm PL D CP KT PD O S(1)(1ES) D(2)(2ES) T(1)(1ES)

Walk No.	Contact name Establishment name Address Region/Postcode	Telephone no. Mobile no. Email Website	OS Map Ref. Dist. from path	Starting price Facilities Room types No. of en-suite rooms
37	Mrs A Stokes Highfield, Carlidnack Lane **MAWNAN SMITH** Falmouth TR11 5HE	01326 250867 avrilstokes@hotmail.com	780 292	 CP O D(1)(1ES) F(2)(2ES) ALL ES
37	Mr & Mrs G Williams Trevarn Carwinion Road **MAWNAN SMITH** TR11 5JD	01326 251245 07877 580321 enquiries@trevarn.co.uk www.trevarn.co.uk	777 284 800m	£35.00 SS PL LSP CP KT PD O S(1)(1ES) D(1)(1ES) T(1)(1ES) ALL ES
37 BUSINESS MEMBER	Mr & Mrs Cook The Rosemary 22 Gyllyngvase Terrace **FALMOUTH** TR11 4DL	01326 314669 stay@therosemary.co.uk www.therosemary.co.uk	810 318 100m	£40.00 SS PL DW D LSP CP KT O S(1)(1ES) D(3)(3ES) T(2)(2ES) F(2)(2ES) ALL ES
37 BUSINESS MEMBER	Ms J Goodchild Falmouth Backpackers 9 Gyllyngvase Terrace **FALMOUTH** TR11 4DL	01326 319996 judi@falmouthlodge.co.uk www.falmouthbackpackers.co.uk	811 319 150m	£19.00 incl. simple breakfast D LSP CP KT O S(1)(0ES) D(1)(1ES) T(2)(0ES)
37 BUSINESS MEMBER	Mrs S Humphreys The Westcott Gyllyngvase Hill **FALMOUTH** TR11 4DN	01326 311309 www.westcottguesthousefalmouth.co.uk	809 317	£35.00 PL D CP KT O S(1)(1ES) D(5)(5ES) T(2)(2ES) F(1)(1ES) ALL ES
37 BUSINESS MEMBER	Ms T Rangecroft Anchor House 17 Harbour Terrace **FALMOUTH** TR11 2AN	01326 317006 07855 722449 tinarange@btinternet.com www.anchorhousebandbfalmouth.co.uk	805 330 150m	£35.00 SS PL EM D LSP CP KT O S(1)(0ES) D(1)(0ES)
37 BUSINESS MEMBER	Mrs T Farthing Trelawney Guesthouse 6 Melville Road **FALMOUTH** TR11 4AS	01326 316607 07792 679553 trelawney@hotmail.co.uk www.trelawney-guesthouse.co.uk	816 321 150m	£35.00 SS, Breakfast extra charge PL D O S(2)(1ES) D(2)(2ES) T(1)(1ES) F(1)(1ES) ALL ES
37 BUSINESS MEMBER	Mr A Oliver The Seaview Inn Wodehouse Terrace **FALMOUTH** TR11 3EP	01326 311359 07805 171018 seaviewinn@hotmail.co.uk www.seaviewinnfalmouth.co.uk	808 326	£70.00 price per room. £55 Single PL EM DW D LSP CP O D(2)(2ES) T(1)(1ES) ALL ES
37	Mr P Lower Gyllyngvase House Hotel Gyllyngvase Road **FALMOUTH** TR11 4GH	01326 312956 info@gyllyngvase.co.uk www.gyllyngvase.co.uk	810 318 50m	£38.00 PL EM D LSP CP KT O S(2)(0ES) D(7)(7ES) T(2)(2ES) F(1)(1ES)
37	Mr & Mrs A Housman The Lerryn Hotel De Pass Road **FALMOUTH** TR11 4BJ	01326 312489 lerrynhotel@btconnect.com www.thelerrynhotel.co.uk	813 319 20m	 PL D CP O EM & DW by prior arrgt S(4)(4ES) D(8)(8ES) T(6)(6ES) F(2)(2ES) ALL ES
37	Mr & Mrs S Davie Dolvean House 50 Melvill Road **FALMOUTH** TR11 4DQ	01326 313658 reservations@dolvean.co.uk www.dolvean.co.uk	809 319 300m	£40.00 SS in D rooms, closed Xmas PL D CP KT O S(2)(2ES) D(6)(6ES) T(2)(2ES) ALL ES
37	Mrs D A Kevern Lynford 20 Avenue Road **FALMOUTH** TR11 4AZ	01326 314258	811 320 200m	£30.00 PL D CP O S(2)(0ES) D(2)(2ES) T(1)(1ES)

Walk No.	Contact name Establishment name Address Region/Postcode	Telephone no. Mobile no. Email Website	OS Map Ref. Dist. from path	Starting price Facilities Room types No. of en-suite rooms
38	Mrs K Moseley Braganza Grove Hill **ST MAWES** TR2 5BJ	01326 270281 078999 67367 braganzak@googlemail.com www.braganza-stmawes.co.uk	846 331 300m	£55.00 CP KT, PL LSP & DW by prior by arrgt 4 S/D/T ALL ES
39	Mr & Mrs M Rawling Treverbyn House Pendower Road **VERYAN** TR2 5QL	01872 501201 info@treverbyn.co.uk www.treverbyn.co.uk	914 393 2 km PD Free local PD, distances charged	£35.00 SS PL D CP KT PD O S(1)(1ES) D(1)(1ES) T(1)(1ES) ALL ES
39	Mrs S Treneary Jago Cottage Trewartha **PORTLOE** TR2 5QJ	01872 501491 jago@roseland.me.uk www.roseland.me.uk	925 396 400m	£35.00 Also self catering for 5 PL EM DW D LSP CP KT O S(3)(3ES) D(3)(3ES) T(3)(3ES) F(1)(1ES) ALL ES
39	Mr & Mrs K Righton Broom Parc Camels **PORTLOE** TR2 5PJ	01872 501803 lindsay@broomparc.co.uk www.broomparc.co.uk	930 390 on path	£46.00 PL DW D LSP CP KT O (Feb-Nov) D(1)(0ES) T(2)(2ES)
39	Mrs B Leach Carradale **PORTLOE** TR2 5RB	01872 501508 barbara495@btinternet.com www.theaa.com	935 394 300m	£35.00 SS PL D LSP CP KT O D(1)(1ES) T(1)(1ES) ALL ES
39	Mr M Swannell The Ship Inn **PORTLOE** TR2 5RA	01872 501356 theshipinnportloe@googlemail.com www.theshipinnportloe.co.uk	936 393 150m	 EM CP D(2)(2ES) T(1)(1ES) ALL ES
39	Mr & Mrs I Lydall Field Cottage Treviskey **PORTLOE** TR2 5PN	01872 501045 injb@btinternet.com	936 404 600m PD	£30.00 continental b'fast only PL D LSP CP PD O D(1)(1ES)
40	Mr R Bennett Lower Penvose PORTHOLLAND Tregony, Truro TR2 5SS	01872 501789 07982 306702 penvose@phonecoop.coop www.penvose.co.uk	949 415 300m	£35.00 PL EM LSP CP KT PD O S(2)(0ES) D(1)(1ES)
40	Mr & Mrs P Calcraft Grenville, 1 Quilver Close **GORRAN HAVEN** PL26 6JT	01726 843243	011 414 300m	£30.00 PL D CP KT O D(1)(1ES) T(1)(1ES)
40	Mrs F Thomas Kervernel 35 Cliff Street **MEVAGISSEY** PL26 6QJ	01726 844656 franormthomas@btinternet.com www.trixology.com/cornwall	015 448 10m	£30.00 SS £5.00 PL D KT PD O T(2)(1ES)
40	Mr & Mrs I Soper Honeycombe House 61 Polkirt Hill **MEVAGISSEY** PL26 6UR	01726 843750 07710 593913 enquiries@honeycombehouse.co.uk www.honeycombehouse.co.uk	015 446 10m	£33.00 SS for D or T D LSP CP O S(1)(0ES) D(3)(0ES) T(1)(0ES)
41	Mrs J Galloway Locksley Church Road **CHARLESTOWN** PL25 3NS	01726 72613 gallowayj265@aol.com	036 521 500m PD	£29.00 PL D LSP CP KT PD O S(1)(1ES) D(1)(1ES)

For Falmouth addresses see West Cornwall B&Bs.

Walk No.	Contact name Establishment name Address Region/Postcode	Telephone no. Mobile no. Email Website	OS Map Ref. Dist. from path	Starting price Facilities Room types No. of en-suite rooms
41	Mrs S Clyne Boslowen 96 Par Green **PAR** PL24 2AG	01726 813720 07980 838578 boslowen@gmail.com www.boslowen.co.uk	079 536 10m	£32.50 £45 single occupancy D LSP CP KT O D(3)(3ES) T(2)(2ES) ALL ES
42	Mr S Hardinge & Mrs A Davis Trevanion Guest House 70 Lostwithiel Street **FOWEY** PL23 1BQ	01726 832602 alisteve@trevanionguesthouse.co.uk www.trevanionguesthouse.co.uk	124 518 500m PD	£37.50 Single £45 PL EM DW D CP PD O LSP by prior arrgt S(2)(1ES) D(3)(3ES) T(3)(3ES)) F(2)(2ES)
42	Mrs S Hoddinott Trekelyn 3 Hanson Drive **FOWEY** PL23 1ET	01726 833375	120 514 200m	£35.00 SS D CP O D(1)(0ES) T(1)(0ES)
42	Mrs P Milbank Mazirah 51 Polvillion Road **FOWEY** PL23 1HG	01726 833339 paulmilbank@gmail.com	120 516 1km	£30.00 £40.00 Single PL D LSP CP O D(1)(1ES)
43	Mrs B Alexander Hormond House 55 Fore Street POLRUAN PL23 1PH	01726 870853 bella@chrisbella.demon.co.uk www.hormondhouse.com	126 508 250m	 DW D KT O S(1)(1ES) T(2)(2ES) F(1)(1ES) ALL ES
43	Mrs P Moore Chyavallon Landaviddy Lane **POLPERRO** PL13 2RT	01503 272788 chyavallon@btinternet.com www.chyavallonpolperro.co.uk	205 510 300m	£34.00 SS mid Feb-mid Nov O D CP PL by arrgt D(2)(2ES)
43	Mr S Shephard The House on Props Talland Street **POLPERRO** PL13 2RE	01503 272310 stephenshephard@btinternet.com www.houseonprops.co.uk	208 509 on path	£40.00 (discounts poss) PL EM DW KT O D(2)(2ES) T(1)(1ES) ALL ES
43	Mr & Mrs C Pidcock Penryn House The Coombes **POLPERRO** PL13 2RQ	01503 272157 enquiries@penrynhouse.co.uk www.penrynhouse.co.uk	205 511 500m	£36.00 PL DW D CP O S(1)(1ES) D(7)(7ES) T(2)(2ES) F(2)(2ES) ALL ES
44 BUSINESS MEMBER	Mr & Mrs D Neal Schooner Point 1 Trelawney Terrace **WEST LOOE** PL13 2AG	01503 262670 enquiries@schoonerpoint.co.uk www.schoonerpoint.co.uk	252 536 150m	£35.00 SS in D room PL D LSP CP KT O S(1)(0ES) D(3)(3ES) T(1)(1ES)
44 BUSINESS MEMBER	Mr & Mrs A Lever Sea Breeze Lower Chapel Street **EAST LOOE** PL13 1AT	01503 263131 07880 701584 seabreezelooe@live.co.uk www.seabreezelooe.com	256 531 100m	£50.00 Price per room CP O LSP by prior arrgt D(4)(4ES) T(1)(1ES) ALL ES
44	Mr E Mawby Marwinthy Guest House East Cliff **EAST LOOE** PL13 1DE	01503 264382 eddiemawby@lineone.net www.marwinthy.co.uk	256 533 on path	£24.00 SS varies DW D O D(2)(2ES)
44	Mr & Mrs D Burton Deganwy Hotel Station Road **EAST LOOE** PL13 1HL	01503 262984 enquiries@deganwyhotel.co.uk www.deganwyhotel.co.uk	254 536 50m	£34.00 Single from £44.00 PL D LSP CP KT O S(2)(2ES) D(4)(4ES) T(3)(3ES) F(2)(2ES) ALL ES

Walk No.	Contact name Establishment name Address Region/Postcode	Telephone no. Mobile no. Email Website	OS Map Ref. Dist. from path	Starting price Facilities Room types No. of en-suite rooms
45	Mrs S Broad Treliddon Farmhouse **DOWNDERRY** PL11 3DP	01503 250288 www.treliddon-farms.co.uk	324 551 1km PD	£30.00 SS £5.00 DW D LSP CP KT PD O S(1)(0ES) D(2)(2ES) F(2)(2ES)
46	Mrs F M Harvey The Bungalow Cliff Road **PORTWRINKLE** PL11 3BY	01503 230334 fiona.harvey334@btinternet.com www.portwrinklebedandbreakfast.co.uk	355 541 220m	£30.00 SS CP KT O PL by prior arrgt D(1)(0ES) T(1)(0ES)
46 BUSINESS MEMBER	Mr & Mrs J Pape Polhawn Cottage **POLHAWN COVE** Whitsand Bay PL10 1LL	01752 822657 polhawn@btinternet.com www.polhawncovecottage.co.uk	213 937 5m	£32.50 SS PL LSP CP PD O D(2)(2ES) T(1)(0ES)
46	Ms A Heasman Cliff House **KINGSAND** PL10 1NJ	01752 823110 chkingsand@aol.com www.cliffhouse-kingsand.co.uk	434 506 20m	£35.00 / also self catering PL EM D CP KT PD O D(2)(2ES) T(1)(1ES)
46	Mrs J King Coombe House B&B Fourlanesend **KINGSAND** PL10 1LR	01752 823925 info@coombehouse-cawsand.co.uk www.coombehouse-cawsand.co.uk	429 512 500m	£37.50 SS D LSP CP KT O D(5)(2ES) T(1)(0ES) F(3)(1ES)
46 BUSINESS MEMBER	Mrs J A Southward The Edgcumbe Arms **CREMYLL** PL10 1HX	01752 822294 info@edgcumbearms.co.uk www.edgcumbearms.co.uk	453 534 on path	£80.00 price per room EM CP O D(3)(3ES) T(1)(1ES) phone for single prices, also SC

Kingsand

Walk No.	Contact name Establishment name Address Region/Postcode	Telephone no. Mobile no. Email Website	OS Map Ref. Dist. from path	Starting price Facilities Room types No. of en-suite rooms
47 BUSINESS MEMBER	Mrs J Kirsop-Taylor Rusty Anchor, 30 Grand Parade, West Hoe **PLYMOUTH** PL1 3DJ	01752 663924 07855 333993 enquiries@therustyanchor-plymouth.co.uk www.therustyanchor-plymouth.co.uk	473 534 on path	£35.00 PL EM DW D CP KT O S(2)(0ES) D(4)(4ES) T(2)(1ES) F(2)(2ES)
47	Mrs A Anderson Sea Breezes, 28 Grand Parade, West Hoe **PLYMOUTH** PL1 3DJ	01752 667205 07790 147505 info@plymouth-bedandbreakfast.co.uk www.plymouth-bedandbreakfast.co.uk	478 537 on path	£40.00 SS PL D LSP CP KT PD O D(4)(4ES) T(3)(3ES) F(2)(2ES) ALL ES
47	Mr & Mrs D Whitfield Squires Guest House 7 St James Pl East, The Hoe **PLYMOUTH** PL1 3AS	01752 261459 info@squiresguesthouse.com www.squiresguesthouse.com	474 541 500m	£26.00 SS for D room D O S(2)(0ES) D(4)(4ES) T(1)(1ES)
47 BUSINESS MEMBER	Mr & Mrs D Radford Rainbow Lodge 29 Atheneum St, The Hoe PLYMOUTH PL1 2RQ	01752 229699 info@rainbowlodgeplymouth.co.uk www.rainbowlodgeplymouth.co.uk	474 545 100m	£24.50 Price for dbl occupancy D CP KT O S(2)(0ES) D(7)(6ES) T(4)(3ES) F(2)(2ES)
47	Ms C M Williams Edgcumbe Guest House 50 Pier St, West Hoe **PLYMOUTH** PL1 3BT	01752 660675 07941 242228 enquiries@edgcumbeguesthouse.co.uk www.edgcumbeguesthouse.co.uk	473 537 10m	£30.00 SS also SC PL DW KT O S(3)(3ES) D(4)(4ES) T(3)(3ES) F(2)(2ES)
47	Mr L Wrench The Riviera 8 Elliott St, The Hoe **PLYMOUTH** PL1 2PP	01752 667379 riviera-hoe@btconnect.com www.riviera-hoe.co.uk	474 540 200m	£30.00 PL DW D LSP CP KT O S(5)(2ES) D(4)(4ES) T(2)(2ES)
47	Mr B Huxley No. 1 The Esplanade The Hoe **PLYMOUTH** PL1 2PJ	07775 798567 barryhuxley@hotmail.com	476 539 on path	£30.00 D O D(2)(2ES)
47	Mrs J Tooze Coombe House The Quay, **ORESTON** Plymstock PL9 7NE	01752 482660 jet-28@hotmail.co.uk	500 534 on path	£30.00 SS PL D CP PD O D(2)(2ES) T(2)(2ES)
47 BUSINESS MEMBER	Mr & Mrs A Elliott The Boringdon Arms **TURNCHAPEL** Plymouth PL9 9TQ	01752 402053 07795 105246 boringdon@btinternet.com www.boringdonarms.co.uk	495 531 5m PD	£25.00 £5.00 SS PL EM DW O D(2)(0ES) T(1)(0ES) F(1)(1ES)
48	Mrs G Shelford Heybrook Bay Guest House Beach Rd **HEYBROOK BAY** Near Wembury PL9 0BS	01752 862345 heybrookgh@btinternet.com	496 488 on path	£29.00 SS PL DW LSP CP KT S(1)(0ES) D(2)(0ES) T(2)(0ES)
48 BUSINESS MEMBER	Mr & Mrs J Pitcher 1 Barton Close **WEMBURY** PL9 0LF	01752 863710 lorraine.pitcher123@btinternet.com	527 494 1km PD	£30.00 PL D LSP CP KT PD O T(1)(1ES)
48	Mrs M R Denby Knoll Cottage 104 Church Road **WEMBURY** PL9 0LA	01752 862036 07803 827165 davidpdenby88@tiscali.co.uk	523 489 500m	£28.00 PL EM LSP CP O S(1)(0ES) D(1)(1ES) T(1)(1ES)

Walk No.	Contact name Establishment name Address Region/Postcode	Telephone no. Mobile no. Email Website	OS Map Ref. Dist. from path	Starting price Facilities Room types No. of en-suite rooms
48	Mrs V Finnegan Old Barton Farmhouse **THORN** Wembury PL9 0EF	01752 863418 oldbartonbnb@hotmail.co.uk www.oldbartonbnb.co.uk	532 490 750m	£30.00 PL EM D LSP CP KT O D(2)(2ES) T(1)(0ES)
48	Mrs J Mills 11 Valley Drive **WEMBURY** PL9 0EZ	01752 862581	523 493 750m	£25.00 D CP O F(1)(1ES)
49	Mrs J Stephenson 38 Yealm Road **NEWTON FERRERS** Plymouth PL8 1BX	01752 872933 davidjstep@btinternet.com	547 480 1km / 1km from Warren Point ferry	£35.00 D CP O T(1)(1ES)
49 BUSINESS MEMBER	Mrs S Spooner Rogers Cellars, Passage Wood Road **NOSS MAYO** PL8 1EU	01752 872771 suespoonerrogers@btinternet.com	534 475 on path	£40.00 PL DW D LSP CP KT O D(1)(1ES) T(1)(1ES) F(1)(1ES)
49 BUSINESS MEMBER	Mrs M Brazier 1 Coastguards Cottages Passage Road **NOSS MAYO** PL8 1EU	01752 872255 07799 433698 coastguardscottages@yahoo.co.uk	534 253	£75.00 Price per room, £60 SO PL D CP KT O D(1)(1ES)
49	Mrs J Barnett Revelstoke Coombe Hannaford Road **NOSS MAYO** PL8 1EJ	01752 872663 mrandmrsbarnett@gmail.com www.nossmayobandb.net	546 469 850m	£40.00 PL DW D LSP CP KT PD O D(3)(1ES) D Rooms can be Twin or Single
49	Mrs J Rogers **WORSWELL BARTON** Noss Mayo PL8 1HB	01752 872977 jackierogers1hb@btinternet.com www.worswellbarton.co.uk	537 470 800m	£35.00 SS Also SC PL LSP CP KT O D(3)(2ES) T(1)(0ES)
49	Mrs J Stockman, Bugle Rocks, The Old School **BATTISBOROUGH CROSS** Holbeton PL8 1JX	01752 830422 stay@buglerock.co.uk www.buglerocks.co.uk	601 473 3km	£37.50 SS PL D LSP CP KT O D(3)(3ES) T(1)(1ES) F(1)(1ES) ALL ES
49 BUSINESS MEMBER	Mr & Mrs R Baker Kimberley **RINGMORE** Near Kingsbridge TQ7 4HJ	01548 811115 info@kimberley-annex.co.uk www.kimberley-annex.co.uk	652 462 1500m, pick up Mothecombe, boat across R. Erme charged	£35.00 D LSP CP KT PD O D(1)(1ES) T(1)(0ES) T room let with D room as family suite
49	Mrs K Purdy Ringmore Vean **RINGMORE** TQ7 4HL	01548 810382 enquiries@ringmorevean.co.uk www.ringmorevean.co.uk	651 459 900m	£40.00 O
49	Mrs P Dolby 1 Coastguard Cottages **CHALLABOROUGH** Nr Kingsbridge TQ7 4HT	01548 810894 patdolby1951@hotmail.co.uk	648 451 50m	£20.00 PL D CP KT O D(2)(2ES)
49	Mr & Mrs A J Roberts Summer Winds Marine Drive **BIGBURY-ON-SEA** TQ7 4AS	01548 810669 07540 533854 pritchard212@btinternet.com	651 443 on path	£32.50 SS £7.50 PL D CP O D(2)(2ES) T(1)(1ES) ALL ES

Walk No.	Contact name Establishment name Address Region/Postcode	Telephone no. Mobile no. Email Website	OS Map Ref. Dist. from path	Starting price Facilities Room types No. of en-suite rooms
50	Mrs E Meldrum Meadow Cottage **WEST BUCKLAND** TQ7 3AF	01548 560759	681 438 1km inland from Bantham ferry.	£30.00 O EM at pub near ferry T(1)(0ES)
50 BUSINESS MEMBER	Mrs S J Howell Beams B&B, 29 Court Park, **THURLESTONE** Kingsbridge TQ7 3LX	01548 562324 07849 154756 fotos967@hotmail.com www.iknowdevon.co.uk	679 431	£37.50 Single £50.00 D LSP CP O D(1)(1ES) T()(1ES) ALL ES
50	Mrs C Righton Cob Cottage **THURLESTONE** TQ7 3NJ	caroline@carolinerighton.com www.southdevontv.com/cob-cottage-thurlestone-bb	676 430	£40.00 SS £10.00 PL EM DW D LSP CP KT O D(1)(1ES) T(1)(0ES)
50 BUSINESS MEMBER	Miss S Ireland The Cottage Hotel **HOPE COVE** Kingsbridge TQ7 3HJ	01548 561555 info@hopecove.com www.hopecove.com	675 401 25m	£55.50 inc. dinner PL EM DW D LSP CP KT O S(2)(2ES) D(24)(24ES) F(5)(5ES) Dbl rooms can be twin
50 BUSINESS MEMBER	Miss S Ireland Tanfield B & B **HOPE COVE** Kingsbridge TQ7 3HJ	01548 561555 info@hopecove.com www.hopecove.com	675 401 300m	£25.00 PL D CP KT O Book in EM & LSP at Cot Hot S(1)(1ES) D(5)(5ES) T(2)(2ES) PL ordered at hotel
51 BUSINESS MEMBER	Miss M L Coleman Sun Bay Hotel **INNER HOPE COVE** Kingsbridge TQ7 3HH	01548 561371 sunbayhotel@btconnect.com www.sunbayhotel-hopecove.co.uk	676 399 on path	£30.00 Phone for single prices PL EM DW CP D(6)(6ES) T()(6ES) F(2)(2ES)
50	Mrs L Dixon Smiley Lodge 9 Weymouth Park **HOPE COVE** TQ7 3HD	01548 561946 enquiries@smileylodge.co.uk www.smileylodge.co.uk	680 403 350m	PL D LSP KT O DW by arrgt D(2)(1ES) KT to Salcombe only
51	Mrs L Hillaby Broad Views Portlemore Close **MALBOROUGH** TQ7 3SX	01548 561478 lynn@lhillaby.wanadoo.co.uk	709 395 3.8 km	£60.00 price per room CP KT O D(1)(1ES) T(1)(0ES)
51	Mr & Mrs R Petty-Brown Rocarno Grenville Road **SALCOMBE** TQ8 8BJ	01548 842732 rocarno@aol.com www.rocarno.co.uk	736 389 500m	£33.00 SS PL CP KT O D(1)(1ES) T(1)(1ES) ALL ES
51	Mrs P Snelson Waverley Devon Road **SALCOMBE** TQ8 8HL	01548 842633 07980 012608 pauline@waverleybandb.co.uk www.waverleybandb.co.uk	738 388 500m	£35.00 SS £15-£20 O S(1)(1ES) D(6)(5ES) T(6)(5ES) F(3)(3ES) also SC
51	Mrs E M Weymouth Motherhill Farm Main Road **SALCOMBE** TQ8 8NB	01548 842552 djweymouth@tiscali.co.uk	730 393 1.5km	£24.00 D LSP CP O S(1)(0ES) D(1)(0ES) T(1)(0ES)
51	Ms A Woodhatch Rainbow's End 11 Platt Close **SALCOMBE** TQ8 8NZ	01548 843654 07974 773451 annwoodhatch@btinternet.com	730 393 1.5km	£28.00 SS PL D LSP CP KT PD O T(1)(1ES) F(1)(1ES) ALL ES

Walk No.	Contact name Establishment name Address Region/Postcode	Telephone no. Mobile no. Email Website	OS Map Ref. Dist. from path	Starting price Facilities Room types No. of en-suite rooms
51 BUSINESS MEMBER	Mr & Mrs R Agar Ashleigh House Ashleigh Road **KINGSBRIDGE** TQ7 1HB	01548 852893 07732 194393 reception@ashleigh-house.co.uk www.ashleigh-house.co.uk	731 439 6km	£40.00 SS £10.00 PL DW D LSP CP O D(5)(5ES) T(2)(2ES) F(1)(1ES) ALL ES
51	Mrs P Jackson 33 Knowle House Close **KINGSBRIDGE** TQ7 1AN	01548 853820 07792 152750 trish.j@hotmail.co.uk	735 446 7km	£30.00 SS £5 in D room PL D LSP KT PD O S(1)(0ES) D(1)(0ES)
52	Mrs J Foss Down Farm **START POINT** Kingsbridge TQ7 2NQ	01548 511234 downfarm@btinternet.com www.downfarm.co.uk	806 377 600m	£37.50 £40 single PL EM D LSP CP KT O D(1)(1ES) T(1)(1ES) F(1)(1ES) ALL ES
52	Mr & Mrs N Heath The Cricket Inn **BEESANDS** TQ7 2EN	01548 580215 thecricketinn@gmail.com www.thecricketinn.com	819 402 on path	£45.00 EM LSP CP KT O D(5)(5ES) T(2)(2ES) F(1)(1ES) ALL ES
52	Mrs V Johnston Valseph The Green, **BEESANDS** Nr Kingsbridge TQ7 2EJ	01548 580650 07890 197673 valseph@btinternet.com www.beesands-bedandbreakfast.co.uk	819 406 on path	£35.00 LSP CP KT O D(1)(1ES)
52	Ms C Ley Linger Lodge **TORCROSS** TQ7 2TJ	01548 580599 ley@lingerlodge.co.uk www.lingerlodge.co.uk	822 421 400m	£45.00 SS D LSP CP KT O D(3)(3ES) ALL ES
53	Mrs Val Mercer Old Walls, **SLAPTON** Nr Kingsbridge TQ7 2QN	01548 580516 val.slapton@gmail.com	823 449 500m	£32.00 SS PL DW D KT PD O S(1)(0ES) D(1)(0ES) T(1)(0ES) F(1)(1ES)
53	Mrs L Sharman Ley Cottage Sands Road **SLAPTON** TQ7 2QN	01548 581376 07854 977852 elizabethsharman@hotmail.com www.leycottage.co.uk	822 449 400m	£30.00 D CP KT O T(1)(1ES)
53	Mr & Mrs C Tonkin Fairholme, Bay View Est STOKE FLEMING Dartmouth TQ6 0QX	01803 770356 stay@fairholmedartmouth.co.uk www.fairholmedartmouth.co.uk	863 488 100m	£30.00 £40.00 SO CP O D(2)(2ES) T(1)(1ES) ALL ES
53 BUSINESS MEMBER	Mr & Mrs R Jordan Cladda B&B & SC Appt. 88-90 Victoria Road & Ford Valley **DARTMOUTH** TQ6 9EF	01803 835957 07967 060003 info@cladda-dartmouth.co.uk www.cladda-dartmouth.co.uk	871 511 750m	£35.00 also self catering PL D CP KT O D(6)(6ES) T(4)(4ES) F(4)(4ES) ALL ES
53 BUSINESS MEMBER	Mr & Mrs A Depledge The Crow's Nest 5A Lower Street **DARTMOUTH** TQ6 9AJ	07920 053580 info@crowsnestdartmouth.co.uk www.crowsnestdartmouth.co.uk	878 512 1km	£30.00 Single £49.00 O D CP LSP 1D 1D/T/F
53	Mrs V Ruddle Estuary View 11 Horn Hill **DARTMOUTH** TQ6 9RA	01803 834066 07950 852014 vjruddle@gmail.com	876 513 200m	£30.00 D KT PD O T(1)(1ES)

Walk No.	Contact name Establishment name Address Region/Postcode	Telephone no. Mobile no. Email Website	OS Map Ref. Dist. from path	Starting price Facilities Room types No. of en-suite rooms
53	Mrs J Wright Camelot 61 Victoria Road **DARTMOUTH** TQ6 9RX	01803 833805 07870 665863 jjwright@talktalk.net	875 514 500m	£30.00 Single £45.00 D O D(2)(1ES) T(1)(1ES)
53	Miss J Robinson The Maitland 28 Victoria Road **DARTMOUTH** TQ6 9SA	01803 835854 enquiries@themaitland.co.uk www.themaitland.co.uk	875 513 500m	£30.00 SS PL DW CP KT O D(3)(2ES)
53	Mr Hammond & Ms White Hill View House 76 Victoria Road **DARTMOUTH** TQ6 9DZ	01803 839372 enquiries@hillviewdartmouth.co.uk www.hillviewdartmouth.co.uk	872 512 1km	£35.00 based on 2 sharing D CP O S(1)(1ES) D(3)(3ES) T(1)(1ES) ALL ES
53	Mrs C B Roberts Brook House 6 Market Street **DARTMOUTH** TQ6 9QE	01803 832920 07818 452421	876 514 40m	SS PL DW D LSP CP O S(1)(1ES) D(1)(1ES) T(1) (1ES) ALL ES
53	Mrs L Worledge Eight Bells South Embankment **DARTMOUTH** TQ6 9BB	01803 839506 07813 803472 lizworledge@hotmail.com www.dartmouthbandb.com	878 511 200m	£35.00 SS £5.00 D CP O S(2)(2ES) D(2)(2ES) T(1)(1ES) F(1)(1ES) ALL ES
54 BUSINESS MEMBER	Mr & Mrs G Sowerby Raddicombe Lodge Kingswear Road, Hillhead **BRIXHAM** TQ5 0EX	01803 882125 stay@raddicombelodge.co.uk www.raddicombelodge.co.uk	904 538 2km	£24.00 possible SS, also SC PL DW D LSP CP KT O S(1)(1ES) D(4)(4ES) T(2)(2ES) F(2)(2ES)
54	Mr & Mrs K Colby Melville Guesthouse 45 New Road **BRIXHAM** TQ5 8NL	01803 852033 info@themelville.co.uk www.themelville.co.uk	920 559 500m	£28.00 PL CP KT O S(2)(2ES) D(8)(8ES) T(2)(2ES) F(2)(2ES) ALL ES
54	Mrs L Goodwill Midhurst B&B 132 New Road **BRIXHAM** TQ5 8DA	01803 857331 www.midhurstbnb.co.uk	917 556 1050m	£30.00 D CP O PL by prior arrgt S(1)(0ES) D(2)(2ES) T(1)(1ES)
54	Mrs C Robinson Westbury Guesthouse 51 New Road **BRIXHAM** TQ5 8NL	01803 851684 info@westburyguesthouse.co.uk www.westburyguesthouse.co.uk	919 560 1km	£30.00 SS £5.00 CP O D(6)(5ES) T(4)(4ES) F(2)(2ES) ALL ES
55	Mrs F Bamford-Dwane The Clifton Hotel 9 & 10 Kernou Road **PAIGNTON** TQ4 6BA	01803 556545 freda@cliftonhotelpaignton.co.uk www.cliftonhotelpaignton.co.uk	891 607 100m	£35.00 SS PL EM D CP O S(6)(4ES) D()(4ES) T(4)(4ES) F(2)(2ES)
55 BUSINESS MEMBER	Ms K Giles, Garway Lodge Guesthouse 79 Avenue Road **TORQUAY** TQ2 5LL	01803 293126 07790 783997 info@garwaylodge.co.uk www.garwaylodge.co.uk	905 646 850m	£35.00 PL D LSP CP KT O S(3)(3ES) D(3)(3ES) T(1)(1ES) ALL ES
55	Mr Adamson & Miss Coombes The Haute Epine 36 Bampfylde Road **TORQUAY** TQ2 5AR	01803 296359 gerryhauteepine@tiscali.co.uk www.haute-epineguesthouse.co.uk	907 642 740m	£23.00 PL EM D O S(3)(1ES) D(3)(3ES) T(1)(1ES) F(1)(1ES)

Walk No.	Contact name Establishment name Address Region/Postcode	Telephone no. Mobile no. Email Website	OS Map Ref. Dist. from path	Starting price Facilities Room types No. of en-suite rooms
55	Mr N D'Allen Orestone Manor Rock House Lane **MAIDENCOMBE** TQ1 4SX	01803 328098 info@orestonemanor.com www.orestonemanor.com	923 670	£50.00 Single £30 PL EM DW D LSP CP O S(2)(2ES) D(11)(11ES) T(3)(3ES) F(2)(2ES) ALL ES
55	Mr & Mrs D Blenkinsopp Aveland House Aveland Road **BABBACOMBE** TQ1 3PT	01803 326622 avelandhouse@aol.com www.avelandhouse.co.uk	921 652 800m	£38.00 O D EM PL CP LSP KT 4D 2T 2S 2F ALL ES ALL ES
55	Mrs S Brewer Coastguard Cottage 84 Babbacombe Downs Rd **BABBACOMBE** TQ1 3LU	01803 311634 07780 661381	927 653 100m	PL D KT O S(1)(1ES) D(1)(1ES) F(1)(1ES) ALL ES
55	Mrs T Howell The Babbacombe Palms Guesthouse, 2 York Road **BABBACOMBE** TQ1 3SG	01803 327087 reception@babbacombepalms.com www.babbacombepalms.com	922 655 100m	£55.00 price per room DW D KT O D(4)(4ES) T(2)(2ES) F(1)(1ES) ALL ES
56 BUSINESS MEMBER	Mr & Mrs P Burdett 10 The Strand **SHALDON** TQ14 0DL	01626 873315 07976 978742 maggieburdett@yahoo.com	934 722 on path	£35.00 SS PL D KT O D(1)(1ES)
56	Ms J Beckett West Wing, Ringmore Lodge, Salty Lane **SHALDON** TQ14 0AP	01626 872754 ringmorelodge@hotmail.co.uk www.stayindevon.co.uk	927 722 1km	£36.00 PL D CP KT PD O D(1)(1ES) T(1)(1ES) F(1)(1ES) ALL ES
56	Mr P Hockings Brunswick House 5 Brunswick Street **TEIGNMOUTH** TQ14 8AE	01626 774102 info@brunswick-house.com www.brunswick-house.com	941 727 50m	£30.00 SS PL D KT O DW by arrgt S(1)(1ES) D(4)(4ES) F(3)(3ES) ALL ES
56	Mrs D Loach Coombe Bank Guest Hse Landscore Road **TEIGNMOUTH** TQ14 9JL	01626 772369 07860 782415 dianne.loach@btopenworld.com www.coombebankhotel.net	935 732 750m	£28.50 SS PL D LSP CP KT O S(2)(1ES) D(4)(3ES) T(2)(2ES) F(1)(1ES)
56	Mr & Mrs J Allan Thomas Luny House Teign Street **TEIGNMOUTH** TQ14 8EG	01626 772976 alisonandjohn@thomas-luny-house.co.uk www.thomas-luny-house.co.uk	939 729 500m	CP O D(2)(2ES) T(2)(2ES) ALL ES
57 BUSINESS MEMBER	Mrs A Ferris The Blenheim, The Seafront, 1 Marine Pde, **DAWLISH** EX7 9DJ	01626 862372 blenheimholidays@btconnect.com www.theblenheim.uk.net	962 765 10m	£35 Variable SS throughout season DW LSP CP KT O S(2)(2ES) D(6)(6ES) T(6)(6ES) F(4)(4ES)
57	Mrs C Logan Carberry Lodge 2 Carberry Avenue **EXMOUTH** EX8 3EH	01395 263869 chris@carberrylodge.co.uk www.carberrylodge.co.uk	002 823 1.8 km	£35.00 PL D CP KT O S(1)(1ES) D(1)(1ES) T(1)(1ES) ALL ES
57	Mrs M Grant Anchoring B & B 106 St Andrew's Road **EXMOUTH** EX8 1AT	01395 268849 07884 017870 anchoring106@yahoo.co.uk www.anchoringbandb.com	995 806 100m KT to Sidmouth only	£35.00 SS CP by prior arrgt LSP CP PD O S(1)(0ES) D(1)(1ES) T(1)(1ES) F(1)(1ES)

Walk No.	Contact name Establishment name Address Region/Postcode	Telephone no. Mobile no. Email Website	OS Map Ref. Dist. from path	Starting price Facilities Room types No. of en-suite rooms
57 BUSINESS MEMBER	Mr & Mrs P Jessen Quentence Farm Salterton Road, **WEST DOWN BEACON** EX8 5BW	01395 442733 palleandrose@hotmail.co.uk www.selfcatering-devon.co.uk	038 820 1km PD	£28.00 SS in D/T rooms DW D LSP CP KT O S(1)(0ES) D(2)(2ES) T(1)(1ES) F(1)(1ES)
58	Mrs H J Simmons Chapter House 6 Westbourne Terrace **BUDLEIGH S'TON** EX9 6BR	01395 444100 07817 849512 janesimmons1952@hotmail.com	059 818 10m	£60.00 SS DW KT O D(1)(1ES) T(1)(1ES) F(1)(1ES) ALL ES
58	Mrs H Morrish Appletree Cottage 23 Victoria Place **BUDLEIGH S'TON** EX9 6JP	01395 445433 hilary@appletreecottagebudleigh.co.uk www.appletreecottagebudleigh.co.uk	061 818 150m	£26.00 SS PL D CP KT O T(3)(1ES)
59	Mrs E Tancock Lower Pinn Farm Peak Hill **SIDMOUTH** EX10 0NN	01395 513733 07774 694776 liz@lowerpinnfarm.co.uk www.lowerpinnfarm.co.uk	096 865 500m	£36.00 SS DW D LSP CP KT O D(1)(1ES) T(1)(1ES) F(1)(1ES) ALL ES
59	Mrs L Lever Larkstone House 22 Connaught Road **SIDMOUTH** EX10 8TT	01395 514345 davidlever22@btinternet.com	125 878 500m	£26.00 DW D CP KT O S(1)(0ES) D(1)(0ES) T(1)(1ES)
59	Mr & Mrs D Haslam Bramley Lodge Guest House Vicarage Road **SIDMOUTH** EX10 8UQ	01395 515710 bramleyowner@btinternet.com	127 880 650m	£34.50 CP KT O EM must be pre-booked S(2)(1ES) D(2)(2ES) T()(1ES) F(1)(1ES)
60	Mrs E D Jordan Lyndhurst Manor Road **SEATON** EX12 2AQ	01297 23490	244 902 800m	£30.00 DW CP O S(1)(1ES) D(1)(1ES) T(1)(1ES)
60	Mr & Mrs B Rosewarne Sea Glimpses Burrow Road **SEATON** EX12 2NF	01297 22664 07527 636687 liz@seaglimpses.fsnet.co.uk	250 899 20m	£30.00 Single £35.00 CP KT O S(1)(1ES) D(1)(1ES) T(1)(1ES)
60	Mrs G Sedgwick Holmleigh House Sea Hill **SEATON** EX12 2QT	01297 625671 gaynorjones_8@hotmail.co.uk www.holmleighhouse.co.uk	243 900 70m	£75.00 Single £55.00 PL D KT O S(1)(1ES) D(2)(2ES) T(1)(1ES) F(1)(1ES)
60	Mrs M Letheren Beach Belles 3 Beach Road **SEATON** EX12 2LZ	01297 23198 07522 809139 beachbelles03@yahoo.com www.beachbelles.yolasite.com	247 899 35m	£30.00 PL EM O S(1)(1ES) D(1)(1ES) T(2)(2ES) F(1)(1ES)
61	Mrs P Trezise Stepps House Stepps Lane **AXMOUTH** EX12 4AR	01297 20679 pattrezise@btinternet.com	260 909 500m PD	£40.00 SS PL D LSP CP KT O D(2)(0ES) T(1)(0ES)

Walk No.	Contact name Establishment name Address Region/Postcode	Telephone no. Mobile no. Email Website	OS Map Ref. Dist. from path	Starting price Facilities Room types No. of en-suite rooms
61	Mrs J Thomson Westley B&B Lyme Road **UPLYME** Lyme Regis DT7 3UY	01297 445104 07982 302038 westleybandb@btinternet.com www.westleybedandbreakfast.wordpress.com	324 934 1.8km	£32.50 SS £5.00 D CP PD O D(2)(1ES) T(1)(1ES)
61	Mr O Lovell Lucerne View Road **LYME REGIS** DT7 3AA	01297 443752 lucernelyme@btopenworld.com	338 923 500m	£35.00 PL D CP O PL by prior arrgt S(1)(1ES) D(3)(3ES) T(1)(1ES) SC(1)(1ES)
61	Mrs G Hatfield Devonia 2 Woodmead Road **LYME REGIS** DT7 3AB	01297 442869 devonia@lymeregisbandb.com www.lymeregisbandb.com	337 925 350m	£42.00 D CP O S(1)(1ES) D(4)(4ES)
62	Ms C Roberts The Cabin, Duck Street **CHIDEOCK** Bridport DT6 6JR	01297 489573 dorsetseagazer@gmail.com www.cabinchideock.com	421 927 1km PD	£30.00 £2.50 SS PL D LSP CP KT O S(1)(1ES) D(1)(1ES) ALL ES
62	Mr J Taylor Brook Cottage Mill Lane **CHIDEOCK** Bridport DT6 6JS	01297 489528 jim@chideockandseatown.co.uk www.chideockandseatown.co.uk	423 926 400m	£37.50 £42.50 with full breakfast D CP KT O S(1)(1ES) D(1)(1ES) T(1)(1ES) ALL ES
62	Mr & Mrs M Kelson Rose Cottage Main Street **CHIDEOCK** DT6 6JQ	01297 489994 enquiries@rosecottage-chideock.co.uk www.rosecottage-chideock.co.uk	423 927 1km	 D CP KT O D(1)(1ES) T(1)(1ES) ALL ES
62	Mr & Mrs C Crawford Mervyn House **CHIDEOCK** Nr Bridport DT6 6JN	01297 489578 callbrig@gmail.com www.chideockandseatown.co.uk	422 928 500m on bus route	£32.50 D CP O S(1)(0ES) T(1)(0ES)
63	Mrs P Bale Highway Farm West Road **BRIDPORT** DT6 6AE	01308 424321 07791 915228 bale@highwayfarm.co.uk www.highwayfarm.co.uk	443 928 1.5km on bus route	£40.00 Self catering available PL D LSP CP KT O D(2)(2ES) T(1)(1ES) F(1)(1ES) ALL ES
63	Mr A Hardy Britmead House West Bay Road **BRIDPORT** DT6 4EG	01308 422941 britmead@talk21.com www.britmeadhouse.co.uk	465 912 500m	 DW CP KT O D(5)(5ES) T(2)(2ES) F(2)(2ES) ALL ES
63	Mrs V A Moore Eggardon View 261 St Andrews Road **BRIDPORT** DT6 3DU	01308 459001 valamoore@hotmail.com www.roundaboutbritain.co.uk	477 941 4km PD	£30.00 D LSP CP KT PD O S(1)(0ES) T(2)(1ES)
63	Mr W Vickers & Ms D Clarke Seacroft, 24 West Bay **BRIDPORT** DT6 4HD	01308 423407 07855 457875 seacroft24@btinternet.com www.seacroftbandb.co.uk	461 905 50m	£32.50 PL D LSP CP KT O S(1)(1ES) D(2)(2ES) T(1)(1ES) F(1)(1ES) ALL ES
63	Mrs L Comley, Bridge Cottage Guest Rooms 87 High St, **BURTON** **BRADSTOCK** DT6 4RA	01308 897222 lizcomley@aol.com www.bridgecottagebedandbreakfast.co.uk	487 893 300m	£32.50 SS, also SC PL DW D CP KT O D(2)(2ES) T(1)(1ES) F(1)(1ES) ALL ES

Walk No.	Contact name Establishment name Address Region/Postcode	Telephone no. Mobile no. Email Website	OS Map Ref. Dist. from path	Starting price Facilities Room types No. of en-suite rooms
63	Mrs EM Edwards Sea Fret Coast Road **PUNCKNOWLE** DT2 9DQ	01308 897435 enquiries@seafret.co.uk www.seafret.co.uk	537 874 1km PD 100m from inland alt route Sect 80	£35.00 Also self-catering PL DW D LSP CP KT PD O D(1)(1ES) T(1)(1ES) ALL ES
63	Mrs S Collier Offley, Looke Lane **PUNCHKNOWLE** DT2 9BD	01308 897044 www.offleybb.com	537 887 400m	£45.00 DW D LSP CP KT O S(1)(1ES) D(1)(1ES) T(1)(1ES)
63 BUSINESS MEMBER	Mrs I Donnelly Cowards Lake Farmhse 13 West Street **ABBOTSBURY** DT3 4JT	01305 871421 cowards-lake@btconnect.com www.cowardslakebandb.com	573 853 800m	£35.00 DW LSP CP KT PD O D(1)(1ES) T(1)(1ES)
63 BUSINESS MEMBER	Mrs L Halfhead Abbotsbury Tea Rooms 26 Rodden Row **ABBOTSBURY** DT3 4JL	01305 871143 atr@uwclub.net www.abbotsbury-tearooms.co.uk	578 852 600m	£75.00 per room PL KT O D(3)(3ES) F(1)(1ES) ALL ES
63	Mrs P Crockett 21 Rodden Row **ABBOTSBURY** DT3 4JL	01305 871465 07925 350023 pat21rr01@hotmail.co.uk	579 855 750m	£27.50 PL O D(1)(0ES) T(1)(0ES)
63	Mrs C Rawlings Upalong, 8 West Street **ABBOTSBURY** DT3 4JT	01305 871882 clarerawlings@sky.com www.yoakibgwestdirset.co.uk	573 853 500m	£30.00 SS £10.00 EM D CP O D(1)(1ES) T(1)(1ES)
63	Mrs M Peach 6 Market Street **ABBOTSBURY** DT3 4JR	01305 871364 enquiries@abbotsburybandb.co.uk www.abbotsburybandb.co.uk	576 853 1200m	£35.00 SS £5.00 KT O S(1)(1ES) D(1)(1ES) ALL ES
65	Mrs J Hunter Turnstones B&B, 6 Ventnor Road, **FORTUNESWELL** Isle of Portland DT5 1JE	01305 824291 07969 040811 info@turnstones.net www.turnstones.net	687 735 500m	£70.00 price p/r, singles £50 p/r D CP KT O D(3)(3ES)
65	Mrs K Smith, Fairview Cottage, 14 Old Coastguard Cottages, **PORTLAND BILL** DT5 2JT	01305 820368 grahamsmith.14@btinternet.com www.portlandbill.net	678 688 on path	£40.00 D CP KT O S(1)(0ES) D(1)(0ES)
66 BUSINESS MEMBER	Mrs D Quick, Harbour Lights Guest House 20 Buxton Road **WEYMOUTH** DT4 9PJ	01305 783273 harbourlights@btconnect.com www.harbourlightsguesthouse.com	673 779 200m	£35.00 D CP KT O S(2)(0ES) D(5)(5ES) T(2)(2ES) F(2)(2ES)
66 BUSINESS MEMBER	Mr M Clark, Oaklands Edwardian Guesthouse 1 Glendinning Ave **WEYMOUTH** DT4 7QF	01305 767081 stay@oaklands-guesthouse.co.uk www.oaklands-guesthouse.co.uk	678 800 500m	£34.00 SS PL EM D CP O D(6)(6ES) T(3)(3ES) F(1)(1ES) ALL ES
66	Ms S Arnold Greenwood Guest Hse 1 Holland Road **WEYMOUTH** DT4 0AL	01305 775626 enquiries@greenwoodguesthouse.co.uk www.greenwoodguesthouse.co.uk	673 793 1km PD	£30.00 PL D CP KT O S(1)(0ES) D(3)(2ES) T(2)(1ES) F(1)(1ES)

Walk No.	Contact name Establishment name Address Region/Postcode	Telephone no. Mobile no. Email Website	OS Map Ref. Dist. from path	Starting price Facilities Room types No. of en-suite rooms
66	Mr Penman Horizon Guest House 16 Brunswick Terrace **WEYMOUTH** DT4 7RW	01305 784916 info@horizonguesthouse.co.uk www.horizonguesthouse.co.uk	682 799 on path	 O S(1)(1ES) D(2)(2ES) T(1)(0ES) F(1)(1ES)
66	Mrs S Leach Sunnyside B&B 15 Brunswick Terrace **WEYMOUTH** DT4 7SA	01305 786358 sunnysideweymouth@hotmail.co.uk www.sunnysideweymouth.com	682 799 10m	£30.00 DW D KT PD O D(1)(0ES) T(1)(0ES) F(3)(3ES)
66	Mr & Mrs J Green Tara Guest House 10 Market Street **WEYMOUTH** DT4 8DD	01305 766235 lesley_john@btinternet.com www.taraweymouth.co.uk	681 787 150m	£30.00 O S(2)(2ES) D(3)(3ES) T(1)(1ES) ALL ES
66	Mr & Mrs Horvath 1 Old Coastguard Cottages, **OSMINGTON** **MILLS** DT3 6HQ	01305 832663 www.heritagecoastbandb.co.uk	736 817 20m	£38.00 No cooked breakfast PL DW LSP KT O S(1)(1ES) D(1)(1ES)
66	Mrs J Laing Tewkesbury Cottage 28 Main Road, **WEST** **LULWORTH** BH20 5RL	01929 400561 07971 426027	823 806 700m	£45.00 Single £55.00 PL DW D CP KT O D(2)(1ES) T(1)(0ES)
67	Mrs G Hole Bradle Farm **CHURCH KNOWLE** Kimmeridge BH20 5NU	01929 480712 07764 950920 info@bradlefarmhouse.co.uk www.bradlefarmhouse.co.uk	930 806 4km PD	£40.00 SS PL D CP KT O EM at cafe owned by farm D(2)(2ES) T(1)(1ES) ALL ES
68	Mrs S Mitchell Alford House, 120 East St **CORFE CASTLE** Wareham BH20 5EH	01929 480156 info@alfordhouse.com www.alfordhouse.com	963 816 2km PD Local PD free Distances charged	£37.50 SS PL D CP KT O DW by arrgt D(2)(2ES) T(1)(1ES) ALL ES
68	Mr D Ensor, Chiltern Lodge 8 Newfoundland Close **WORTH MATRAVERS** BH19 3LX	01929 439337 07906 508125 densor@btopenworld.com www.chilternlodge.co.uk	976 778 1.5km	£30.00 SS PL EM D CP KT O D(1)(0ES) T(1)(0ES)
69	Mr & Mrs A Preston Sunny Bay House 17 Cluny Crescent **SWANAGE** BH19 2BP	01929 422650 gill@sunnybay.co.uk www.sunnybay.co.uk	031 784 1km	£30.00 CP S(1)(0ES) D(1)(1ES) T(1)(1ES) F(1)(1ES)
69	Mrs K Gibson Harmony House 93 Kings Road West **SWANAGE** BH19 1HN	01929 427255 07837 403892 harmonyhouse-swanage@hotmail.com	022 789 800m PD	£34.00 PL D KT PD O D(2)(2ES) T(1)(0ES)
69	Mr & Mrs M Anderson Danesfort Hotel 3 Highcliffe Road **SWANAGE** BH19 1LW	01929 424224 reception@danesforthotel.co.uk www.danesforthotel.co.uk	031 798 25m	£35.00 PL LSP CP KT O EM by arrgt S(1)(1ES) D(3)(3ES) T(1)(1ES) F(3)(3ES) ALL ES
70	Mrs C Rose Shell Bay Cottage Glebe Estate **STUDLAND** BH19 3AS	01929 450249 info@shellbaycottage.com www.shellbaycottage.com	037 817 500m	£49.50 D CP O KT & PD by arrgt D(1)(0ES) T(1)(1ES)

The Mayflower Steps, Plymouth

Exmoor Campsites

Walk No.	Contact name Establishment name Address Region/Postcode	Telephone no. Fax / Reservation / Mobile no. Website Email	OS Map Ref. Dist. from path	Starting price Months Open Facilities Info
1	Holiday Site Manager Camping & Caravanning Club Site, Hill Road North Hill, **MINEHEAD** TA24 5LB	01643 704138 Reservations Tel: 0845 1307633 www.campingandcaravanningclub.co.uk/minehead enquiries@thefriendlyclub.co.uk	958 471 550 mts	£4.75 May-Sept T S LY CP DW non-members welcome
1	Mr P R Weaver Sparkhayes Farm Camp Site Sparkhayes Lane **PORLOCK** TA24 8NE	01643 862470 www.porlock.co.uk/camping	886 469 on path	£7.00 Apr to Oct O T S LY G CP LSP DW KT 300 coast bus route
2	Holiday Site Manager Camping and Caravan Club Lynton, Caffyn's Cross **LYNTON** EX35 6JS	01598 752379 www.campingandcaravanningclub.co.uk/lynton enquiries@thefriendlyclub.co.uk	703 480 2 km	£5.35 21 Mar-30 Sept T S LY CP DW
2	Mr C Onley Sunny Lyn Camp & Caravan Site, **LYNBRIDGE LYNTON** EX35 6NS	01598 753384 www.caravandevon.co.uk info@caravandevon.co.uk	719 485 800mts	£6.00 Mar-Oct T S LY G CP LSP DW

Goats along North Walk

For Combe Martin addresses see Exmoor Campsites.

North Devon Campsites

Walk No.	Contact name Establishment name Address Region/Postcode	Telephone no. Fax / Reservation / Mobile no. Website Email	OS Map Ref. Dist. from path	Starting price Months Open Facilities Info
3	Mr & Mrs Mortimer Lower Campscott Farm **LEE**, Ilfracombe EX34 8LS	01271 863479 www.lowercampscott.co.uk holidays@lowercampscott.co.uk	495 455 2 km	£6.00 O T S LY CP LSP DW
5	Mr & Mrs B Gilbert North Morte Farm Campsite **MORTEHOE** Devon EX34 7EG	01271 870381 01271 870115 www.northmortefarm.co.uk info@northmortefarm.co.uk	459 455 500 mts	£6.00 Apr-Oct T S LY G CP LSP DW
5	Mrs H Lethbridge Damage Barton **MORTEHOE** Woolacombe EX34 7EJ	01271 870502 www.damagebarton.co.uk enquiries@damagebarton.co.uk	476 457 2 km	£11.00 Mar-Nov T S LY G CP DW
11	Mr & Mrs R Croslegh Robin & Lesley Steart Farm Touring Park **HORNS CROSS** EX39 5DW	01237 431836 www.steartfarmtouringpark.co.uk steartenquiries@btconnect.com	356 229 1 km	£11.00 Easter-Sept T S LY CP LSP DW

Morte Point

North Cornwall Campsites

Walk No.	Contact name Establishment name Address Region/Postcode	Telephone no. Fax / Reservation / Mobile no. Website Email	OS Map Ref. Dist. from path	Starting price Months Open Facilities Info
15	Mr C Heard Lower Pennycrocker Farm **BOSCASTLE** PL35 0BY	01840 250613 07967 605392 www.pennycrocker.com karyn.heard@yahoo.com	124 925 500 mts	£6.00 Apr-Oct T S CP DW
17	Holiday Site Manager Bude Camping & Caravanning Club Site, Gillards Moor **ST GENNYS**, Bude EX23 0BG	01840 230650 Reservations Tel: 0845 1307633 www.campingandcaravanningclub.co.uk enquiries@thefriendlyclub.co.uk	176 943 5 km	£5.95 May-Sept T S LY CP DW non-members welcome
20	Mrs C Pawley Carnevas Farm Holiday Park **PORTHCOTHAN BAY** PL28 8PN	01841 520230 www.carnevasholidaypark.co.uk carnevascampsite@aol.com	862 728 800 mts	£10.50 Apr-Oct T S LY G DW
21	Mrs L Lightfoot Magic Cove Touring Park **MAWGAN PORTH** Newquay TR8 4BZ	01637 860263 www.magiccove.co.uk magic@magiccove.co.uk	850 679 300 mts	£6.00 Easter-Sept T S LY DW G 250 mts from site
21	Holiday Site Manager Camping & Caravan Club Tregurrian, **NEWQUAY** TR8 4AE	01637 860448 www.campingand caravanningclub.co.uk enquiries@thefriendlyclub.co.uk	853 654 500 mts	£7.35 21 Mar-4 Nov T S LY CP DW
21	Mrs S Eastlake Treago Farm Caravan & Camping Site, **CRANTOCK** Newquay TR8 5QS	01637 830277 www.treagofarm.co.uk info@treagofarm.co.uk	781 600 400 mts	£5.00 T S LY G CP DW Easter-early Oct G from May-Sept
24	Ms J Sawle Beacon Cottage Farm Touring Park, Beacon Drive **ST AGNES** TR5 0NU	01872 552347 Mobile 07879 413862 www.beaconcottagefarmholidays.co.uk beaconcottagefarm@lineone.net	705 505 400 mts	£7.00 Apr-Sept T S LY CP LSP DW
24	Mrs P Williams Presingoll Farm Caravan & Camping Park **ST AGNES** TR5 0PB	01872 552333 www.presingollfarm.co.uk pam@presingollfarm.co.uk	720 495 1.6 km	£7.00 Easter-Oct T S LY G CP LSP DW

Trevaunance Cove

Walk No.	Contact name Establishment name Address Region/Postcode	Telephone no. Fax / Reservation / Mobile no. Website Email	OS Map Ref. Dist. from path	Starting price Months Open Facilities Info
28	Miss K Morgan Ayr Holiday Park **ST IVES** TR26 1EJ	01736 795855 01736 798797 www.ayrholidaypark.co.uk recpt@ayrholidaypark.co.uk	511 405 350 mts	£12.00 O T S LY LSP DW price based on 2 sharing
28	Mr E J Coak The North Inn **PENDEEN** TR19 7DN	01736 788417 www.thenorthinnpendeen.co.uk ernestjohncoak@aol.com	383 344 1 km	£4.00 O T S CP LSP DW Also B&B
28	Mr & Mrs Blaken Trevaylor Caravan & Camping Park **BOTTALACK** TR19 7PU	01736 787016 www.cornishcamping.co.uk trevaylor@cornishcamping.co.uk	370 328 500mts	£5.00 Mar-Oct T S LY G DW
28	Mr & Mrs A Collinson Secret Garden Caravan & Camping Park, Bosavern House **ST JUST IN PENWITH** TR19 7RD	01736 788301 www.secretbosavern.com mail@bosavern.com	371 305 1 km	 Mar-Oct T S LY CP Also B&B
28	Mr K Hall Treen Farm Campsite **TREEN** TR19 6LF	01736 810273 Mobile: 07598 469322 www.treenfarmcampsite.co.uk	392 228 200 mts	£7.00 Apr-Oct T S LY G CP DW
28/ 29	The Site Manager, Sennen Cove Camping & Cavavanning Club, Higher Tregiffian Farm **SENNEN COVE** TR19 6JB	01736 871588 Reservations Tel: 0870 243 3331 www.campingandcaravanningclub.co.uk enquiries@thefriendlyclub.co.uk	378 276 2.4 km	£5.95 15 Mar-4 Nov T S LY CP DW non-members welcome
32	Mrs L Garthwaite Kenneggy Cove Holiday Park, Higher Kenneggy, **ROSUDGEON** Penzance TR20 0AU	01736 763453 www.kenneggycove.co.uk mgarthwa@aol.com	561 287 500 mts	 15 May-Sept T S LY G DW
32	Mr & Mrs M Wallis Penrose Campsite **PORTHLEVEN** TR13 0RB	01326 572714 www.campingcornwall.net martin@newpotatoes.net	636 259 1 km	£5.00 July-August T S CP LSP DW KT PD price per adult
33	Mr S Cook, National Trust, Teneriffe Farm Campsite, Predannack **MULLION** TR12 7EZ	01326 240293 www.nationaltrust.org.uk teneriffefarmcampsite@nationaltrust.org.uk	672 167 1km	£7.50 22 Mar-3 Nov T S LY CP LSP DW
33	Mr & Mrs N Whittle Silver Sands Holiday Park Gwendreath, **KENNACK SANDS,** Helston TR12 7LZ	01326 290631 www.silversandsholidaypark.co.uk info@seliversandsholidaypark.co.uk	729 169 1km	£12.50 Mar-Oct T S LY DW
34	Mr & Mrs R H Lyne Henry's Campsite Caerthillian Farm **THE LIZARD** TR12 7NX	01326 290596 www.henryscampsite.co.uk	701 125 500 mts PD	£7.00 O T S LY G CP LSP DWKTPD Open all year
35	Mr & Mrs Flynn Little Trevothan Caravan and Camping Park **COVERACK** TR12 6SD	01326 280260 www.littletrevothan.com sales@littletrevothan.co.uk	770 180 750 mts	£8.00 Mar-Oct T S LY G CP DW

South Cornwall Campsites

Walk No.	Contact name Establishment name Address Region/Postcode	Telephone no. Fax / Reservation / Mobile no. Website Email	OS Map Ref. Dist. from path	Starting price Months Open Facilities Info
39	Holiday Site Manager Camp & Cara Club Site, Veryan Camp & Cara Club, Tretheake, **VERYAN** TR2 5PP	0845 1307633 Reservations: 0845 1307633 www.campingandcaravanningclub.co.uk/veryan enquiries@thefriendlyclub.co.uk	934 414 1.7 km	£5.95 15 Mar-4 Nov T S LY CP DW non-members welcome
40	Dr J Whetter Trelispen Caravan & Camping Park, **GORRAN HAVEN** PL26 6NR	01726 843501 www.trelispen.co.uk trelispen@care4free.net	005 421 1 km	£10.00 Apr-Oct T S LY CP LSP DW
40	Seaview International Campsite **BOSWINGER** Gorran, PL26 6LL	01726 843425 www.seaviewinternational.com holidays@seaviewinternational.com	989 412 500 mts	£7.00 Mar-Oct T S LY G CP DW
41	Mrs D Best Broad Meadow House Quay Road **CHARLESTOWN** PL25 3NX	01726 76636 www.broadmeadowhouse.com stay@broadmeadowhouse.com	039 517 100 mts	£12.00 Pre-booking essential Easter-Oct T S CP LSP DW lux tent & bfast avble; drying facility.
43	Mr & Mrs K Cox Polruan Camping & Caravanning **POLRUAN** PL23 1QH	01726 870263 www.polruanholidays.co.uk polholiday@aol.com	132 507 250 mts	£13.00 Apr-Sept T S LY G DW
43	Mrs J Williams Great Kellow Caravan & Campsite, **POLPERRO** PL13 2QL	01503 272387 www.bestofsecornwall.co.uk kellow.farm@virgin.net	200 521 500 mts	£5.00 Mar-Jan 3rd T S CP LSP DW
44	Mr D Byers Polborder House Caravan & Campsite, Bucklawren Road **ST MARTIN**, Looe PL13 1QS	01503 240265 www.polborderhouse.co.uk reception@polborderhouse.co.uk	283 555 2 km	£11.00 O T S LY G CP DW DW by prior arrangement
44	Mr S R Cox Camping Caradon Park Trelawne, **LOOE** PL13 2NA	01503 272388 01503 272858 www.campingcaradon.co.uk enquiries@campingcaradon.co.uk	542 218 2.4 km	£12.00 O T S LY G CP DW Nov-Mar booking essential
45	Mrs C Petherick The Old Coach House Windsworth, **ST MARTIN BY LOOE, MILLENDREATH** PL13 1NZ	01503 262671 www.thelabyrinth.org.uk caroline@thelabyrinth.org.uk	282 543 on path	£15.00 T CP LSP KT O DW Camping Barn for up to 8 with cooking facilities

Looe Island from Hore Point

Walk No.	Contact name Establishment name Address Region/Postcode	Telephone no. Fax / Reservation / Mobile no. Website Email	OS Map Ref. Dist. from path	Starting price Months Open Facilities Info
49	Mr J Tucker Mount Folly Farm **BIGBURY ON SEA** Devon TQ7 4AR	01548 810267 www.bigburyholidays.co.uk info@bigburyholidays.co.uk	661 447 on path	£6.00 Open All Year O T S CP LSP DW
52	Mrs M Tucker Higher House Farm Little Holloway **EAST PRAWLE** TQ7 2BU	01548 511422 www.eastprawlefarmholidays.co.uk marilynjtucker@btinternet.com	781 365 250 mts	£5.00 June-Sept T CP LSP DW tel for opening times, G 250mts
53	Holiday Site Manager Slapton Camp & Carav Club Middle Grounds, **SLAPTON**, Kingsbridge TQ7 1QW	01548 580538 Reservations Tel: 0845 1307633 www.campingandcaravanningclub.co.uk/slaptonsands enquiries@thefriendlyclub.co.uk	825 450 400mts	£5.95 21 Mar-4 Nov T S LY CP DW non-members welcome
53	Holiday Site Manager Dartmouth Camp & Carav Club, Deer Park, Dartmouth Road, **STOKE FLEMING** TQ6 0RF	01803 770253 www.campingandcaravanningclub.co.uk/dartmouth enquiries@thefriendlyclub.co.uk	864 491 600 mts	£7.35 15 Mar-15 Nov T S LY G CP DW
54	Mr & Mrs W Hosking Upton Manor Farm Camping St Mary's Road **BRIXHAM** TQ5 9QH	01803 882384 www.uptonmanorfarm.co.uk uptoncamp@aol.com	549 926 650 mts	 Easter - Sept T S LY CP
56	Mrs Mann Long Meadow Farm Combe Road, Ringmore **SHALDON** TQ14 0EX	01626 872732 01626 872323 www.longmeadowfarm.co.uk anne@longmeadowfarm.co.uk	922 721 2 kms	£10.00 Easter-Sept T S LY CP LSP DW Also self catering
57	Mr A Bulpin Leadstone Camping Warren Road **DAWLISH** EX7 0NG	01626 864411 www.leadstonecamping.co.uk post@leadstonecamping.co.uk	974 782 800 mts	£7.50 7June-Aug T S LY G CP DW Also self catering
58	Ms M Marsden Prattshayes Farmhouse Maer Lane **LITTLEHAM** EX8 5DB	01395 276626 mary.marsden@nationaltrust.org.uk	025 807 1.5 km	£12.00 Apr-Oct T S CP DW

Ness Cove from Bundle Head

Walk No.	Contact name Establishment name Address Region/Postcode	Telephone no. Fax / Reservation / Mobile no. Website Email	OS Map Ref. Dist. from path	Starting price Months Open Facilities Info
62	Mr M Loosmore Manor Farm Holiday Centre **CHARMOUTH** DT6 6QL	01297 560226 www.manorfarmholidaycentre.co.uk enquiries@manorfarmholidaycentre.co.uk	368 937 500 mts	£15.00 Open All Year O T S LY G CP LSP DW
62	Mr M J Cox Golden Cap Holiday Park **SEATOWN** Chideock DT6 6JX	01308 422139 01308 425672 www.wdlh.co.uk holidays@wdlh.co.uk	425 919 50 mts	£13.70 End Mar-Early Nov T S LY G DW
63	Mr & Mrs Cox Highlands End Holiday Park **EYPE** DT6 6AR	01308 422139 01308 425672 www.wdlh.co.uk holidays@wdlh.co.uk	453 916 100 mts	£13.70 End Mar-earlyNov T S LY G DW
63	Mr R Condliffe Freshwater Beach Holiday Park, **BURTON** **BRADSTOCK** DT6 4PT	01308 897317 01308 897336 www.freshwaterbeach.co.uk enquiries@freshwaterbeach.co.uk	898 479 on path	£14.00 mid Mar-mid Nov T S LY G CP DW
63	Mr R Cox Graston Copse Holiday Park Annings Lane, **BURTON** **BRADSTOCK** DT6 4QP	01308 426947 01308 425672 www.wdlh.co.uk holidays@wdlh.co.uk	497 899 2 km	£12.35 mid Apr-Sept 8 T S LY CP DW
64	Mrs K Kennedy Bagwell Farm Touring Park **CHICKERELL** Weymouth, DT3 4EA	01305 782575 01305 780554 www.bagwellfarm.co.uk sw@bagwellfarm.co.uk	634 812 1 km	£13.00 O T S LY G CP LSP DW
64	East Fleet Farm Touring Park, **CHICKERELL** Weymouth DT3 4DW	01305 785768 www.eastfleet.co.uk enquiries@eastfleet.co.uk	641 795 on path	£14.50 mid Mar-Oct T S LY G CP LSP DW KT
66	Mrs M Green Rosewall Camping, East Farm Dairy, **OSMINGTON** **MILLS**, Weymouth DT3 6HA	01305 832248 01305 835251 www.weymouthcamping.com holidays@weymouthcamping.com	733 824 50 mts	£10.00 Apr-Oct T S LY G CP LSP DW
69	Mr & Mrs J Wootton Toms Field Campsite & Shop, Toms Field Road **SWANAGE** BH19 3HN	01929 427110 As Phone www.tomsfieldcamping.co.uk tomsfield@hotmail.com	995 785 1.5 km	£15.00 mid Mar-Oct T S LY G CP DW Walkers Barn also avble, open all year

Dancing Ledges

Newquay - The Island

Youth Hostels

There is an amazing variety of Youth Hostels along the South West Coast Path, 19 in total and all offering comfortable, friendly accommodation.

Prices start from £9.95 (U18) £12.95 (Adult) per night, including bed linen, the use of self-catering kitchens, drying rooms and cycle sheds. The YHA is a membership organisation, however non-members are welcome to join on arrival at the hostel. Membership enables you to take advantage of more than 4000 Youth Hostels world wide, and discounts at with online and high street retailers and local tourist attractions.

YHA annual membership costs are currently:
Under 26 - £9.95, Individual - £15.95, Family (2 adults & children) - £22.95

The meals are excellent value, at around £4.65 for breakfast, Packed Lunches £4.50 to £5.50 and evening meals are also available.

Book directly with the Youth Hostel of your choice or for further assistance, please contact YHA Customer Services, Tel: 01629 592700, or why not visit their website at www.yha.org.uk

YHA (England & Wales), Trevelyan House, Dimple Road, Matlock, Derbyshire, DE4 3YH
Email: customerservices@yha.org.uk

Youth Hostels

Town	Address	Phone	OS Ref
Minehead	Alcombe Combe MINEHEAD TA24 6EW	0845 371 9033	973 442
Elmscott	Hartland, BIDEFORD EX39 6ES *Self Catering Only*	01237 441367	231 217
Boscastle	Palace Stables BOSCASTLE PL35 0HD	0845 371 9006	096 915
Tintagel	Dunderhole Point TINTAGEL PL34 0DW *Self Catering Only*	0845 371 9145	047 881
Treyarnon	Tregonnan Treyarnon PADSTOW PL28 8JR	0845 371 9664	859 741
Perranporth	Droskyn Point PERRANPORTH TR6 0GS *Self Catering Only*	0845 371 9755	752 544
Portreath	Nance Farm, Illogan, PORTREATH TR16 4QX	01209 842244	668 443
Land's End	Letcha Vean ST JUST TR19 7NT	0845 371 9643	364 305
Penzance	Horneck, PENZANCE TR20 8TF	0845 371 9653	457 302
Lizard	The Lizard HELSTON TR12 7NT *Self Catering Only*	0845 371 9550	704 116
Coverack	Parc Behan, School Hill HELSTON TR12 6SA	0845 371 9014	782 184
Boswinger	GORRAN PL26 6LL	0845 371 9107	991 411
Golant	Penquite House, Golant FOWEY PL23 1LA	0845 371 9019	116 556
Salcombe	Sharpitor SALCOMBE TQ8 8LW	0845 371 9341	728 374
Beer	Bovey Combe, Townsend SEATON EX12 3LL	0845 371 9502	223 896
Litton Cheney	Litton Cheney DORCHESTER DT2 9AT *Self Catering Only*	0845 371 9329	548 900
Lulworth Cove	School Lane WEST LULWORTH BH20 5SA	0845 371 9331	832 806
Portland	Castle Road, Castle Town PORTLAND DT5 1AU	0845 371 9339	685 741
Swanage	Cluny Crescent SWANAGE BH19 2BS	0845 371 9346	031 785

Tourist Information Centres

Town	Address	Phone	Fax
Porlock	West End, Porlock TA24 8QD	01643 863150	01643 863014
Lynton	Town Hall Lee Road EX35 6BT	01598 752225	01598 752755
Combe Martin	Sea Cottage Cross Street EX34 0DH	01271 883319	01271 883319
Ilfracombe	The Landmark The Sea Front EX34 9BX	01271 863001	01271 862586
Woolacombe	The Esplanade EX34 7DL	01271 870553	
Braunton	The Bakehouse Centre Caen Street EX33 1AA	01271 816400	01271 816947
Barnstaple	36 Boutport Street EX31 1RX	01271 375000	01271 374037
Bideford	Victoria Park The Quay EX39 2QQ	01237 477676	01237 421853
Bude	Visitor Centre The Crescent EX23 8LE	01288 354240	01288 355769
Padstow	Red Brick Building North Quay PL28 8AF	01841 533449	01841 532356
Boscastle	The Harbour, Boscastle PL35 0HD	01840 280010	
St Ives	The Guildhall Street an Pol TR26 2DS	01736 796297	01736 798309
Penzance	Station Approach, Penzance TR18 2NF	01736 335530	
Falmouth	11 Market Strand, Prince of Wales Pier TR11 3DF	01326 312300	01326 313457
Fowey	5 South Street PL23 1AR	01726 833616	01726 833616
Mevagissey	St. George's Square Mevagissey PL26 6UB	01726 844857	01726 844857
Looe	The Guildhall, Fore Street PL13 1AA	01503 262072	01503 265426
Plymouth	Plymouth Mayflower 3-5 The Barbican PL1 2LR	01752 306330	01752 257955
Ivybridge	The Watermark PL21 0SZ	01752 897035	
Salcombe	Council Hall Market Street TQ8 8DE	01548 843927	01548 842736
Dartmouth	The Engine House, Mayors Avenue TQ6 9YY	01803 834224	01803 835631
Kingsbridge	The Quay TQ7 1HS	01548 853195	01548 854185
Brixham	The Old Market House The Quay TQ5 8TB	01803 852861	01803 852939
Paignton	The Esplanade TQ4 6ED	01803 558383	01803 551959
Torquay	Vaughan Parade TQ2 5JG	01803 297428	01803 214885
Teignmouth	The Den, Sea Front TQ14 8BE	01626 215666	01626 778333
Dawlish	The Lawn EX7 9EL	01626 215665	01626 865985
Exmouth	Alexandra Terrace EX8 1NZ	01395 222299	01395 269911
Budleigh Salterton	Fore Street EX9 6NG	01395 445275	01395 442208
Sidmouth	Ham Lane EX10 8XR	01395 516441	01395 519333
Seaton	The Underfleet EX12 2TB	01297 21660	01297 21689
Lyme Regis	Guildhall Cottage Church Street DT7 3BS	01297 442138	01297 443773
Bridport	47 South Street DT6 3NY	01308 424901	01308 421060
Weymouth	King's Statue The Esplanade DT4 7AN	01305 785747	01305 788092
Swanage	The White House Shore Road BH19 1LB	01929 422885	01929 423423
Wareham	Trinity Church South Street BH20 4LU	01929 552740	01929 554491
Poole	Tourism Centre, The Quay BH15 1BW	01202 253253	01202 684531

Land's End

We are sometimes asked what we have achieved and have set out below some of the things in which we have been involved in one way or another. We do as well send a steady flow of reports on path deficiencies, both as regards maintenance and the route of the path to the local authorities and the Natural England and the South West Coast Path Team.

1973 Official Formation in May. Attendance Cornish opening at Newquay. First information sheets produced.

1974 Attendance at South Devon and Dorset opening in September at Beer. Registration as a Charity.

1975 Clematon Hill, Bigbury, small new section of Coast Path agreed at SWWA's instigation.

Attendance at opening of so-called Exmoor Coast Path.

Bideford Public Enquiry - successful opposition to golf course on the Coast Path at Abbotsham.

Hartland Point success in getting path south from Hartland Point over Blagdon and Upright Cliffs.

Lulworth walk the new range Coast Path.

1976 First Footpath Guide issued. Thurlestone Diversion opposed.

North Cliffs improvements between Portreath and Hayle secured, thanks to National Trust.

Watermouth consulted by Devon County Council. Abbotsbury consulted by Dorset County Council.

1977 Evidence presented to Lord Porchester's Exmoor study.

Evidence given to Devon County Council for Taw/Torridge Estuary survey.

1978 Westward Ho! Attendance at Somerset/N. Devon opening.

Hartland new path seaward of radar station obtained, thanks to South West Way Association.

1979 Evidence given at Public Enquiries at Abbotsbury and Lulworth Cove.

First printed News Letters and Descriptions (illustrated)

1980 Dialogues with Countryside Commission about path deficiencies.

Alternative Coast Path open Glenthorne Estate, Somerset

1981 Path improvements at Watermouth; Braunton to Barnstaple; Dean Quarry; Clematon Hill; Bigbury; Mothecombe and Maidencombe.

1982 Further openings at: Cleave Farm (N Cornwall) Pentewan and Mount Edgcumbe, (S Cornwall) Higher Brownstone Farm, Kingswear and a short section west of Berry Head in South Devon.

Also agreement for a high tide route at Mothecombe (S Devon).

1983 Opening of the Widmouth Head section (N Devon), Kingswear and Mansands (S Devon) Crackington Haven (N Cornwall) with major improvements to path on the western side.

1984 New Sections of path opened on the east bank of the mouth of the River Dart near Kingswear giving access to Mill Bay Cove. And Trebarwith Strand to Backways Cove (N Cornwall).

1985 Culbone - Foreland Point - path at the Glenthorne Estate waymarked as official route.

Pinehaven - Port Quin (N Cornwall) new path opened.

1986 Minehead - Porlock Weir New path between North Hill and Hurlstone Point waymarked.

Black Head (Cornwall) purchased by the National Trust so allowing a coastal route.

1987 Barnstaple/Bideford/Northam new route completed along old railway track.

Bude - attendance at Public Enquiry to prevent development adjacent to footpath.

Chynhalls Point path moved to seaward of hotel.

Branscombe - Attendance at Public Enquiry for true coast path - route adopted.

Bidna/Northam - sea wall breached, acceptable diversion negotiated.

1988 Woody Bay- Trentishoe - Devon County Council adopts our recommended, nearer the coast route.

1989 Fire Beacon Point/Pentargon Cornwall County Council installs new path.

Wembury - attend public meeting to successfully oppose erection of locked gates across Coast Path by Royal Navy.

1991 Buckator - at our request Cornwall County Council re-route official path around the headland.

1992 Watcombe and Maidencombe Our recommended route installed by Devon County Council.

Worthygate Wood - our suggested path installed by National Trust.

1993 Foreland Point - successful opposition to stop closure of path on west side.

Buck's Mills - success with our request for a Path to avoid the holiday complex.

Port Quin - our suggested path installed by National Trust.

Reverse Guide from Poole to Minehead introduced.

1994 Invited by Countryside Commission to become a member of the South West Coast Path Steering Group to review the management of the South West Coast Path.

1995 Culbone - section re-opened by Exmoor National Park.

Association details on the Internet. See details on page 2.

1996 Path Descriptions for the whole Coast Path published.

Lyme Regis - golf course route reinstated by Dorset County Council.

1997 The SWCP Project published its strategy for the future management of the Coast Path.

The Association becomes a member of the SWCP Management Group.

1998 Our Silver Jubilee Year (25 years old).

The Association launches its Silver Jubilee Appeal to raise funds towards markers at each end of the Coast Path.

Mount Batten, Plymouth - Coast Path opened

1999 Name changed to South West Coast Path Association.

2000 Crock Pits - Exmoor National Park installs a coastal route recommended by Association.

Bolt Tail South Devon

2001 Eight Winter Cliff Falls Disrupt Dorset Coast Path.

Celebratory marker installed at Minehead.

Foot & Mouth Crisis - whole Coast Path closed for 3 months.

11 August - Whole Coast Path walked on one day by Association members to celebrate the re-opening of the Coast Path.

2002 Celebratory marker installed at South Haven Point, Poole Harbour.

St German's Beacon - True coastal route installed between Downderry & Portwrinkle

2003 South West Coast Path Association is 30 years old

Easter Saturday - Association arranges 'Walk the whole path in one day' to celebrate the 25th anniversary of the official inclusion of the Somerset and North Devon sections

Chynhalls Cliff -desired realignment is installed by Cornwall County Council.

Isle of Portland - Countryside Agency accepts the route around the Island.

Tregantle Cliff - desired realignment throughout the rifle ranges is installed by the MoD as permissive path. For this we award the MoD our Annual Award.

2004 Annual award presented to Brian Muelaner and National Trust Team for their work at Lansallos.

2005 Strete to Stoke Fleming - realigned Coast Path opened.

Wembury Point -Association donates £1000 to National Trust fundraising to buy this land.

2006 After 33 years in members' homes, our Administration department moves to new office at Lee Mill.

Cain's Folly -Path reinstated after 6 years of an unsatisfactory diversion.

2007 Minehead - Porlock Marsh - Thatcher Point -our requested realignments installed.

Watermouth - Major funding pledged by Association for off road Path realignment.

Porthallow - Design and artists chosen for the halfway marker.

2008 Association On-Line Shop opened.

5000th Member - Jill Fletcher, of Portishead given a presentation at Minehead.

2009 Honorary Secretary, Eric Wallis, listed in New Year's Honours, to receive MBE for his voluntary service to this registered charity.

Porthallow Halfway marker unveiled in May.

2010 Death of Eric Wallis MBE Hon Secretary since 1986 after short illness.

Coast Path re-routed around Cape Cornwall

Planning for new style Annual Guide.

Planning and surveying the first stretch of the new English Coast Path from Portland to Lulworth commenced by Natural England.

2011 Association moves to larger office at Lee Mill.

2012 Association funding is used to help progress no fewer than twelve improvement projects around the Coast Path, at Baggy Point, near Northam, between Westward Ho! and Bucks Mills, at Hartland, at Trevaunance Cove (St Agnes), in West Cornwall at Trevega, Tregerthen and Trevean Cliffs, near Millendreath (Looe), at Challaborough (South Devon), at St Mary's Bay (Torbay) and at Durlston near Swanage.

The Association Shop

To order:

- Order at **www.swcp.org.uk** or by telephone **01752 896237**. You can use a credit/debit card.
- Alternatively please send details of the sizes of garments and/or quantity of items required, together with a cheque made payable to: The South West Coast Path Association to the Administrator. Non UK orders: extra postage will be taken to a maximum of £4.00 depending on the number of items ordered.

Log Book

Keep a day by day record of your walk in an easy to carry, pocket size booklet, with a page per section in which to record your journey around some of the most beautiful countryside in the British Isles. Supplied with Waterproof Cover.

£3.50 including postage

Front Row Top

Zip neck sweatshirt, 100% cotton, looped back terry with peached finish. Contrast tape to neck and left hem. Panel detail to body sides. Available in navy/white or red/navy both with embroidered Coast Path logo. Sizes: XS, S, M, L, XL, XXL

£35.00 including postage

Sweat Shirt

In Bottle Green or Jade embroidered with the Peninsula map on the left side, with 'South West Coast Path' around it (70% polyester/30% cotton). Sizes: S, M, Large, XL, XXL.
Other colours are available on request.

£25.00 including postage

Baseball Cap

Available in Dark Green or Stone Colour.
100% cotton with embroidered logo.
One size adjustable to fit.

£9.95 including postage

Sleeveless Fleece

In Bottle Green with the Peninsula map on the left side and two zip pockets. 100% pill resistant polyester and unlined. Sizes: S, M, L, XL, XXL.
Other colours are available on request.

£25.00 including postage

Legionnaires Cap

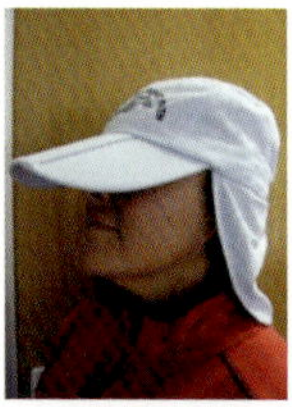

100% plush cotton, available Black, Bottle, Natural, Royal Blue, Sky Blue and White.
Sun protector neck flap. One size fits all.

£10.00 including postage

If in Salcombe you may like to visit Salcombe Embroiderers who stock all the Association clothing with the Coast Path logo. You will find them at Hannaford's Landing, Island Street, Salcombe, TQ8 8FE telephone: 01548 842115

We accept the following credit/debit cards:

To order online, visit our shop at www.swcp.org.uk

Polo Shirt

In an attractive Jade Green, with the Peninsula map embroidered on the shirt, with 'South West Coast Path' embroidered around it. A good quality garment, easy to wash (65% polyester/35% cotton). Sizes: S, M, L, XL and XXL. Other colours are available on request.

£19.25 including postage

Morf Snoods

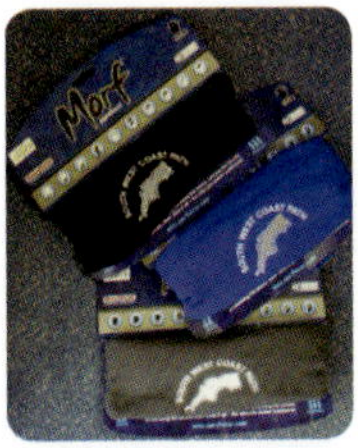

Morf Suprafleece multi-function snood/hat/neckwarmer/headband. 100% polyester microfibre, anti-microbial. Available in Black, Royal, Red or Grey. Embroidered with the Coast Path logo.

£9.00 including postage

Neck Warmer

100% polyester Suprafleece, pill resistant. Unique dual purpose design can be used as a hat or neck cowl. Elasticated drawcord with toggle, embroidered with Coast Path logo. Available in Black, Navy, Charcoal or Sky.

£8.00 including postage

Cloth Badge

Good quality cloth badge, showing the Peninsula map, with 'South West Coast Path' embroidered below, approximate size 4" x 3" (10cm x 8cm). Suitable for sewing onto shirt or rucksack.

£3.00 including postage

Polar Fleece Jacket

In Bottle Green with the Peninsula map on the left side and two zip pockets. 100% pill resistant, unlined, elasticated hem and cuffs. Sizes: S, M, L, XL and XXL. Other colours are available on request.

£29.00 including postage

Tea Towel

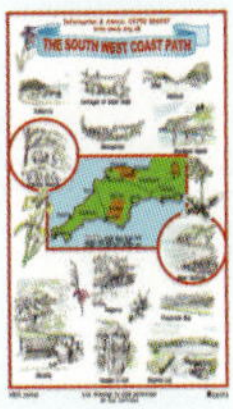

Full cotton tea towel 48cm x 78cm, depicting the end markers and scenes and flowers from locations on the trail. In the centre is a clear map of the whole South West Coast Path.

£3.85 including postage

To order:

- Order at **www.swcp.org.uk** or by telephone **01752 896237**. You can use a credit/debit card.
- Alternatively please send details of the sizes of garments and/or quantity of items required, together with a cheque made payable to: The South West Coast Path Association to the Administrator. Non UK orders: extra postage will be taken to a maximum of £4.00 depending on the number of items ordered.

Plymouth Waterfront Walk Book

A 32-page fully illusrated bboklet describing the South West Coast Path through the City of Plymouth

Free of charge but £1.50 postage

Marker Postcards

Depicting the magnificent markers at Minehead and South Haven Point.

30p each including postage

Beer Tankard

One pint glass tankard engraved with Association Peninsula logo

£15.00 including postage

Tumbler

Cut glass tumblers with the Peninsula map sand-blasted on the glass. Suitably packaged.

£16.00 each including postage

Certificate

These lovely colour certificates are available to people who have walked the whole path. Contact the Administrator. Members can have them presented by the Chairman at our next AGM.

FREE (members)
£3.50 (non-members including postage)

Map Poster

A large sized map poster showing the South West Coast Path with the path printed in white enabling walkers to mark off sections walked. Size 64cm x 45cm (251/4" x 173/4").

£5.75 including postage

We accept the following credit/debit cards:

To order online, visit our shop at www.swcp.org.uk

Self Catering Booklet

Contact information on Self Catering accommodation recommended by Coast Path walkers. Arranged in path order.

£1.50 including postage

Walking Holiday Companies

A booklet listing walking holiday companies offering walks based on the South West Coast Path.

£1.50 including postage

Reverse Guide

REVISED 2011 A trail description of the whole 630 miles in the direction Poole to Minehead.

£4.00 including postage

2013 Association Calendar

Twelve gorgeous pictures in full colour. (2013 calendar pictured). Available from June each year.

£7.50 including postage

Also available direct from the artist...

A Calligraphic Map of the South West Coast Path

This quality calligraphic map of the South West Coast Path has been designed, illustrated and written by James Skinner of Gloucester.

The printed calligraphic map has been written entirely by hand, complemented by fine pen and ink drawings illustrating many of the sights to be found whilst walking the path.

The calligraphic map would make a superb gift, or an ideal memento for anyone having walked part or all of the path.

Overall size: approx 560 mm deep x 760 mm wide (22 inches x 30 inches)

£10.99 including free postage and packing

View the map at www.jamesskinnercalligrapher.co.uk or telephone 01452 611614 for further details

Membership

You may be one of those who have either bought this guide from us or a book shop. You can guarantee receipt of next year's updated, revised edition by joining the Association.

The South West Coast Path Association is a charity which represents all users of the Coast Path, be they serious hikers or afternoon strollers.

As well as producing information guides about the Coast Path, the Association raises money to help the authorities provide the best possible standard for Coast Path walkers.

If you would like to join the Association, and see your subscription go towards improving the path and its publications, you would be very welcome. Membership includes a free copy of the updated annual guide each year.

This annual guide is updated every year and published at the end of February.

Annual Subscriptions:

Single	**£13.50**
Joint	**£15.00**
Associations & Local Authorities	**£23.00**
Life Membership	**£205.00**
Joint Life Membership	**£227.00**
Non-UK Membership	**£21.00**
Business Membership	**£23.00**

To join online visit www.swcp.org.uk or telephone 01752 896237

The Lizard

I wish to join the South West Coast Path Association for 2014.

Name ____________________

Address ____________________

____

____

Postcode ____________________

Telephone ____________________

Email ____________________

Payment Details:

Payment made by:

☐ Cheque ☐ Amex ☐ Visa/Mastercard

Valid From ________/________ Expiry ________/________ Issue No ______

Card Number ____________________

Gift Aid

Under the Gift Aid Scheme the Association can reclaim the income tax paid on any donation or membership subscription received, provided you are a UK tax payer. If you would like to help us in this way then please indicate below and sign. All that we ask is if you cease to pay income tax in the future, please let us know.

I am a UK tax payer and would like South West Coast Path Association to reclaim the tax paid on any subscriptions or donations that I make to them.

Signature(s) Date

Please send completed form to:
The Administrator, South West Coast Path Association, Bowker House, Lee Mill Bridge, Ivybridge PL21 9EF • Tel: 01752 896237 • Fax: 01752 893654

PLEASE DETACH HERE

Whilst walking on the path, or on any other occasion, should you meet someone interested in this book, the Association, or the Coast Path, do not worry if no one has a pencil and paper, just tear off one of these:

The South West Coast Path Association was formed 39 years ago to promote the interest of users of our Coast Path. We continue to press the authorities to maintain it properly and to complete the path. An annually updated guide to the whole 630 miles (1014km) of the South West Coast Path is issued to members every Spring. They also receive newsletters that provide the latest news about the state of the path.

For information about membership and how to obtain this annual guide contact:
South West Coast Path Association, Bowker House, Lee Mill Bridge, Ivybridge PL21 9EF
T: 01752 8961237 **F:** 01752 893654 **E:** info@swcp.org.uk **W:** www.swcp.org.uk

The South West Coast Path Association was formed 39 years ago to promote the interest of users of our Coast Path. We continue to press the authorities to maintain it properly and to complete the path. An annually updated guide to the whole 630 miles (1014km) of the South West Coast Path is issued to members every Spring. They also receive newsletters that provide the latest news about the state of the path.

For information about membership and how to obtain this annual guide contact:
South West Coast Path Association, Bowker House, Lee Mill Bridge, Ivybridge PL21 9EF
T: 01752 8961237 **F:** 01752 893654 **E:** info@swcp.org.uk **W:** www.swcp.org.uk

The South West Coast Path Association was formed 39 years ago to promote the interest of users of our Coast Path. We continue to press the authorities to maintain it properly and to complete the path. An annually updated guide to the whole 630 miles (1014km) of the South West Coast Path is issued to members every Spring. They also receive newsletters that provide the latest news about the state of the path.

For information about membership and how to obtain this annual guide contact:
South West Coast Path Association, Bowker House, Lee Mill Bridge, Ivybridge PL21 9EF
T: 01752 8961237 **F:** 01752 893654 **E:** info@swcp.org.uk **W:** www.swcp.org.uk

The South West Coast Path Association was formed 39 years ago to promote the interest of users of our Coast Path. We continue to press the authorities to maintain it properly and to complete the path. An annually updated guide to the whole 630 miles (1014km) of the South West Coast Path is issued to members every Spring. They also receive newsletters that provide the latest news about the state of the path.

For information about membership and how to obtain this annual guide contact:
South West Coast Path Association, Bowker House, Lee Mill Bridge, Ivybridge PL21 9EF
T: 01752 8961237 **F:** 01752 893654 **E:** info@swcp.org.uk **W:** www.swcp.org.uk

The South West Coast Path Association was formed 39 years ago to promote the interest of users of our Coast Path. We continue to press the authorities to maintain it properly and to complete the path. An annually updated guide to the whole 630 miles (1014km) of the South West Coast Path is issued to members every Spring. They also receive newsletters that provide the latest news about the state of the path.

For information about membership and how to obtain this annual guide contact:
South West Coast Path Association, Bowker House, Lee Mill Bridge, Ivybridge PL21 9EF
T: 01752 8961237 **F:** 01752 893654 **E:** info@swcp.org.uk **W:** www.swcp.org.uk

PLEASE CUT ALONG DOTTED LINES